£10.99

)0

2000

001

MAY 20

2 MAR 2002

THE TEMPEST

THEORY IN PRACTICE SERIES

General Editor: Nigel Wood, School of English, University of Birmingham

Associate Editors: Tony Davies and Barbara Rasmussen, University of Birmingham

Current titles:

Don Juan
Mansfield Park
A Passage to India
The Prelude
The Tempest
The Waste Land

Forthcoming titles include:

Antony and Cleopatra
Hamlet
Henry IV
Measure for Measure
The Merchant of Venice
To the Lighthouse

THE TEMPEST

EDITED BY
NIGEL WOOD

OPEN UNIVERSITY PRESS
BUCKINGHAM·PHILADELPHIA

Open University Press
Celtic Court
22 Ballmoor
Buckingham
MK18 1XW

and
1900 Frost Road, Suite 101
Bristol, PA 19007, USA

First Published 1995

A catalogue record of this book is available from the British Library

ISBN 0 335 15688 6 (pb)

Library of Congress Cataloging-in-Publication Data
The tempest / Nigel Wood (ed.).
    p. cm. — (Theory in practice series)
  Includes bibliographical references (p.   ) and index.
  ISBN 0–335–15688–6
  1. Shakespeare, William, 1564–1616. Tempest. 2. Tragicomedy.
I. Wood, Nigel, 1953–   . II. Series.
PR2833.T46 1994
822.3′3—dc20

                                                                          94–19659

Typeset by Colset Pte. Ltd., Singapore
Printed in Great Britain by St Edmundsbury Press,
Bury St Edmunds, Suffolk

Contents

vi CONTENTS

The Editor and Contributors

HOWARD FELPERIN has lectured on Shakespeare and critical theory for more than twenty-five years at several universities on four continents. He is the author of *Shakespearean Romance* (1972); *Shakespearean Representation* (1977); *Beyond Deconstruction* (1985); and *The Uses of the Canon* (1990).

CHARLES H. FREY teaches Shakespeare in the Department of English at the University of Washington in Seattle. He has authored and edited numerous books and articles on Shakespeare and other subjects, including *Shakespeare's Vast Romance: A Study of 'The Winter's Tale'* (1980) and *Experiencing Shakespeare: Essays on Text, Classroom, and Performance* (1988).

JOHN TURNER is lecturer in English at Swansea University. He is the author of *Wordsworth: Play and Politics* (1986), co-author of *Shakespeare: The Play of History* (1988) and *Shakespeare: Out of Court* (1990), and author of *Macbeth* (1992). He is currently editing D.H. Lawrence's *The Trespasser* for Penguin.

RICHARD P. WHEELER is professor of English at the University of Illinois at Urbana-Champaign. He is the author of several essays on Shakespeare and psychoanalytic approaches in particular, including *Shakespeare's Development and the Problem Comedies* (1981) and *The*

Whole Journey: Shakespeare's Power of Development (co-authored with C.L. Barber) (1986).

NIGEL WOOD is lecturer in English at the University of Birmingham. He is the author of a study on Jonathan Swift (1986), and of several essays on literary theory, has co-edited essays on John Gay (1989), edited a selection from Fanny Burney's diaries and journals (1990), and is editor of the *Theory in Practice* volumes on *Don Juan, The Prelude, Mansfield Park* (all 1993), *The Waste Land* and *A Passage to India* (both with Tony Davies) (1994).

Editors' Preface

The object of this series is to help bridge the divide between the understanding of theory and the interpretation of individual texts. Students are therefore introduced to theory in practice. Although contemporary critical theory is now taught in many colleges and universities, it is often separated from the day-to-day consideration of literary texts that is the staple ingredient of most tuition in English. A thorough dialogue between theoretical and literary texts is thus avoided.

Each of these specially commissioned volumes of essays seeks by contrast to involve students of literature in the questions and debates that emerge when a variety of theoretical perspectives are brought to bear on a selection of 'canonical' literary texts. Contributors were not asked to provide a comprehensive survey of the arguments involved in a particular theoretical position, but rather to discuss in detail the implications for interpretation found in particular essays or studies, and then, taking these into account, to offer a reading of the literary text.

This rubric was designed to avoid two major difficulties which commonly arise in the interaction between literary and theoretical texts: the temptation to treat a theory as a bloc of formulaic rules that could be brought to bear on any text with roughly predictable results; and the circular argument that texts are constructed as such merely by the theoretical perspective from which we choose to regard them. The former usually leads to studies that are really just footnotes to the adopted theorists, whereas the latter is effortlessly self-fulfilling.

It would be disingenuous to claim that our interests in the teaching of theory were somehow neutral and not open to debate. The idea for this series arose from the teaching of theory in relation to specific texts. It is inevitable, however, that the practice of theory poses significant questions as to just what 'texts' might be and where the dividing lines between text and context may be drawn. Our hope is that this series will provide a forum for debate on just such issues as these which are continually posed when students of literature try to engage with theory in practice.

Tony Davies
Barbara Rasmussen
Nigel Wood

Preface

Thanks are due to Robert Smallwood for much help (direct and indirect), Patricia Smith for many large mercies, and also the students in the Bread Loaf School of English *Shakespeare: Page and Stage* classes (Oxford, 1992–4) for their enthusiasm, sense of challenge and commitment. I would also like to record my appreciation of the enterprise and forbearance of the contributors, who have been tactful and extraordinarily helpful.

Nigel Wood

How to Use
this Book

Each of these essays is composed of a theoretical and a practical element. Contributors were asked to identify the main features of their perspective on the text (exemplified by a single theoretical essay or book) and then to illustrate their own attempts to put this into practice.

We realize that many readers new to recent theory will find its specific vocabulary and leading concepts strange and difficult to relate to current critical traditions in most English courses.

The format of this book has been designed to help if this is your situation, and we would advise the following:

(i) Before reading the essays, glance at the editor's introduction where the literary text's critical history is discussed, and

(ii) also at the prefatory information immediately before the essays, where the editor attempts to supply a context for the adopted theoretical position.

(iii) If you would like to develop your reading in any of these areas, turn to the annotated further reading section at the end of the volume, where you will find brief descriptions of those texts that each contributor has considered of more advanced interest. There are also full citations of the texts to which the contributors have referred in the references. It is also possible that more local information will be contained in notes to the essays.

(iv) The contributors have often regarded the chosen theoretical texts as points of departure and it is also in the nature of theoretical discussion to apply and test ideas on a variety of texts. Turn, therefore, to question and answer sections that follow each essay which are designed to allow contributors to comment and expand on their views in more general terms.

A Note on
the Texts Used

All quotations from *The Tempest* have been taken from the Oxford
University Press edition, ed. Stephen Orgel (1987). In addition, the
following Shakespeare editions have been consulted:

As You Like It	ed. Alan Brissenden (Oxford, 1993)
The Comedy of Errors	ed. T.S. Dorsch (Cambridge, 1988)
Cymbeline	ed. J.M. Nosworthy (London, 1955)
Hamlet	ed. Philip Edwards (Cambridge, 1985)
Henry V	ed. Gary Taylor (Oxford, 1982)
The Second Part of King Henry IV	ed. Giorgio Melchiori (Cambridge, 1989)
Julius Caesar	ed. Martin Spevack (Cambridge, 1988)
The Tragedy of King Lear	ed. Jay L. Halio (Cambridge, 1992)
The Tragedy of Macbeth	ed. Nicholas Brooke (Oxford, 1990)
Measure for Measure	ed. N.W. Bawcutt (Oxford, 1991)
The Merchant of Venice	ed. Jay L. Halio (Oxford, 1993)
A Midsummer Night's Dream	ed. R.A. Foakes (Cambridge, 1984)
Pericles	ed. F.D. Hoeninger (London, 1963)
King Richard II	ed. Andrew Gurr (Cambridge, 1984)
The Sonnets and Love's Complaint	ed. John Kerrigan (Harmondsworth, 1986)

Twelfth Night   ed. Elizabeth Story Donno (Cambridge, 1985)

The Winter's Tale   ed. J.H.P. Pafford (London, 1963)

Introduction

NIGEL WOOD

'Where should this music be? – i'th' air or th' earth?', exclaims Ferdinand on his first entrance, drawn into the action by an 'invisible' Ariel, 'playing and singing' (I.ii.388; stage direction (s.d.) 374). His consternation arises not just from the question as to the source of this music but also as to where it *ought* to be located, and whether he any longer enjoys freedom of action: 'Thence I have followed it,/Or it hath drawn me rather . . .' (I.ii.394–5). An audience might now echo this sentiment. In what could be termed 'uniquely a musical play among Shakespeare's writings' (according to Gurr 1989: 92), we may run the risk of harbouring inappropriate expectations of the text. There seems a deliberate lack of clarity about Prospero's cell and his art. Is the island intended as an enclave of the mind and the whole action a projection of Prospero's psyche, or is it merely *terra incognita*, lying just off the charts, yet earthly, quotidian stuff, transfigured only by his painfully acquired magic tricks? Certainly, in the few hours' traffic of the stage, during a performance, Prospero's magic ordains most of the action, and we could conclude that the illusions and/or transformations that so confound the protagonists are eventually no more than theatricality, and, within the terms of the narrative, little more than just well-judged expediency to help Prospero regain his dukedom.

The mere mention of the alternatives 'air' and 'earth' would seem to lock any further reading of the play into the consideration of a binary opposition that comprises Ariel and Caliban. Certainly, the action, as we shall see, is often generated by stark contrasts (among others, innocence/experience, art/nature and power/subservience). Ferdinand's wonder is comprehensible, as Ariel's song, while it starts melodiously ('Come unto these yellow sands,/And then take hands;') is eventually twice shot through with the calls of 'watch dogs' and also the 'strain' of a 'strutting Chanticleer', which substitute onomatopoeia ('Bow-wow'/'Cock a diddle dow') for poetry (I.ii.374–86). The Folio stage direction that accompanies these calls is 'Burthen dispersedly', which points to a spectacle wherein the 'sweet sprites' charged with chanting the refrain or undersong do it disjointedly, even discordantly. Is this the kind of melody that would allay 'fury and . . . passion', the 'sweet air' that Ferdinand hears (I.ii.393–4)? Similarly, Ferdinand might understand this music as the accompaniment for 'Some god o'th' island' (I.ii.390), and yet we know that that divinity is Prospero, whose powers in fact come attended with and even derive from a 'magic garment' (I.ii.24) and his copious library.

Before involving other items in this review it might be useful to advance two basic interpretative propositions: first, that it is an inescapable fact that there will be embedded irony in performing a play text; and second, that an 'audience' is a very nominal referent in the analysis of drama, recourse to which often hides more than it reveals. Hamlet's soliloquizing may provide the most memorable verse in the play of that name, but the net effect of such lines is dependent on the whole play – the action of which he is but a part – and the implied audience. Taken out of context, Gonzalo's cheering words to Alonso about the plantation of the island, the prospect of a 'commonwealth', where 'All things in common nature should produce/Without sweat or endeavour' (II.i.145; 156–7) might illustrate some nostalgia about a Golden Age.[1] Is he just cheering his king up, every inch the 'honest old councillor'? Or is there an implicit absurdity in the berobed courtier, envisioning a state where there would be 'No occupation, all men idle, all' (II.i.152), that may well bring to mind the levelling tempest of the first scene, and, in its midst, the idleness of authority identified by the Boatswain? This is to say nothing of the sardonic commentary to Gonzalo's vision provided by Sebastian and Antonio, in whose eyes we find the Arcadians merely 'whores and knaves' (II.i.164). Similarly, when Miranda first sees these satirists, she concludes that mankind is indeed 'beauteous' and thereby welcomes a 'brave new world', and yet Prospero immediately reminds us that it is 'new' to her only (V.i.183–4). This 'showing' has often a complexity that theatrical 'telling' cannot match.

Dramatic analysis can thus only barely proceed without the invocation of 'audience'. As soon as we attempt to come to terms with the intricacies of dramatic representation we involve ourselves with what, to a lesser or a greater degree, is a public document, that is, one that is directly transitive in its net effect, and that derives from an intricate nexus of collaboration whereby the commissioning company influence the eventual shape of the play as well as its recorded author. Peter Brook's location of the Deadly Theatre as one where outmoded, ritualized gestures are disguised as a return to 'basic' simplicities is a telling one: it is mostly one-way traffic, implying that there should be a passive, reified audience listening to the (all too) unambiguous signals transmitted from the author via the director. Such 'messages' rarely have the desired result, because the play text just does not supply the fixed point required of the Deadly paradigm:

> When I hear a director speaking glibly of serving the author, of letting a play speak for itself, my suspicions are aroused, because this is the hardest job of all. If you just let a play speak, it may not make a sound. If what you want is for the play to be heard, then you must conjure its sound from it. This demands many deliberate actions and the result may have great simplicity. However, setting out to 'be simple' can be quite negative, an easy evasion of the exacting steps to the simple answer.
>
> (Brook 1968: 43)

Context need not just summon up historical distance, for, as Charles Frey points out, the dramatic experience need not involve a thinking *about* the play, but actually absorbing *in the present* its sensuous signals (pp. 73–9). For those who inevitably encounter the play text as 'set text' and not as a formulation that will eventuate as a particular theatrical event with its own acquired set of production values, the prime goal must also be to avoid this 'glibness'. While still maintaining some contact with a text that can give rise to multiple (although related) meanings, we need to explore the conditions under which dramatic texts can achieve meaning in performance *and* note that that inevitably involves a notion of 'context' that is variable.

The Unserene *Tempest*

> But Shakespear's Magick could not copy'd be,
> Within that Circle none durst walk but he.
> ('Prologue', *The Tempest,* or *The Enchanted Island,*
> 11.19–20 (Dryden 1955–   , 10: 6))

Dryden's Shakespeare is such a 'strong' and influential author that when he agreed to help Sir William Davenant to remould *The Tempest* in 1667 it was deemed prudent to admire him yet do otherwise. Davenant's royal warrant to attempt a 'reformeinge' and 'makeinge ... fitt' (Nicoll 1952–9, 1: 352–4) of eleven Shakespeare plays, granted on 12 December 1660, testifies to a confidence that now seems presumptuous. Shakespeare possessed a genius that was wild and uncultivated and, although succeeding ages might not be capable of repeating such untutored brilliance, they could curb some of its excesses and faults of taste. The play that Davenant started and Dryden completed, indeed, bears small resemblance to the original. Both Miranda and Caliban have sisters, Dorinda and Sycorax, and, as a counterpart to Miranda's innocence, there is the introduction of an equally naïve Hippolito, who, Prospero learns from an astrological projection, will die if he sights a woman. If this sounds potentially tragic, then it is as well if we remember the work's sub-title: 'A Comedy'. Sycorax is no longer the shadowy evil presence still capable of haunting the island, and the opportunities for music and dance are seized avidly. Ariel even dances a 'Saraband' with a female spirit, Milcha, at the close of the play (Dryden 1955– , 10: 102). It comes as no surprise to learn that Thomas Shadwell adapted this text for opera in 1674.

There is perhaps little to admire about the conversion of reverence for chastity to urbane or witty variations on virginal themes, and of the self-doubt of Prospero to the schemes of a rather more marginal ringmaster. The extra bodies on stage and an inevitably more episodic plot replace the original's focus on individual motivation. For Prospero there is no hint that the revels end and no intense confrontation with Antonio, whose blood freely pleads for pardon (V.ii.148; Dryden 1955– , 10: 99). Within months of *The Tempest* becoming an opera, Thomas Duffett had burlesqued it with his *The Mock-Tempest, or The Enchanted Castle*, wherein Caliban becomes a bullish hireling, Hectoro, and Prospero the keeper of Bridewell prison. Dryden/ Davenant's lowering of the moral tone may be regrettable, yet there is also here a significant rereading of what is itself hardly taken seriously by Shakespeare: the querulous political debates between Trinculo, Mustacho, Stephano and Ventoso as to what might replace Prospero's dominion.[2] Recently, the possibility of a coded comment on kingship and its 'rights' has been uncovered by Katharine Eisaman Maus and Matthew H. Wikander. Whereas Maus (1982: 206) notes the enhanced role afforded a 'loyal, resourceful subject' (Ariel), instead of the island's 'benevolent monarch' in the play's more Whiggish conclusion, Wikander (1991: 97) is alive to the net effects of diluting Prospero's overall authority: 'The restoration play withholds from Prospero his Stuart absolutist dimension. The idea of the self-mastering sage, father, and monarch is absorbed in the general atmosphere of guilt and repentance'. It is surely no idle fact to discover that one of the earliest interests in *The Tempest*, although no allegory, included an interest in extrinsic political matters.

The Enchanted Island may now be regarded more as a cul-de-sac than part of the high road of Shakespearian appreciation but it is an instructive instance of what may happen to the text when the symbolic value of both Caliban and Prospero is discounted. Caliban, throughout the play's eighteenth-century stage history, is frequently a stock figure of fun, deployed for a scene or two but never allowed to be anything other than functional. As Alden and Virginia Vaughan have discovered, Caliban was a grotesque and Prospero's totalitarian potential thereby excused (see Vaughan and Vaughan 1991: 177–9). Some of this determination to remove him to the periphery derived from the basic fact that his 'unnatural' qualities confronted the highest forms of mimesis with unassimilable details. Dryden's Preface to his adaptation of *Troilus and Cressida* (1679) simply regards Caliban as monstrous, an individually drawn monster ('a Species of himself'), but still the 'product of unnatural Lust' (Dryden 1955– , 13: 239–40). Nicholas Rowe, in his *Account* of 1709, was so taken with the play's 'very Solemn and very Poetical' magic that Caliban is merely evidence of Shakespeare's 'wonderful Invention' (Vickers 1974– , 2: 197) and Joseph Warton's similar reverence for such 'boundless imagination' leads to applause for the 'romantic, the wonderful, and the wild' which leads to a 'pleasing extravagance'. Ariel is safer material, exhibiting a 'wildness of fancy, and yet with equal propriety' (*The Adventurer*, no. 93 (1753), in Vickers 1974– , 4: 61).[3] Four numbers of *The Adventurer* later and Warton finds a place for Caliban in much the same terms as Rowe; he is a 'fiend' of whom little is to be expected (Vickers 1974– , 4: 65).

It is symptomatic of Dryden and Davenant's influence that their *Tempest* enjoyed revivals as more of an annual pantomimic treat throughout the 1730s. As Michael Dobson (1991: 103–5) points out, at the same time as the 'colonial plot' was all but invisible, the installation of 'Shakespeare' as a national monument attracted, on the other hand, many overt identifications of him with Prospero (a fuller context is given in Dobson 1992: 38–61). Formal cohesion demanded that, as Warton put it, the unities of plot as well as of time and place be observed, and that this be 'one, great, and entire, the restoration of

PROSPERO to his dukedom' (Vickers 1974–   , 4: 68). The demands of this formal unity prepared the way for the renewed acceptance of Shakespeare's text; it was gradual for, although James Lacy claimed to offer the original at Drury Lane in 1746, Shadwell's fulsome fifth-act masque of Neptune and Amphitrite was retained. It was not until 1757 that David Garrick attempted to provide an unvarnished text; even then, over 400 lines were cut, most of them from the first introduction of the shipwrecked court in Act II, scene i. It was left to William Charles Macready, in 1838, to present a *Tempest* that stood first and foremost as a dramatic experience. Even then, Ariel still sung some interpolated Shadwell numbers, in flight across the stage.

The characteristic response to the play until well into the Victorian period was that it was a Shakespearian flight of fancy, a holiday from more problematic reflections on human duty and social kinship (see Parker 1989: 112–26). Samuel Johnson regarded Prospero as an enchanter, in his note to I.ii.250 in the edition of 1765, and this meant that Ariel and his companions were

> evidently of the fairy kind, an order of beings to which tradition
> has always ascribed a sort of diminutive agency, powerful but
> ludicrous, a humorous and frolick controlment of nature . . .
>   (note to I.ii.396; Bronson and O'Meara 1986: 61, 64–5)

This is consistent with Johnson's steadfast view in the Preface that Shakespeare's pre-eminent virtue was his 'just' representations of 'general nature' (Bronson and O'Meara 1986: 10). This is easily misunderstood as a liking for abstractions at the expense of red-blooded detail, but Johnson is clear that generality is an effect, not always a rhetorical means. The ability to reach the common mind must exclude banal stereotypes as well as unmotivated and eccentric symbolism. Caliban, however, was a difficult case; such rough-cast 'brutality of sentiment' could only be recuperated by regarding it natural to any being placed so disadvantageously (note to I.ii.321; Bronson and O'Meara 1986: 63).

The lack of seriousness granted to its fairies and monsters might be partially explained by the operatic versions of the play that were firmly installed in the eighteenth-century repertory. With the Romantic reappraisal of Shakespeare's talents *The Tempest*'s more purely theatrical virtues were rediscovered. In his ninth lecture on Shakespeare (*Lectures on Shakespeare and Milton* (1811)) Coleridge's apparently uncontroversial distinction between those characters 'in which the ideal is most prominent' and those cases where we are deluded into believing them 'real' actually has far-reaching consequences. His prime example of the former species is *The Tempest*. Shorn of such mimetic responsibility, the play has an 'organic regularity' of its own, which is obedient to some *immanent* law 'which all the parts obey, conforming themselves to the outward symbols and manifestations of the essential principle'. Life does not supply a reliable yardstick of artistic quality so much as this derived 'principle' which is addressed to the imagination, and which does not need to adhere strictly to original, worldly states of being. Consequently, the play might not even be *actable* in the accepted sense. On the bare stage, the text was likely to have been 'recited rather than acted':

> that is to say, description and narration supplied the place of visual exhibition: the audience was told to fancy that they saw what they only heard described; the painting was not in colours, but in words.
>
> (Coleridge 1960, 2: 130–1)[4]

Where poetry supplanted drama, the tendency was for Prospero to dominate less. Caliban and Ariel had their poetry, too. Later, when Coleridge focused on the 'improbability' of the plot in his *Literary Remains* (published in 1836) it is counted almost as a virtue, for 'a purely romantic drama' is the stuff of imagination, not history, 'or the natural connexion of events' (Bate 1992: 529).

It is tempting to conclude that *The Tempest*, under these critical influences, came to be regarded as more symphonic in form. In a sense, this was certainly the case – for the purposes of a purely formal approach. It is a peculiar trait of the period that matters of abstract form could be matters of political debate. Jonathan Bate reminds us that while Prospero could be almost an archetype of the Romantic artist for Coleridge among others (see Bate 1986: 61–2, 69, 157–8), he could in some quarters be touted merely as a tetchy autocrat (see Bate 1989: 178–80). In 1818 Coleridge's lecture on *The Tempest*, with its perception of Caliban as the 'original and caricature of Jacobinism' (Coleridge 1987, 2: 124), had a galvanizing effect on William Hazlitt, who, in the next issue of the radical *Yellow Dwarf* (14 February 1818), turned Coleridge's allegorizing back on him:

> Caliban is so far from being a prototype of modern Jacobinism, that he is strictly the legitimate sovereign of the isle, and Prospero and the rest are usurpers, who have ousted him from his hereditary jurisdiction by superiority of talent and knowledge.
>
> (Hazlitt 1930–4, 19: 207)

Hazlitt is not at this juncture merely supplying an opportunistic piece, as Caliban had been granted a more prominent stature in his *Characters of Shakespeare's Plays* (1817). While 'the essence of grossness', he does not express one 'particle of vulgarity', as his portrayal of a 'brutal mind' is still 'in contact with the pure and original forms of nature . . . uncramped by any of the meannesses of custom' (Hazlitt 1930–4, 4: 239). This Romantic discovery of a Caliban both significant and even pathetic places Prospero's character in a different light. As we shall see, its introduction of irony in Act 1, scene ii has been taken up in many contemporary readings.

As Griffiths (1983) has made plain, the problem of just what might happen to Caliban at the end of the play was often shelved. Does he resume the husbandry of the island? How can he be 'wise hereafter,/ And seek for grace' (V.i.294–5)? The text leaves him in Prospero's cell, the schoolboy truant in the head's study. Two developments by the end of the century in both criticism and staging shift the attention on to Caliban: the recognition of the post-colonial possibilities once Prospero's power is rolled back from the island, and, as is clearly explored in texts such as Daniel Wilson's *Caliban: The Missing Link* (1873), the Darwinian hypothesis that Caliban is not just influenced by nature but rather constitutes essential humanity (see Vaughan and Vaughan 1991: 183–9).[5] On the one hand, audiences could be presented with a closing tableau of Caliban once again at his ease, sunbathing, as in John Ryder's Queen's Theatre production (1871), but on the other, Caliban could be some aboriginal as in F.R. Benson's gibbering monkey in Stratford (1891) and even a central ingredient of the closing of the play, as directed by Beerbohm Tree (1904) (see Nilan 1972).

If Prospero comes to control the emotional centre of the play much less, then his rule also becomes a far less dangerous force. Sprague (1944) has traced the replacement of a Faustian Prospero by an ultimately beneficent stage manager. This is attended by a renewed interest in the psychology of power. Orgel's summary (1987: 79–87) neatly captures the significance of casting him as either a return to *King Lear* or *Henry IV*, a weary Shakespeare or the chastened just ruler. Dowden (1875: 415) traced a powerful sense of relief when 'Shakspere's final period' hove into sight, for then there was a sense of artistic maturity: 'a clear yet tender luminousness', redolent of a wise pathos, shed over 'the beauty of youth and the love of youth'. It is significant how Dowden's verdict depended on a Prospero who can not only preside over the island but also win our admiration for so doing. Thus he was a 'great enchanter' and possessed a 'grave harmony . . . calm validity of will . . . [and] unfaltering justice', the very qualities he imagined that the mature Shakespeare himself must have possessed: 'Prospero is a harmonious and fully developed *will*'. Awarding him 'the higher levels of moral attainment' (Dowden 1875: 417–18), Dowden was in little doubt that his usurpation of Caliban's birthright was merely a right ensured by civilized *mores*, wherein the 'great master' overcame 'the rights of the brute-power Caliban' (Dowden 1875: 420). Dowden pursued a quest of isolating 'Shakspere's' particular set of mind, and this took him to identify within him 'some of the elements of English conservatism' (Dowden 1875: 421), that is, the portrayal of honourable service (Ariel), on the one hand, and desperate would-be communards (Stephano, Trinculo and Caliban), on the other. Prospero/Shakspere is the linchpin; the others, reflections of his personal quest.

Dowden, however, looks forward as well as back. He is one of the first critics to find contrary impulses in the Epilogue, 'forgiveness and freedom', a dichotomy that is borne out in Shakespeare's own life in the passage from artist to an 'English country gentleman' (this from a professor of English literature at Trinity College, Dublin). Prospero's 'ending' lay not in despair, but in a 'truth': that the 'highest freedom' lay in the 'bonds of duty' (Dowden 1875: 423). This response at least renders Prospero's progress a coherent one. He starts out to educate others, yet eventually discovers that he has educated himself. As we will see, the most coherent critical versions of the play need a Caliban akin to the 'brute-power', and an Ariel who wins his own release by obedience. It therefore forms a parabolic meditation on the mutually enforcing rights of a civil society.

Dowden's appreciation of such psychological power is squared with its symbolic and cultural signs. This is a fragile arrangement, for where earlier readings of the 'Last Plays' had claimed Shakespeare as the poet of Nature, those after took up the poet of unreality – a romanticist's last statement – and it has not been until very recently that the possibilities for a political reassessment have been reopened. This contemporary interest leads to the allegorizing of the action – not necessarily in every scene, but as a recurrent possibility. In 1936, J. Middleton Murry (in *Shakespeare*) found this tendency anti-intuitive, yet still confessed to finding the play's symbolic arrangement intended, providing 'an imaginative paradigm of Shakespeare himself in his function as poet', a well-disposed influence, especially for Ferdinand who is made the acceptable ruler by Prospero's design (Murry 1936: 391). Similarly, Tillyard (1938: 58) highlights the betrothed couple's paramount significance for the completion of Prospero's full design:

> Not only do Ferdinand and Miranda sustain Prospero in representing a new order of things that has evolved out of destruction; they also vouch for its continuation. At the end of the play Alonso and Prospero are old and worn men. A younger and happier generation is needed to secure the new state to which Prospero has so painfully brought himself, his friends, and all his enemies save Caliban.

Unexpectedly, this is a tragic pattern, the faint tracing of a new, but as yet unrealized, redemption.

It is tempting to find in this closing consolation (for all, that is, except Caliban, note) the contemporary need, especially in Europe, for art to stand distinct from strife and for authority to promote beneficent ends. In 1947, G. Wilson Knight could grasp hold of Prospero-as-Shakespeare as very much an internal affair, with no 'objective story' to stand as an external yardstick or source. Shakespeare 'spins his plot from his own poetic world entirely' (Knight 1947: 204). Dramatic power is equated with a contained textual order, and Brower's (1951) close examination of the play's metaphors finds most of them analogous to episodes that may seem distant in the plot and in narrative function. The point is to put in place a gradually unfolding network of figures suggestive of the 'atmospheric unity' of Romantic poetry (Brower 1951: 104). Repeated mention of clouds, tempests, strangeness and sea-changes prepares us for the closing narrative metamorphoses, the most telling being Prospero's final 'discasing' (V.i.85) and abjuration of magic. The same attention to textual detail had been shown in Brower's acknowledged model, *The Shakespearean Tempest* (Knight 1932), but here the full effect is less watertight. Brower may have faith in a 'total design', but Ovidian metamorphosis is not wholly reassuring: 'In a world where everywhere may become something else, doubts naturally arise, and in the swift flow of change the confusion about what is and what is not becomes fairly acute' (Brower 1951: 120). Is this still all carefully preordained, or is it actually, in the last analysis, oxymoronic to equate poetry with design?

In Frank Kermode's seminal account, in his Introduction to the Arden edition of 1954, the play is best put in its Renaissance context by stressing the contrast and strife between Art and Nature, Prospero and Caliban. The former exercises honourable self-discipline, the self-knowledge traditionally expected of the good ruler, whereas the latter exhibits all the unregenerate desperation of rude and unlettered savagery, which implicitly endorses the rights of centralized authority (Kermode 1957: esp. xlix–lix). Kermode shows an impatience with the proverbial tag for Shakespeare of 'natural poet' as it encourages a neglect of 'the conscious philosophical structure of his plays'. It is often forgotten that he clearly realizes that poetry is historical, and, instead of providing a 'commonplace' rendition of Art/Nature contrasts, he ends his account by a gesture towards the unique qualities of the play, 'beyond the last analysis of criticism' (Kermode 1957: lxxxviii). If ever one were put to find a prefiguration of what has come to be called (loosely) 'deconstruction', this would be a strong contender: that is, the perception that, in attempting to frame the meaning of writing, one cannot help entering that very frame and have the text conform to patterns that it always surpasses by an inevitable figurative excess. No matter how sophisticated the construction of our approaches, there is always a surplus of unaccountable signification that will challenge their universal validity; there will always be, for example, details, or 'supplements', to any identified 'core' meaning (what we can identify of an author's intention or the text's historical situation), that are so unsettling that they end up 'deconstructing' the authority of such readings, often designed to supply 'real', valid and exhaustive meaning.

The desire to account for the play's integrity is conventional critical wisdom, and yet *The Tempest* has recently proved a text particularly resistant to such cohesion. One of the difficulties in taking Prospero at his own estimate is Caliban and, less obviously, Ariel, both of whom have been released for the purposes of critical analysis from their master's rhetoric. Contemporary evidence has been sifted to provide a picture of early colonialism and Europe's encounters with new worlds (see below, pp. 45–6) that offer an image of Prospero less as a mage than as a governor-general, thereby rendering the island culture radically misunderstood and unjustly dismissed by what now come to be seen as his prejudices. As early as 1969, however, Harry Berger Jr was alive to the ironic possibilities in the delineation of Prospero's character. In admitting that one can trace a 'renunciation pattern', Berger does not at the same time find that it explains the play as a *drama*: 'There are too many cues and clues, too many quirky details, pointing in other directions, and critics have been able to make renunciation in this simple form the central action only by ignoring these details' (Berger 1969: 254). In posing several difficult and, as some would have to say, literal-minded questions, he inexorably exposes the enabling fictions on which the purification of Prospero (and his support) rests. To what extent is he responsible for his own usurpation? Was it not the case that Gonzalo must have played a part in Alonso's elevation to power? Does he now repent, or has he always acted in the best interests of the Milanese state, even when ridding it of an ineffective bookish recluse? Why is there a gap between Prospero's view of Caliban and an audience's? Why was Ariel bound in a tree in the first place? Why does the Epilogue give off so many contradictory signals? In seeking these answers we also discover a Prospero less secure in his call on the audience's approbation. Perhaps the Epilogue is merely a carefully staged detaining of the audience. Divorce the last couplet from the main body of the speech – 'As you from crimes would pardoned be,/Let your indulgence set me free' (V.i.338–9) – then Prospero is far less sunk in *anomie*; Berger (1969: 279) notes that it 'points the finger' rather than just requests an audience's sympathy, a prologue to a re-engagement with reality as much as evidence of a deathwish.[6]

This revision of the Epilogue as interpretable gesture rather than more or less coherent statement may stand for a wider reappraisal of the whole play. As John O'Toole has recently made clear, dramatic process presupposes a collective management of the text's fictional context. This is expressed according to a medium of exchange which comprises both a particular theatrical medium and the specific needs of an audience – its 'real context' (O'Toole 1992: 217; see also 14–25). No matter how much the play reaches out for romantic and utopian myths, these cannot be understood accurately without reference to the specific culture within which the acting space is located and the spectators find initial definition.

Prospero and a Jacobean *Tempest*

One of the most suggestive propositions about the early theatre history of the play is that it is likely that its audience was a courtly one. The Revels Accounts for 1611 mention it as a 'Hallowmas nyght' entertainment at Whitehall before 'the kinges Maiestie' and it figures in a list of fourteen Court performances as part of the festivities in 1613 immediately before James I's daughter, Elizabeth, married the Elector Palatine.[7] This promotes at least two related approaches to the play: first, one that perceives it as coded advice to all rulers (and so, specifically to James); and second, one that treats large passages as a parody or affectionate homage to courtly culture. On the other hand, as Orgel (1987: 2–4) – among others – has pointed out, the mere fact that it was performed at Court does not indicate that it was tailored for these occasions. In any case, the records just could not show the degree to which the Folio version might have been revised to suit such an event. According to John Dryden, in the Preface to *The Tempest, or the Enchanted Island* (1670; performed 1667), the play was certainly put on by the King's Men at the Blackfriars Theatre. Both considerations lead us to assume that Shakespeare was probably exploiting theatrical opportunities that were relatively new to him.

Ever since Bentley's (1948) trenchant reminder of the changed conditions for drama that obtained at the Blackfriars Theatre,[8] criticism has tended to regard the last phase of Shakespeare's writing career as given over to theatrical spectacle and thus to works where Romance elements could be given freer rein. Certainly, *The Winter's Tale*, *Cymbeline* and *Pericles* (probably written with George Wilkins), all incorporate episodes where complex effects (specialized lighting and flying machinery, to name two) are needed. Less obvious is the possibility that a Blackfriars audience would also be a more polite one. Back in 1584 John Lyly's boys' company put on *Campaspe* preceded by a Prologue that concluded by complimenting the taste and politeness found there exclusively: 'wishing that although there bee in your precise judgementes an universall mislike, yet wee maye enjoy by your woonted courtisies a general silence' (Lyly 1902, 2: 315). Lyly, however, perhaps refers here to a more exclusive clientele, in a private theatre, than probably frequented the refurbished Blackfriars of the Jacobean period. When Richard Burbage was planning to convert it to a 'comon playhouse' in 1596, the Privy Council received a petition from the inhabitants of Blackfriars, objecting to the change on several counts: it would bring the threat of plague, disturb the peace 'in tyme of devine service and sermons' and also bring the area into disrepute, instigating 'a very great annoyance and trouble ... to all the noblemen and gentlemen thereabout inhabiting' by attracting 'all manner of vagrant and lewde persons' (Chambers 1923, 4: 320). After a hiatus of four to five years Burbage finally succeeded in re-opening in 1600, again with a children's company, the Children of the Chapel Royal. The petitioners' fears seemed not to have been well founded. Such performances were definitely a cut above those produced on 'public' stages, although this second auditorium was still open to anyone who could afford the prices. Its superior reputation rested initially on its being (technically) a private house, and therefore not subject to City regulations (see Smith 1966: 175–85; Orgel 1975: 5–36).

Shakespeare was doubtless aware of this distinction. When Rosencrantz announces the Players to Hamlet, he portrays a company whose popularity is definitely on the slide, due in no small part to the rage for 'little eyases' who were beginning to infiltrate 'the common stages' (*Hamlet*, II.ii.315, 317).[9] Certainly, by 1616, it had become a place to view others and to be seen yourself. Fitzdotterel, the Norfolk squire, in Ben Jonson's *The Devil is an Ass*, can parade there before 'Ladies' (I.vi.37).[10] The acquisition of the site by the King's Men in 1609 fulfilled Burbage's original scheme of 1596: an adult acting company, using an indoor space, convenient for the law students and gallants that populated the Inns of Court area (see Gurr 1987: 164–9). Accordingly, prices increased sixfold over the Globe Theatre's minimum, while the capacity was just over 2000 less (at Irwin Smith's estimate, 516; see Smith 1966: 296–301). The King's Men, moreover, were in the process of dignifying the activity of acting. Not only did they enjoy royal patronage, after 1612 they were regularly chosen for the Christmas masques, a more formal understanding derived from occasional seasons at Court, for example, between 26 December 1607 and 7 February 1608, when they are on record as having performed there thirteen times (see Thomson 1983: 80). This is a far cry from what had been the recent view of theatre as an employer of vagabonds.[11]

This unpacking of the play's early stage history works by implication in matters of interpretation. What we discover is the distinct possibility that *The Tempest* did not have to be designed directly as a courtly entertainment to include in its address courtly issues. Masques, or at least close allusions to them, and masque interludes were part of the new conventions that the King's Men took over from the Children of the Chapel Royal, along with modest seating on the stage, act intermissions, greater opportunities for music and dancing in performance and the apparatus for flights across the stage. While there is an evident difference between actual Court occasions and non-courtly masques, allusions to the genre could imply, and generate comment upon, its often tacit cultural assumptions. The masque often rendered these apparent and *performed* them. John Turner (in this volume, pp. 122–3) reminds us that its power is not just political, as it taps and extends a deep recognition of myth. For Stephen Orgel, the whole illusionistic spectacle took in the audience as well, to make them 'living emblems of the aristocratic hierarchy' and the ensuing scenic vistas testified to 'royal liberality, exemplifying the princely virtue of magnificence'. Hence there arose a performative power in a masque, where the 'stage was not the setting for a drama, but was itself the action' (Orgel 1975: 36, 37). Strictly speaking, then, a masque was no drama, as, far from exploring contradiction and conflict, it rehearsed the foreknown, but rarely expressed, *copia* of regal power that, at the climactic moment, embraced with grace and magnanimity the watching Court. Kings crossed the allegorical line to become the heroes which their power indeed ensured, and the noble spectator ultimately became a participant in the courtly dance of dependence and differential privilege when he/she accepted the closing invitation to join the dance of masquers.[12]

Divorce this gesture from its precisely calculated context, and what ensues? Could it survive transplantation, even to an apparently sympathetic Blackfriars? An audience may not know just what its cultural touchstones might be or even care whether it can accommodate contradictions in its collective ideologies or its aesthetic preferences. Just as a courtly masque constructed its audience, first as wide-eyed spectators and then as 'willing' participators in a ritual of power and service, so drama can accomplish a similar feat, especially when it addresses an auditory that conceives of itself, in its collective responses, as a homogeneous mass (even if this, on closer inspection, elides important cultural differences). The model for this transaction is significantly different from the one-sided *monologic* discourses so prevalent in popular theatre criticism, where either we think we have discovered what the author intended and plot our course as an 'official' audience accordingly ('I know that I wasn't supposed to find Ariel sinister, but I did . . .') or, because we have mined a rich vein of contextual evidence about the regular Blackfriars clientele, we feel duty-bound to define some standardized 'world-picture' capable of passing through the particular theatrical experience relatively unscathed ('Londoners would have been principally impressed by Prospero as a magus and Caliban as a threatening savage, and would have responded accordingly'). These are exclusive positions, and doubtless help form certain common terms of debate, but they both oversimplify the work of rendering dramatic experience in a theatre, which thrives on a *dialogue* between expectation and realization, between the shared 'truth' which exists as a largely unexamined notion when we enter the playhouse and the process of reversal and test that is provoked by immediate theatrical power. In this there are no fixed points, just an always fluid sense, when analysed, of historical or cultural limits.

An example might be instructive here. One of the scenes that has always been regarded as both apparently significant and yet problematic is Prospero's theatrical 'trick', that 'vanity' of his art, that is 'Bestow[ed] upon the eyes' (IV.i.37, 40–1) of Ferdinand and Miranda. Prospero is thus out to impress the lovers, and, with a potent display of skill, even cow Ferdinand into a fearful regard for chastity before marriage, a no less 'holy rite' than the donation of his daughter (IV.i.17). This moral interest is in keeping with the aspirations of the Jonsonian masque, especially his *Hymenaei* (1606) and *The Golden Age Restored* (1615), which both present regal dominion over the seasons (see Orgel 1965: 103–7; Limon 1990: 78–9; and the remarks by David Norbrook in Lindley 1984: 97–9). Here the obviously staged action includes a span of spring (the 'flat meads thatched with stover' (winter provender) that characterize 'spongy April' (IV.i.63, 65)), summer (Ceres's celebration of 'Earth's increase, foison plenty,/Barns and garners never empty' (IV.i.110–11), and autumn (the labour of harvest-time suggested in Iris's address to the 'sunburned sickle-men, of August weary' (IV.i.134)). That the reassuring circle of the seasons is not completed is a significant detail, for, before the reapers and nymphs can complete their 'graceful dance' (s.d. IV.i.138), the outside world importunes Prospero when he remembers the 'foul conspiracy' against his life, 'Of the beast Caliban and his confederates' (IV.i.139–41). Winter is not contained within the artful frame and play is interrupted. The deeper mythical references to the redemption of Proserpine from the under-world, and the banishment of less welcome deities that attend a mature relationship (Venus and Cupid, found in Ovid's *Metamorphoses* V), are similarly suspended, and, as Howard Felperin summarizes (in this volume, pp. 57–8), there is a strong reading of this moment that traces the return of repressed colonial anxiety.

Is this a portrayal of Prospero's mastery? If we were to find in the sudden dispersal of his attendant spirits an invulnerable ease, then we might agree with Stephen Orgel's verdict that 'the masque's world is able to banish even winter' when Ceres summons a 'Spring' that would 'come to you at the farthest,/In the very end of harvest!' (IV.i.114–15). He continues:

> Appropriately, it is at this point that the magician interrupts his creation to recall himself and the play to the other realities of the world of action . . . Prospero's awareness of time comprehends both masque and drama, both the seasonal cycle of endless fruition and the crisis of the dramatic moment. This awareness is both his art and his power, producing on the one hand his sense of his world as an insubstantial pageant, and on the other, his total command of the action moment by moment.
>
> (Orgel 1975: 46–7)

In a pageant that Prospero does *not* construct, however, we see exactly just how he could have lost his dukedom to Alonso, for here is also represented that neglect of 'worldly ends' (I.ii.89) and immersion in the pursuit of the 'liberal arts' (I.ii.73), a vignette that lies outside the world cranked into place by the masque's elaborate stage machinery, and of which Prospero is no longer the complacent artificer. Stephano, Trinculo and Caliban *do* have an effect on this palace of art; well may Ferdinand be impressed with this spectacle as a 'most majestic vision' and 'harmonious charmingly' at lines 118–19, but by lines 143–4 he is more impressed by Prospero's 'strange' behaviour and his 'passion/That works him strongly' when he dismisses the vision. From 'graceful' measures, the dancing that supplies that seamless passage from the masque's *hubris* to the self-fulfilling participation of actors and audience, degenerates, according to the Folio stage direction, with 'a strange hollow and confused noise' into a most unwilling exit (as they 'heavily vanish') (s.d. IV.i.138). The audience, as well as Ferdinand and Miranda, do not participate and Prospero becomes the direct object of our gaze and involved in our 'real' and wider considerations of the dues Art has to pay to Life.

In contrast to Orgel's understanding that order is rescued within the dramatic action of the play, we might place Howard Felperin's appreciation of Prospero's plight, caught in an 'endless and dizzying dialectic between self-mystification and self-demystification, to which no stable synthesis seems possible', which is very much part of the work of displacement from the 'ritually sanctioned forms of romance' to a less framed 'theatrical self-consciousness' ('Romance and romanticism: Some reflections on *The Tempest* and *The Heart of Darkness*', in Kay and Jacobs 1978: 68). The stress may perhaps fall here on *less* framed, for this dissipation of Prospero's rhetorical calculation promotes the sober self-analysis of his much anthologized (and often isolated) speech of consolation, initially to Ferdinand, but possibly as much to himself (IV.i.146–63). Here Prospero notes the end of 'revels' (technically the masque's closing dance that consolidates courtly self-images) and the dissolution of the 'cloud-capped towers' that are the stuff specifically of masque illusion. This stage-play world is thus renounced before Prospero's Epilogue, faded to an 'insubstantial pageant' (IV.i.148–56). Minus this sustaining project, now almost come to fruition, Prospero talks of 'infirmity', 'weakness' and a 'troubled' brain (IV.i.160, 159).

It is debatable whether Shakespeare's allusions to or use of masque features ever resolve narrative complications. When the masque of Hymen comes to 'bar confusion' in the last scene of his *As You Like It* (*c.* 1600) (V.iv.120), it appears to close the action of the main plot (with the dance and Rosalind's epilogue to follow). Suddenly 'earthly things . . ./Atone together' (V.iv.104–5), and it is specifically *Hymen* who 'must make conclusion/Of these most strange events' – but with a significant rider: 'If truth holds true contents' (V.iv.121–2, 125). The ordered verbal patterns that Hymen instigates certainly banish Touchstone's tortuous (and prosaic) sub-courtly wit that has held the stage too long from line 38, but the more we dwell on its dramatic positioning and effect the more the *use* of the courtly format is no simple endorsement of a 'civilizing' alternative. The Duke Senior is hardly the centrepiece of the masque action; indeed, it is unlikely that, without this *deus ex machina* (or, if one doubts Hymen's transcendent status, Rosalind's ingenuity), such order would have been ordained by courtly authority. In the 'wedlock hymn' in praise of Juno, Hymen 'peoples' and is 'god' of 'every *town*' (V. iv. 138, 141; emphasis added). The Duke Senior ushers in the closing festivity with a plea that the dancers 'forget this new-fallen dignity' (the sudden Romance conversion of Duke Frederick who has bequeathed the crown to his brother) and that they 'fall into our rustic revelry' (V.iv.171–2). Here is no courtly conclusion, especially when you consider Jacques's parody of the ritual acceptance of Hymen's influence (V.iv.111–19, cf. 181–8). The closing dance cannot embrace Jacques, who does not stay to see such 'pastime' (V.iv.190). Like the suddenly religious Duke Frederick, Jacques stays to learn and partake of the retired life that the courtiers-in-exile now rush to relinquish.

When a masque forms part of and functions within a larger narrative unit, its metaphysical claims are often destined to be questioned. Absolute power cannot be framed. Where a masque audience is encouraged to comment on the masque action, as Will Summers does, the presenter of Thomas Nashe's *Summer's Last Will and Testament* (1592–3), this is often merely the prelude to his being taken over by empathic power. Where once he scoffed, he proceeds to sympathize and excuse. As Martin Butler notes, under these circumstances, 'it was the occasion that shaped the play . . . and the show was not so much a performance as an event' ('Private and occasional drama' in Braunmuller and Hattaway 1990: 128). The process of presenting before a more public eye a form originally designed for private show opens its images and symbols up to less predictable and shared assumptions. To some extent, the masque could anticipate objections. For example, often in Jonson's hands, perhaps commencing with his greatly influential *Masque of Queens* (1609), the convention of the 'antemasque' (prefatory material) was extended to portray potentially anarchic or doubtful forces throughout the main action that the royal effulgence had to eclipse, an 'antimasque'. In his *Love Restored* (1612), one of the antimasquers is a puritan who voices widespread concern about the masque's conspicuous consumption; in *Oberon* (1611) its humorous and ribald satyrs learn not to disturb the Fairy King's progress, yet they are still present when he achieves his closing apotheosis. In his *The Somerset Masque* (1613), Thomas Campion even introduced an antimasque after the masque proper. The force, then, of *The Tempest*'s allusions to the courtly masque is not immediately clear. Extension and variation need not entail parody and distance.

In a very important sense our view of Prospero is structured by just how an audience is encouraged to regard his power and his right to it. If the masque is indeed a 'vanity' and a 'trick' then, as he fears at IV.i.127, the spell will indeed be 'marred' not just for the young lovers but as a wider trope that the whole drama promotes because our willing suspension of disbelief as an audience will be affected, and yet Prospero does maintain to Ferdinand that the vision includes actual 'spirits' which have been called from their 'confines ... to enact/[His] present fancies' (IV.i.120-2), one of whose number is certainly Ariel who confesses later to his 'commander' that he 'presented' the part of Ceres (IV.i.167). Doubtless, the magic summoned by culling spirits on to the stage seems potent enough, and yet Shakespeare cannot refrain from advancing the proposition that they are directed by art and showing us how linked such raising of shapes can be to staged illusionism. When we are asked to place this masque material historically and so come to understand its conventions, we may bear in mind the fact that an 'antimasque' need not detract from the ingenuities of the masque proper, as if theatrical representation were an equation that should balance out. If this is accepted, Ariel's portrayal of the Harpy with attendant shapes at III.iii.52-82 (or, throughout, the unholy trio of Caliban, Stephano and Trinculo) might be just a well-judged reminder of the anarchy that the prudent ruler has to overcome.

The doubt remains, however, as to whether Prospero actually resolves much outside the restitution of his own temporal power. No penance is won from Antonio; the stage is not filled with final visual images of continuity, acceptance and a society newly empowered – just Prospero in an Epilogue, with 'faint' strength and 'charms ... o'erthrown' (V.i.319-21). Here is no affirmation after climactic dramatic action that so marks *Cymbeline* or *The Winter's Tale*.[13] To take the post-Romantic line, we see here *ecce homo*, unaccommodated man, and a Shakespeare bidding farewell to the stage.[14] This is at best a partial reading. For W.H. Auden, narrating Antonio's closing antiphonal verdict in his *The Sea and the Mirror* (1945), Prospero's 'all is partial' and cannot touch Antonio's will, who remains 'by choice [himself] alone' (Auden 1968: 212). When Stephen Mullaney compares Prospero's closing confession to the Duke's similar equivocal gesture in *Measure for Measure*, he concludes that he is driven to 'license what he cannot control, in a magnanimous gesture meant to turn the manifest embodiment of his own limits into a display of his power to issue such a license' (Mullaney 1988: 115). Power is here not absolute.

It is surely not a contingent factor that the early staging of this representation of power and its relation to strenuously acquired magic rather than innate quality reached both a courtly audience and one that was a self-consciously 'modern' one, placed in a twilight zone between 'public' access and exclusive 'private' identity. From this perspective, there is very much more to be said about the characterization of Prospero than that it appears to be Shakespeare in confessional mode or even an autonomous three-dimensional creation, more an object of disinterested contemplation than an aspect of directed comment on the assumptions of an audience. In Bakhtin's terms, the 'dialogic' takes into account (here, possibly in Voloshinov's wording[15]) a 'territory *shared* by both addresser and addressee, by the speaker and his interlocutor' (Voloshinov 1973: 86), and hence a series of speech acts that are never completely finished and delivered entities. Prospero may advance a plea that he is detained from Milan by the 'spell' of the audience (V.i.326), and that their applause will signal his own return to the dystopia of rule and responsibility, but what might the delivery of such power signify *as part of a dialogue* (then as now)? Primarily, it stages a surrender of what had seemed up until then as unassailable dominion. Without an awakened faith in the objects of its mastery, authority is a failed 'spell', yet the net dramatic effect of this coda is not free of a rhetorical design. As Joseph Westlund makes clear, Prospero must 'prosper' in his aims, 'for they establish, or so he apparently hopes, his sense of greatness and worth'. That which needs shoring up or parading cannot go without saying. Here we are given the chance to 'bestow on Prospero the compassion which he so parsimoniously offered to others . . . As father, ruler, and magician Prospero remains unneedy, distant, and superior' ('Omnipotence and reparation in Prospero's Epilogue', in Layton and Schapiro 1986: 72) – and, we may add, isolated. Can we divorce this closing appeal from his other designs, in order to grant freely the common consent that applause conventionally entails?

To return to what may be most historically specific about this moment: it has become clear in most recent research on Jacobean debates about the nature of authority that James's declaration of a free monarchy, based on absolutist principles, did not go unchallenged.[16] In his *The Trew Law of Free Monarchies* (1598), republished to herald his English reign, James found himself the sole recipient of divine favour, and yet in the midst of an orthodox absolutist apology for his right to rule, he takes upon himself a different persona, that of benevolent father: 'And as the Father by his fatherly duty is bound to care for the nourishing, education and uertuous gouernment of his children; euen so is the king bound to care for all his subjects' (McIlwain 1918: 55). Jerzy Limon, among others, has found that James was particular about his own roles in masques and elsewhere, almost to the point where an assumed image usurped a deeper sense of historical and cultural reality. The mask came to fit (see Limon 1990: 44–5, 85–6, 99–100; Tennenhouse 1986: 147–86). Whatever the rhetoric, it is also evident that James could not be financially self-sufficient without the will of the Commons. In his address to Parliament on 21 March 1610, his attempt at persuasion brought forth not only the claim that 'Kings are . . . GODS Lieutenants vpon earth, and sit vpon GODS throne' (that is, they are virtual gods themselves), but also (the more acceptable face of this patriarchy), that they may be compared to 'Fathers of families: for a King is trewly *Parens Patriae*' (McIlwain 1918: 305). The impact of this appeal may be judged by simply reflecting upon the currency in late Elizabethan political theory of the justification of power in its derivation from the people. Tracts such as *De Presbyterio* (1591) by Matthew Sutcliffe, Dean of Exeter, explicitly traced such regal largess from an act of transference by the people, and in Richard Hooker's eighth book of his seminal *Of the Laws of Ecclesiastical Polity* (written 1591–93; Book VIII pub. 1648), the independence of choice that marks out a political class is truly free:

> First unto me it seemeth almost out of doubt and controversy that every independent multitude before any certain form of regiment established hath under *God's* supreme authority full dominion over itself . . . That the *Christian* world should be ordered by kingly regiment the law of *God* doth not anywhere command. And yet the law of God doth give them right which once are exalted to that estate, to exact at the hands of their Subjects general obedience in whatsoever affairs their power may serve to command. So God doth ratify the works of that Sovereign authority which *Kings* have received by men.
>
> (Hooker 1989: 141–2)

It is perhaps no surprise that how kings gain such divine sanction (along with the obedience of their subjects) is not in the nature of things; it comes *de facto* rather than *de iure*, rather like Prospero's dominion on 'his' island. This may have been known only by repute, and James's position may have been outlined by both the Convocations of York and Canterbury in 1606, but the debate common to both natural law theorists (that *public* welfare should be the proper task of the commonwealth) and loyal divine righters (that it was in the public interest for power to be concentrated in the Court) centred on just what a 'commonwealth' and the 'public' might be: spectators or providers of the divine right to authority? (See Sommerville 1986: esp. 9–39, 57–85; Eccleshall 1978: 30–46, 97–125; Underdown 1985: 1–43.)

There is no more marked witness to the rift between required performance and personal belief than in the career of Ben Jonson. The Court admired the part-creator and impresario of masque entertainment. A passing acquaintance with his poetry would provide us with a fuller picture. When admiring the Sidney estate at Penshurst, he commends the fact that it was not built for 'envious show,/... nor canst boast a row/Of polished pillars, or a roof of gold' ('To Penshurst' (1611–12; pub. 1616), ll. 1–3). Instead, it provides 'better marks, of soil, of air,/Of wood, of water: ...' (7–8). When addressing John Selden in the 'Epistle' (1614), he notes with relief that he knows exactly whom he is addressing:

> I know to whom I write. Here, I am sure,
> Though I am short, I cannot be obscure:
> Less shall I for the art or dressing care;
> Truth, and the Graces, best when naked are.
>
> (ll. 1–4)

Here there seems no pretext for the address. In the past, Jonson may have erred in praising 'some names too much', but that was 'with purpose to have made them such' (ll. 21–2). This performative rhetorical action is an integral ingredient of the masque, and the resonance of this sentiment is louder once one remembers that the addressee, Selden, was a staunch advocate of limited monarchy, and who in his *Titles of Honor* (1614), drew a clear distinction between the 'Oeconomique rule' necessary over the family circle, and that over the 'common state'. This led him to depict the origins of monarchical privilege as an outcrop of some measure of political maturity: where the family developed into the 'Popular state'. Power placed in one person, the king, was thus not an original state of political organization, for one had to presuppose 'a Democracie, out of which . . . a Monarchie might have originall' (Selden 1614: 2–3).[17]

There might now be some unease at this line of interpretation. Jonson is not Shakespeare, but then we have little direct evidence as to how and on what bases we are to draw clear lines of cultural difference between them. To dwell too exclusively on matters of conscious intention, what Shakespeare 'must have' meant, is to pursue an unduly 'monologic' course which might eventually reduce the text to a form of more or less covert polemic, where its signs point just one way. For Bakhtin, a 'dialogue' does not involve a resolution or even a synthesis of the voices that any specific historical moment holds in suspension. A writer can signify far more than we can ascribe to an original individual opinion, as his/her work passes into the public domain, indeed, is often *designed* with this in view. Furthermore, what if the sum of those very intentions that traditionally make up personality is composed of unconscious drives, radically opposed discourses or responses that cannot quite be defined apart from the symbols in which we now encounter them, where the 'official' and 'unofficial' are near neighbours? For Raymond Williams (1977: 113), adopting Voloshinov's linguistic perspectives, enquiries into the politics of writing do not stand or fall on the identification of doctrine:

> The reality of any hegemony . . . is that, while by definition it is always dominant, it is never either total or exclusive. At any time, forms of alternative or directly oppositional politics and culture exist as significant elements in the society . . . their active presence is decisive, not only because they have to be included in any historical . . . analysis, but as forms which have had significant impact on the hegemonic process itself.

Consequently, 'individuality' can be understood as a 'social capacity', a necessary and inevitable 'means of realization' that takes into account 'the fully social fact of language (whether as "outer" or "inner" speech)': 'Consciousness, in this precise sense, is social being' (Williams 1977: 41–2).

In practice, both Bakhtin and Williams/Voloshinov refuse to deduce a separable 'inner intention' that can be clearly divined from 'outer' language. It might very well have been the case that Jonson wanted to address Selden in a purely personal capacity, to avoid his 'public' political image, yet, however intimate the discourse may appear, the poem's appearance in the *Underwoods* collection shows Jonson interested in its preservation for a reading public's understanding.[18] Similarly, one could claim that the praise of Penshurst is purely conventional, a playful pastoral exercise, yet such play gestures to a family and seat that have 'public' significance, knowledge of which relates Jonson's desire to portray them as an organic community to a much wider spectrum of cultural alternatives and possible readers that no amount of close quotation or analysis of the text would provide.[19] It is no doubt quite likely that the distrust of courtly corruption that could be picked out from certain of Shakespeare's sonnets has a conventional aspect, yet the care taken with the 1609 edition's text of the *Sonnets* and *A Lover's Complaint* testifies to a determination to have them take on a 'public' role. Hence it is that, say, the terms in which the transience of human affections is figured in Sonnet 64 may simply summon an indistinct sense of apparently impregnable material well-being doomed to eventual decay:

> When I have seen by Time's fell hand defaced
> The rich proud cost of outworn buried age,
> When sometime lofty towers I see down-razed,
> And brass eternal slave to mortal rage;

(ll. 1–4)

There is nothing to prevent our concluding, on the other hand, that the references to luxury, those 'lofty [or cloud-capped?] towers' with their 'rich proud cost', do not only function as signifiers (the rhetorical means to signify something else) but *at the same time* as specific signified material in their own right. For Bakhtin, all textual references to reality are inescapably virtual ones, deflected from direct mimesis by the infinite capacity of readers to 'misread' and for writers to express more than they can intend.

The Staging of Power and Its Subjects

Prospero's power is perhaps designed not to stand up well to close scrutiny. In this, the play moves between his cell and larger spaces of responsibility and authority, that take in part-references to James, early colonialism, the responsibilities of the artist and the role of fathers, to name only the most prominent. It is nearly always depicted as power exerted to some end, and, when that end is in sight, 'virtue' supplants 'vengeance', 'nobler reason' resists 'fury' (V.i.26–8) and his eyes, on renewing acquaintance with Gonzalo, 'ev'n sociable to the show of thine,/Fall fellowly drops' (V.i.63–4). Virtue, reason and fellowship are a dream ticket, in every sense. In Richard Wheeler's formulation (this volume, p. 155), however, this embrace of a 'vantage point in which action no longer matters' is as much a defensive as a 'rational' gesture. Prospero treads foreign ground as a consequence of the very stratagem that was at first designed merely to bring about a counter-reformation. In Kermode's (1957: li) terms, he 'expresses the qualities of the world of Art, of the *non vile*', and so achieves a marriage in his own life of the 'active and contemplative lives'. How altruistic is he? In the Introduction to his 1987 edition, (1987: 54–6) Orgel gives a detailed account of what will in fact be the result of Miranda's marriage to Ferdinand, the son of his enemy. On his death, Milan will be engrossed by Naples, Antonio forever banished from ducal power and the responsibility for Miranda's future discharged. He concludes that 'giving away Miranda is as much a means of preserving Prospero's authority as of relinquishing it' (Orgel 1987: 55). He is still the narcissist in the closing humility, and, when we applaud, we now do so because he has loaded that conventional gesture with his own meaning.

Exploring the varied nature of how *The Tempest* offers a dialogue with an audience entails an account of how ambiguous our responses to Prospero's absolutism and/or closing abasement might be. Not all allusions are functional ones in this encounter, yet even without recourse to the enchantress Medea's speech in Ovid's *Metamorphoses* (vii, 197–209) as a source for Prospero's renunciation of magic at V.i.33–57, we may find the exact identity of the forsworn 'rough magic' (V.i.50) ill-defined. The critical literature on this passage, although profuse, tends to divide into just three emphases: first, that Prospero is the mage having to renounce magic in order to reassume his stately role (the fall on an audience's capacity for prayer that might '[assault]/Mercy itself' (V.i.335–6) is part of a final movement in the whole play towards an orthodoxy of belief); second, the action displays his power as black as well as white magic (Medea's accents hover uneasily over these closing passages to remind us of Sycorax's sorcery); and last, passages from Golding's translation of Ovid's *Metamorphoses* (1565–7) were adopted simply for their formal qualities (we should not therefore import too much of our knowledge of the source text into our appreciation of the speech's dramatic power). If our approach to the text takes account of Bakhtin's perception that elements of *intertextuality* are inescapably traced in all expression, then, instead of the image of the controlling artistic hand, deftly shaping language to just the correct 'inner' specifications, we might consider how the inevitable encounter with a 'fully social' language tends to provide a medium of expression shot through with hybridity and potential irony. In short, it was (and still is) entirely possible for an audience to find that they respond in all three of the above ways *simultaneously*, admiring the poetry while noting the mix of danger and conformity in the theatrical gesture that it helps compose.

For those literate enough to trace Ovid's Medea in Prospero's lines, the parallel is hard to mould into a concerted or well-executed trope. Prospero's 'rough magic' has always apparently been attended by 'heavenly music' (V.i.52), and this conjuration has to be distinct from the malevolent spells (as he often tells us) of Sycorax. What he has attempted, however, has been of dubious provenance, for there is an admixture of paganism in this righting of wrongs. One thinks of the shoreline 'elves' chasing 'the ebbing Neptune', post-curfew spirits raised from their graves 'at [his] command', and thunder deployed to rive 'Jove's stout oak/With his own bolt' (V.i.33–5, 48, 45–6). Does the end justify questionable means? Or rather, is it at all possible to arrive at honourable conclusions by totally honourable procedures? There is also a certain generic indeterminacy about the speech: is it a soliloquy or part of a formal ritual of renunciation? The stage direction at V.i.57 indicates that the courtiers who enter at that point 'stand charmed' in a 'circle which Prospero had made' – but when? John Dover Wilson's additional direction at V.i.32 (in his 1921 edition) has Prospero trace 'a magic circle on the stage with his staff' at Ariel's exit, and this may account for the sudden patterning of speech thereafter, but it would be just as viable to count the lines as part of the newly confessional Prospero (compare this with the sonority of the farewell to 'revels' at IV.i.148–63).

It is tempting to find Sycorax within the allusive weave of these lines. As de Grazia (1981) has discovered, Prospero's precursor on the island is not always safely absent. Indeed, she infiltrates Prospero's act of closure, as he is reminded of her when confronting Caliban for the last time:

> This misshapen knave,
> His mother was a witch, and one so strong
> That could control the moon, make flows and ebbs,
> And deal in her command without her power.

> (V.i.268–71)

The verbal echo of Medea/Prospero's 'ebbing Neptune' and the 'moonshine', wherein 'midnight mushrooms' appear (V.i.35, 37, 39), may appear unexpected and perhaps unwelcome, but it merely follows the allusions and close tracing of Medea already embedded in the abjuration. The passage most consulted by Shakespeare at this point is uttered by Medea at Iolcos as she invokes the help of Hecate and night in her attempts to rejuvenate Jason's father, Aeson, by bathing him in a magic herbal broth (Ovid 1961: 141–2 (ll. 244–86)). Niece to Circe, she is a type of female enchantress that is immediately distracting to male pioneers – and potentially threatening, too. In Euripides' tragedy (431 BC) Jason's quest takes them to Corinth. By that time, she has already murdered Jason's uncle, Pelias; and at Corinth, in a sexual rage, to deny Jason, she adds the deaths of King Creon and his daughter, plus those of her own children. This is largely the theme of Seneca's tragedy of Medea (c. AD 62–3), which, perhaps coincidentally for Shakespeare's (or Gonzalo's) purposes, contains a prophetic vision of the discovery of new worlds beyond *ultima Thule* (l. 379).[20] Sycorax commands, it should be noted, without her own magic powers, suggesting the help of outside agents, probably diabolical ones.

The more detailed the review, the less we may be convinced that the patriarchal hold Prospero has on his island community is omnipotent. This is perhaps most revealing in his dealings with his daughter, who, after all, is being primed for an arranged marriage, and who, in principle, is just as subjected as is, say, Hermia by Egeus at the start of *A Midsummer Night's Dream* (I.i.22–127). In his relation to Miranda of their landfall on the island, Prospero ascribes the marvellous to 'providence divine' (I.ii.159), as does Ferdinand later in the play (V.i.189). Learning may do much, but the opportunity to wield magical sway over Alonso's court he puts down to 'accident most strange, bountiful Fortune' (I.ii.178), and, although his 'prescience' (I.ii.180) is a necessary ingredient, this only informs him that his

> zenith doth depend upon
> A most auspicious star, whose influence
> If now [he] court[s] not, but omit[s], [his] fortunes
> Will ever after droop.
>
> (I.ii.180–4)

The moment is an auspicious and a critical one – all the more so when one realizes that Prospero, though immensely learned and in control within his limited island space, may perceive limits to such authority. When he then proceeds to relate his tale to Miranda, we may wonder just why the scene proceeds as a communication to another of the *dramatis personae*, within the framework of the dramatic action, and not by direct address, by soliloquy. The pragmatic answer would be to point out how much necessary exposition is here staged; we see their own particular form of affiliation, and learn of Miranda's innocence. On the other hand, there are hints of a lack of complete dependence or rule.

The information Prospero here imparts informs Miranda about her public self ('my daughter, who/Art ignorant of what thou art; . . .' (I.ii.17–18)). As an instinctive being, her immediate compassion for any victims of the tempest delineates her natural self. To Prospero's surprise, she does indeed remember a time before their exile, when she had women, and not Prospero, to attend her (I.ii.46–7). He also feels the need to check whether she is listening with the right degree of attention ('Dost thou attend me?' (I.ii.78), 'thou attend'st not!' (87), 'Dost thou hear?' (106)), as well as enforce his role as 'schoolmaster' (172). When she seems to fall asleep quite naturally, Prospero reminds us that she cannot choose to do otherwise (186). Miranda starts the play as much manipulated by his art as the opening storm. When confronted by Caliban, however, she shows a vituperative side to her character that has caused many a director and adaptor/editor (Dryden, for example) to reassign the lines to Prospero (350–2). Furthermore, she is not above a measure of disobedience, as she defends Ferdinand to her father (458–60, 467–9) and goes against explicit instructions not to speak with him (III.i.36–7, 57–9).

The difference the inclusion of a wife for Prospero would have made is radical – enough to summon up the image of a totally different play. Such an absence places full power and its isolating obligations on the father-figure.[21] Do we see evidence of Prospero stooping to enjoy the 'fresh springs, brine pits, barren place and fertile' that make up Caliban's island (I.ii.338)? Or a display of a fully rounded 'tender' and 'human' individual, the 'natural' image that Ariel instructs his master to recognize (V.i.17–24) – a recognition no less telling than that forced on him when he is brought to acknowledge Caliban's 'darkness' as his own (V.i.275–6)? For Adelman (1992: 237–8), there is a dark underside to this assumption of power, a compulsion to wield authority over 'the maternal body of nature' that is as much a force for 'good' as the means by which Prospero, recently emerged from the study, defines himself. Caliban, by being returned to the 'body' of his island at the close of the play, becomes estranged from his natural self. Having learned the pigeon-holes provided by language, he can only now divide his experience up and file it. He is left with dreams that only cause him to cry upon awakening (III.ii.133–41). When Stephano foresees a 'brave kingdom', where he will have the delight of its music 'for nothing', Caliban immediately warns him that this can only come about 'when Prospero is destroyed' (III.ii.142–4). The value of such experiences cannot be priced. If a Romance is the embodiment of wishes vicariously fulfilled, Prospero's Epilogue is its radical alternative: the display of a death that attends such fruition.

CHAPTER 1

Political Criticism at the Crossroads: The Utopian Historicism of *The Tempest*

HOWARD FELPERIN

[Howard Felperin's reading of *The Tempest* draws on the Hegelian Marxist positions offered by Fredric Jameson's *The Political Unconscious* (1981). Marxist theories of literature are varied in detail but stem more or less directly from the view that, while art may seem to be produced just by individuals, we might learn much more about their work if we identify (a) the artist's 'ideology', that is, not a set of codified beliefs, but rather an unphilosophical reflection of how individuals see their roles in class society and the values, symbols and ideas that help explain that role to such individuals and which therefore ties them all the more securely to their inherited context; and (b) the basic conditions under which such art can be produced (for example, conditions of patronage, growth of the mass market, availability of new technologies of production) which establish inexorable limits to the apparent freedoms of artistic activity.

Marx's (and Engels's) terms still provide the original inspiration for Marxist interpretation. In Marx and Engels's *The German Ideology* (1845–6) the 'production of ideas, of conceptions, of consciousness is at first directly inter-woven with the material activity and the material intercourse of men'. Thus, thought is the 'direct efflux' of this 'material behaviour', and individuals must be brought to realize that they, in fact, have a hand in the production of their own conceptions, 'real, active men, as they are conditioned by a definite development of their productive forces'. The conclusion is inescapable that 'life is not determined by consciousness, but consciousness by life' (Marx and Engels 1959: 287–8). This is given more specific focus in the Preface to *A Contribution to the Critique of Political Economy* (1859), where it is held as a condition of the 'social production' of one's own life that one enters 'into definite relations that are indispensable and independent of [one's] will, *relations of production* which correspond to a definite stage of development of [one's] material productive *forces'*. This forms 'the economic structure of society, the real foundation, on which rises a legal and political superstructure and to which correspond definite forms of social consciousness' (Marx and Engels 1959: 84). This model seems particularly deterministic, and most recent Marxist analysis regards this 'base–superstructure' divide as a preliminary move, one which, if carried through without extra sophistication, reduces all art to its modes of production, a position that makes it particularly difficult to account for individual variations.

The 'definite forms of social consciousness' group themselves in analysis as *ideology*. In order to render such awareness as narrow and partisan (that is, stemming from a class identity, not 'nature' or 'common sense'), there is a need to compare it with some greater entity or notion that proceeds from a more 'scientific' grasp of the total system of social relationships. 'Ideology' was often, then, equated with 'false consciousness'. More recently, 'ideology' has come to be associated with *all* forms of social perception, without which we could not function as members of society. In the work of Louis Althusser the role assigned to art is a major one, for he claims that it is only through the depiction of a process of thought in literary form that the work of ideology can be inspected with sufficient detachment. In his essay 'Ideology and ideological state apparatuses' (1969), Althusser finds ideology integral to *all* thought processes. It supplies a focus for definitions, even if actually based on biased premises. The state apparatuses (Church, political party, university and the legal system) 'interpellate' us (encourage us to believe) that we are free individuals, and therein lies their attraction and power (see Althusser 1971: 123–73).

This tendency to differentiate literary from non-literary expression is obviously fraught with the difficulty of defining just what the 'literary' might be, and Felperin here illustrates the apparent divide that opens up between formalist and materialist criticism, between investigations of how literary form might structure response across historical boundaries and the conviction that attempts at transcendence can always be related to a specific historical moment. Without some notion of just how aesthetic form refracts history, it is entirely possible that Marxist criticism would become reductive.

Jameson's great popularity stems from his ability to accommodate the private with the public sphere of analysis, the formal and the historical. He takes seriously the influential codification of recurrent myths and archetypes that Northrop Frye undertook in 1957 in *The Anatomy of Criticism*. This project to add discipline to literary study ran in the face of the prevailing critical orthodoxy (loosely termed 'New Criticism') that regarded texts as best analysed as separate and self-sufficient units. On the contrary, literature was not 'a simple aggregate of discrete works but a conceptual space which can be coherently organized'. Consequently, literary texts were not merely bags 'stuffed [with] a specific number of beauties or effects' which it was the duty of the critic to unpack one by one (Frye 1957: 16, 17–18). The net effect of Frye's syntheses, however, was ultimately to direct critical attention back on to the individual response and away from historical process, that is, how cultural forces, directly, or indirectly, subject to historical changes, alter and sometimes actually reconstitute these pervasive types of narrative or satisfactions of desire.

A critical engagement with Frye's ideas, however, has a salutary result. For Jameson it is necessary that history is not merely 'context' or 'background', but rather something far less unitary; it is perceived in 'ideologies' and several alternative points of access for the researcher. Hegel argued in his *Philosophy of Fine Art* (1835) that there was a very gradual unfolding in particular events of a history which was seen as stages in the development of a 'world-spirit' or an 'idea' or 'absolute', an idealist concept which pointed towards a time (post-capitalist) when form and content might eventually form a harmonious unity. In the work of Georg Lukács and Lucien Goldmann there is an attempt to breathe new life into this perspective, by regarding art as the production of a whole social group whose 'trans-individual mental structures' (Goldmann's term, indicating the group's aspirations and how it makes sense of them) are transposed by the most valuable artists into eventually unified and recurrent structures. For Goldmann, in studies such as *The Hidden God* (1964), structural relations are sought between the literary text, the 'world-view' of the artist's social grouping and its particular historical situation. The tendency is towards an achieved totality of view that can take in something wider than history is more traditionally taken to be. Jameson (1981: 50–7) emphasizes this concept of the 'totality' as a standard of judgement, not as a predicted future state. Ideology confirms a constricted horizon by 'strategies of containment' where limits to reference created by mimetic means (for example, Prospero's island and the restricted range of its population) enforce an unnecessary frontier to discourse in the interests of 'coherence' or just simply intelligibility. Reading texts as 'symbolic acts' entails 'the will ... [to] grasp them as resolutions of determinate contradictions'. Interpretation becomes a rewriting of the rhetorical text 'in such a way that the latter may itself be seen as the rewriting or restructuration of a prior historical or ideological *subtext*' which is only ever available by self-conscious analytical (re)construction (Jameson 1981: 80–1).

In short, texts never 'tell' us their history; they must be made to do this, and this involves breaking out of what Jameson (1972: 195–216) called the 'prison-house of language' and re-engaging with a history which contains several coexistent 'histories' and competing ideologies – see his 'Marxism and Historicism' (1979) in Jameson (1988, 2: 148–77). To place the text within the 'totality' is thus also to express what it cannot. *The Tempest*'s romance structure cannot ensure an evasion of history.]

NIGEL WOOD

> *Constant revolutionising of production, uninterrupted disturbance of all social conditions, everlasting uncertainty and agitation distinguish the bourgeois epoch from all earlier ones. All fixed, fast-frozen relations, with their train of ancient and venerable prejudices and opinions, are swept away, all new-formed ones become antiquated before they can ossify. All that is solid melts into air, all that is holy is profaned, and man is at last compelled to face with sober senses his real conditions of life, and his relations with his kind.*
>
> (Karl Marx, *Manifesto of the Communist Party* (1848)
> (Mark and Engels (1959: 52))

Theory: 'The Political Unconscious'

Every product of culture must, as something *made*, be the outcome of a process and thereby have a history. Moreover, as a product made to serve a purpose within its culture, it must also have a place within some larger, more comprehensive history, if only that of its particular culture. This should be as true of works of art and literature as it is of more obviously material or utilitarian products of culture such as sailing ships or the British East India Company that once commissioned and employed them. Yet the historical dimension of art and literature has not proved easy to situate and specify to the satisfaction even of those engaged in the attempt, and even to the point where some have questioned whether the very enterprise of a historical criticism or a literary history is possible at all, and not a contradiction in terms. This debate has emerged once again in recent years under the prompting of a 'new historicism' in literary studies, and Shakespeare's *The Tempest* has come to occupy, for reasons we shall go into, the very centre of contention.

The special difficulties of historicizing works of literature doubtless have to do with the difficulties of historicizing in general – so much of the enterprise hinges on what is by its very nature lost, unavailable, or speculative – but they also have to do with the particular qualities of works of literature. For the best of these the classic or canonical texts whose historical dimension remains, by virtue of their cultural centrality, of greatest interest to us, seem to inhabit a kind of eternal present – as the grammatical tense in which we discuss their characters and actions attests – despite the obvious marks of cultural difference and historical distance they undeniably bear. As one modern critic writes:

We read the *Iliad* or the plays of Sophocles or Shakespeare, and they come so close to our hearts and minds that they put to rout, or into abeyance, our instructed consciousness of the moral life as it is conditioned by a particular culture – they persuade us that human nature never varies, that the moral life is unitary and its terms perennial, and that only a busy intruding pedantry could ever have suggested otherwise.

(Trilling 1972: 2)

Such works as *The Tempest* – reinterpreted and reproduced as it continues to be – seem to speak to us, with most miraculous organ, across history and cultures, to render all but irrelevant their own historical origins and cultural uses, and to occupy a timeless and transcendent space to which we are granted, with a minimum of instruction, almost immediate access.

How do we account for the paradoxical experience most readers have had of the contemporaneity of texts that we simultaneously know to be historically embedded and culturally encoded? Modern critical theory has been divided in its response to this question of the apparent timelessness of the literary text, a division that might be said to structure critical theory itself into two large and opposed camps: one traditionally termed 'idealist' or 'formalist'; the other 'materialist' or 'historicist'. While each of these broad perspectives has its own long history and encompasses a range of distinct and diverse critical movements and positions, their underlying orientations toward literary texts and their status and function within culture are so fundamentally opposed as to seem irreconcilable, not least to their respective proponents. In fact, criticism of *The Tempest* in the latter half of the twentieth century would seem to illustrate, in the most explicit and spectacular terms, just how irreconcilable these different critical viewpoints are in their assumptions, aims and methods.

Yet my contention in this essay will be that these two traditional viewpoints of idealism and formalism on the one side, and materialism and historicism on the other, are not finally irreconcilable; that they find their respective justifications and mutual reconciliation within a larger view, a version of Fredric Jameson's theory of the 'political unconscious' of literature. *The Tempest*, a text that lies well outside the range of Jameson's more immediate concerns, will serve as a paradigm case in testing and, on the whole, validating the utility and power of this theory to explain and illuminate the cultural operations of literary texts.

Before turning to Jameson's theory and its application to *The Tempest*, let us consider the two traditional positions in some detail, beginning with the one that is much older, more familiar, and more thoroughly ingrained and naturalized within our culture, namely the idealist or formalist position. We have already seen one of its basic assumptions reflected in the admirable passage quoted above, that great works of literature 'persuade us that human nature never varies', that they represent back to us an 'essential human nature' that transcends particular historical cultures.

The idea of 'mimesis' or imitation – of 'life', 'action', 'experience', or even 'reality' or 'truth' – as the 'work' of literature goes all the way back to Plato and Aristotle; and from the beginning what was at stake in the idea of 'imitation' was very much the imitation of an 'idea'. That is to say, epic or tragedy or comedy – or even more modern forms like the masque or the novel – were not conceived at any level of sophistication as imitating 'life' or 'the world' or 'experience' in themselves, but the 'form' or 'idea' that lies hidden in them, that which was not directly available to observation. Their true essence or meaning, their inner logic or ideal form, was always located somewhere else than in the mere appearances of people or events as they unfold to us in history. Hence the need for, and emphasis on, *form*, genre and technique in this tradition of criticism, on everything we think of as distinguishing 'art' from 'life'. These are the means of unconcealing what lies beyond or beneath phenomenal 'reality' and participates in the eternal and universal – be it divine or human.

The artistic process, thus conceived, always involves a certain idealization, a reconstruction of appearances in order that something essential and eternal may, through the working of form and symbol, be represented or revealed to us, 'mirrors' or 'lamps' being the favoured metaphors for this process within traditional idealist poetics. Clearly, there is not really much room here for the historical or cultural context of art as such, history and culture either dropping altogether out of account, or being subordinated to the status of mere background or 'raw material' from which the finished work emerges. The artist, on such a view, becomes a kind of prophetic intermediary who expresses the eternal and universal through his inspired manipulation of the all but sacred forms at his disposal. Thus, a history of *forms*, such as Erich Auerbach's *Mimesis* (1953), or Northrop Frye's *Anatomy of Criticism* (1957) is about all that can be written from this position, a criticism or a poetics that from the other viewpoint is only gesturally historical. Perhaps paradoxically, it is only since the Romantic period – which coincides with the Industrial Revolution, the rapid expansion of capitalism, the rise of the bourgeoisie as the dominant economic and social class – that formalist and idealist poetics have undergone their most detailed elaboration.

Yet at the same moment the alternative position of historicism and materialism, which found its strongest underpinnings in the economic and historical theories of Karl Marx, began to be developed. The materialist address to the question of the apparent timelessness of the text – a question Marx himself raised in connection with ancient Greek literature and never satisfactorily answered[1] – is by way of history, of the text's inescapable relations not merely to a continuum of forms but to the changing material, social and political conditions of its production and reception. It would be a mistake, however, to regard the text as reflecting or reproducing these directly – as an older, 'vulgar' Marxism tended to do – for if it did, a text so embedded in its own historical conditions could never exert a continuing appeal or even continue to make sense to those of us who inhabit different ones. Rather, the historical dimension of the literary text has more recently been located, not in direct relation to the basic, ultimately economic, structure of society, but in relation to the 'ideological' superstructure erected upon it. The concept of 'ideology' has a long history of its own within materialist thought, and in recent years has become all but indispensable within critical theory.

In its early Marxian sense, 'ideology' refers to the 'false consciousness' or collective delusions that work to conceal or falsify the real material conditions – and the real positions we occupy within them – that constitute a given social system, and thereby to legitimate and perpetuate that system. In classic Marxism it is ideology – in the forms of law, religion, morality, and so on – that operates indirectly, along with more direct and material forces of repression such as the military and police, to prevent the working class from achieving consciousness of its real condition and acting upon it to overthrow its oppressors. Yet in his later writings Marx himself uses the term in a somewhat different way, and it is this later sense of 'ideology' that has been much discussed and elaborated in recent critical theory. For Louis Althusser, as for Jameson who follows him, 'ideology' is less a matter of 'false consciousness' than of 'consciousness' itself. That is, it is not something like a bad dream or a state of hypnosis from which we can wake up or snap out of on being told the truth, because it is redefined as 'the imaginary representation of the subject's relationship to his or her real conditions of existence' (Althusser 1971: 162). It already *is* a kind of truth, albeit the truth of imagination. In so far as we must always live within material conditions, and imagine our relation to them, there can be no escape or awakening from ideology.

Yet there is another, even stronger sense in which ideology becomes doubly inescapable, one which may help explain its tenacity within even the most oppressive and exploitative social and economic regimes. The direct knowledge of our real condition under such regimes would simply be too painful to bear. From a Marxist standpoint, history is a succession of systems of exploitation – of slave by master, serf by lord, worker by employer – that would, if clearly and fully apprehended as such, be too traumatic to be experienced, let alone knowingly perpetuated, by either side in the continuing class struggle. Hence the psychological necessity of ideology, for that collective repression which enables us to misapprehend the real conditions of social existence and thereby survive them more or less unhappily. Particular ideologies, such as religion, nationalism and racism, seem to those who hold, or are held by, them to be *natural* – as distinct from 'constructed' or imposed by the powers that be – and by so seeming, to take on a certain invisibility or inevitability to those within their grip. They thus work to induce an acceptance or passivity towards systems of domination to which we would not consent if we could see them for what they are. Essential to ideological structures is the imaging of an 'eternal human nature' that they at once project and reflect, thus reproducing a subject to whom the very idea of radical change seems inconceivable or futile.

The importance of this definition of ideology for literary studies is its relocation of literature partly outside the ideological complex that keeps us mystified or stupefied by virtue of its representation of it – that is, by offering a certain distance from it, rather than simply extending its domain of 'containment'. Though not quite a representation of the historical *real* – which, for Althusser, is the 'absent cause' that can never be directly represented – literature is not simply another reflex of ideology either.[2] The full work of demystification made possible by the text, however, requires a 'theoretical practice', a kind of reading focused on the 'gaps' and 'fissures' of the text's apparent unity to reveal the 'marks' of the social and historical formations it incompletely conceals and into which it can then be 'reinserted'. As these metaphors of hard surfaces and mechanical operations might suggest, such procedures presuppose a 'materialism' for both textuality and history that is rather more literal in the work of Althusser's disciples than in that of Althusser or Jameson (see, for example, Macherey 1966; and Eagleton

(1976a)). Jameson, in fact, characterizes the work of ideological critique and unmasking that makes up most Marxist textual analysis, as a 'negative hermeneutic', which, however necessary, still leaves a lot to be desired, as we shall soon see.

Whatever its own limitations, ideological critique views idealist criticism as itself a form of ideology, or more precisely, an ideology of form, in so far as literary form is not something autonomous or unchanging but itself an ideological projection of social and material formations always already in place. From this materialist standpoint, the paradoxical contemporaneity of historical texts – the problem with which we began – is an effect of the persistence of ideology. What we recognize in the characters and action of the literary text, in the 'world' encapsulated by its form and apparently sealed off from history, is not some essential form of our deeper selves with which we are said to 'identify'; rather, the ideological forms of our lived existence, represented in the text, 'hail' or 'summon' us – as a policeman might hail someone in a crowd – through the process Althusser terms 'interpellation'. They offer us, that is to say, an 'identity', a place within their structures, a sense of belonging to the group or class whose interests and values they represent and, up to a point, legitimate. The 'eternal presence' of literature, and its illusion of an eternal human nature, are made possible by the persistence of the ideological structures represented in the text and their congruence with or similarity to those dominant in the society outside it. This illusion is only reinforced and reproduced by formalist and idealist – from this Marxist viewpoint, 'bourgeois' – criticism, and a potentially liberating knowledge thereby strategically contained.

But Jameson's project of unconcealing the 'political unconscious' that literary form all but occludes goes beyond Althusser's and his disciples' attempts to theorize the ideological functions of the 'cultural text'. In fact, Jameson's characteristic use of this term – in contradistinction to the 'literary text' of a more traditional formalism and Marxism alike – signals at once an expansion of horizons and a unique responsiveness to the dynamic interplay of 'cultural' and 'textual' dimensions. Arguably, the method he develops is inspired less directly by Marx (despite its obviously political emphasis) or even by Freud (despite its projection of an 'unconscious') than by Marx's main philosophical forerunner, Hegel. While Marx is commonly credited, at least by Marxists, with having stood Hegel 'on his feet', that is to say, with having supplied a materialist basis for the historical change that Hegel had located in the dialectical operations of a 'World-Spirit', it is the Hegelian principle of 'truth is totality', carried over by Marxism, that is fundamental to Jameson's working method of 'metacommentary'.

Let us consider 'metacommentary', which Jameson explains and illustrates in his opening chapter, in some detail. He writes:

> Interpretation is here construed as an essentially allegorical act, which consists in rewriting a given text in terms of a particular interpretive master code . . . Their juxtaposition [of such codes as 'the ethical, the psychoanalytic, the myth-critical, the semiotic, the structural'] with a dialectical or totalizing, properly Marxist ideal of understanding will be used to demonstrate the structural limitations of the other interpretive codes, and in particular to show the 'local', ways in which they construct their objects of study and the 'strategies of containment' whereby they are able to project the illusion that their readings are somehow complete and self-sufficient.
>
> (Jameson 1981: 10)

'Metacommentary', that is to say, does not take up competing approaches to a text in order to refute or invalidate them; on the contrary, it grants them a local or 'sectoral' validity, while at the same time situating them historically and thereby accounting for their limitations: 'The authority of such methods springs from their faithful consonance with this or that local law of a fragmented social life, this or that subsystem of a complex and mushrooming cultural superstructure' (Jameson 1981: 10).

In alluding to 'the "pluralism" of the intellectual marketplace today', to 'a fragmented social life', and to 'a complex and mushrooming cultural superstructure' – all of which the present volume is an example or symptom – Jameson gestures towards the basis of his own ambitious claims: the unique capacity of Marxism, as a theory of history and society, to account for its own emergence and existence, as well as those of its competitors. For Jameson, Marxism is nothing less than the 'untranscendable horizon' that subsumes their 'apparently antagonistic or incommensurable critical operations'.

> It projects a rival hermeneutic to those already enumerated; but it does so . . . not so much by repudiating their findings as by arguing its ultimate philosophical and methodological priority over more specialized interpretive codes whose insights are strategically limited as much by their own situational origins as

by the narrow or local ways in which they construe or construct
their objects of study.

(Jameson 1981: 21)

Psychoanalytic method is, for Jameson, a crucial example. He writes:

The conditions of possibility of psychoanalysis become visible
only when you begin to appreciate the extent of psychic fragmentation since the beginnings of capitalism, with its systematic
quantification and rationalization of experience, its instrumental
reorganization of the subject just as much as of the outside world.

(Jameson 1981: 62)

Despite the claims of Freud, and of subsequent Freudians, to have
systematized the workings of the psyche in its eternal and universal
aspects, it is only the workings of the *bourgeois* psyche under *capitalism* –
the social class and historical era we still cohabit with Freud – that have
actually been systematized, with a validity that is increasingly open to
question – and not surprisingly from a historical standpoint ever more
remote from the moment of origin of psychoanalysis.

Even more revealing of the explanatory claims and ambitions of
Jameson's metacommentary – and more relevant for our impending
application of it to *The Tempest* – is his analysis of the interpretative
system of Northrop Frye. According to Jameson (1981: 69):

The greatness of Frye, and the radical difference between his work
and that of the great bulk of garden-variety myth criticism, lies
in his willingness to raise the issue of community and to draw
basic, essentially social, interpretive consequences from the nature
of religion as collective representation.

In his highly systematic decoding of modern, that is to say, post-
medieval, literature as a secular scripture, as a displacement of divine
myth in a human direction with the great romances of Spenser,
Shakespeare and Milton at its centre, Frye more or less openly recasts
the typological exegesis performed on the Bible by medieval commentators. 'Frye's work comes before us as a virtual contemporary reinvention of the four-fold hermeneutic associated with the theological
tradition' (Jameson 1981: 69).

Yet Frye's modern reconstruction of medieval methods of reading
entails a crucial change.

His 'Theory of Symbols' rewrites the older fourfold scheme as
four 'phases': the Literal and Descriptive; the Formal; the

> Mythical or Archetypal; and the Anagogic . . . It is only at the third level, the Mythical or Archetypal, on which the concepts of both desire and society make their appearance, that we reach interpretation proper.
>
> (Jameson 1981: 69)

But Frye has here reversed the priorities of his medieval predecessors. Whereas medieval theology located on the fourth or anagogic level of the text its reference to the collective history and destiny of society as a whole as extending and completing the third or moral level of the progress of the individual soul, Frye sees the completion of textual meaning in his fourth or anagogic level of the 'libidinal body' of fulfilled individual desire, which arises only after his third or archetypal level of the community. 'The essentially historical interpretive system of the church fathers has here been recontained, and its political elements turned back into the merest figures for the Utopian realities of the individual subject' (Jameson 1981: 74). This shift is a function of Frye's historical position, 'a significant strategic and ideological move, in which political and collective imagery is transformed into a mere relay in some ultimately privatizing celebration of the category of individual experience' – the role to which literary experience has been largely relegated under bourgeois capitalism.

It is particularly clear from the case of Frye – or from Jameson's intensive reading of Frye – that the repression of the political dimension of the text is at least as much a function of our historically conditioned methods of reading texts as it is of the texts we read. And in the extended case studies of Balzac, Gissing and Conrad that comprise the central chapters of *The Political Unconscious*, it is often difficult to distinguish between the two in so far as the 'ideology of form' developed and deployed by the novelists under study increasingly overlaps with what might be termed the 'ideology of formalism' developed and deployed by modern criticism to interpret their work. Yet as we move with Jameson from the proto-realist Balzac to the pre-modernist Conrad, it becomes clear that the 'political' understanding obscurely and obliquely encoded in their texts is becoming increasingly fragmented and displaced, partly as an effect and partly as a cause of formal change, even to the point where the 'perfected poetic apparatus of high modernism represses History' almost completely, and 'the political, no longer visible in the high modernist texts, any more than in the everyday world of appearance of bourgeois life, and relentlessly driven underground by accumulated reification, has at last become a genuine Unconscious' (Jameson 1981: 280).

Jameson's identification of 'the perfected poetic apparatus of high modernism' as symptomatic of a politicality repressed to the point of becoming 'a genuine Unconscious' holds important implications for his theory and for its application to *The Tempest*. The modernist text, mutually generated by an artistic and a critical ideology responding to – and in the main reacting against – the privatization, commodification and alienation of advanced capitalism, becomes in effect an *alternative world*, a vicarious compensation for desires so fragmented and frustrated in the social world as to become, in its developed intensities and complexities of form, an almost viable and habitable, but completely depoliticized, version of its 'original'. And with the cultivation by both modernist author and modern critic of a formalism so exalted and autonomous comes the retrospective celebration of 'art' as the one remaining mode of civility, community and even 'salvation' in a world of accelerating fragmentation and alienation; and the simultaneous illusion – or ideology – on the rise since the Romantics, that it was always this way, that in every age and culture art has been a refuge for the sensitive individual from the brutality of the social process at work around him, an island of civilization precariously afloat in a sea of barbarism, a soothing interlude in the nightmare of history from which we cannot seem to awake.

Hence the necessity of unmasking the political dimension repressed in 'literary' texts that were and are always already 'cultural' in a deeper than usual sense, in order that the history recovered from them may be turned from the mode of barbarism and nightmare into something else. It is therefore hardly surprising that Jameson opens the concluding chapter of *The Political Unconscious* – in many respects, and certainly for our present purposes, its most original and provocative contribution to Marxist cultural theory – with an epigraph, from Walter Benjamin's 'Theses on the Philosophy of History' (1940), that asserts in the strongest terms what must be the central tenet of left-political criticism today:

> As in all previous history, whoever emerges as victor still participates in that triumph in which today's rulers march over the prostrate bodies of their victims. As is customary, the spoils are borne aloft in that triumphal parade. These are generally called the cultural heritage. The latter finds a rather distanced observer in the historical materialist. For such cultural riches, as he surveys them, everywhere betray an origin which he cannot but contemplate with horror. They owe their existence, not merely to the toil of the great creators who have produced them, but equally

to the anonymous forced labor of the latter's contemporaries. There has never been a document of culture which was not at one and the same time a document of barbarism.

(Benjamin 1968: 253)

It has been the work of *The Political Unconscious* up to this point to explore the implications of Benjamin's luminous and withering insight. Yet in this final chapter, Jameson seeks to supplement, in his characteristically Hegelian way, the agenda of the ideological critique so far pursued; and at this point that agenda turns, through a startling dialectical reversal, into its apparent opposite: what he terms a 'utopian hermeneutic'. For this 'utopian hermeneutic' is only the other side of the ideological critique he has been practising all along.

Countering the charge that Marxism must, by its very logic, adopt an 'instrumental' or 'functional' – and to that extent reductive and demeaning – view of 'culture' as a system of values always at the service of dominant interests, of the classes or groups which in the last analysis support and patronize culture, Jameson seeks a more positive basis for a Marxist understanding of culture than that of ideological critique. In so doing, he attempts to 'rewrite certain religious concepts – most notably Christian historicism and the "concept" of providence – as anticipatory foreshadowings of historical materialism', to grasp afresh in specifically Marxian, that is, collective and class, terms, 'the revolutionary power of that *promesse de bonheur* most immediately inscribed in the aesthetic text', a formulation that hints 'at a variety of options for articulating a properly Marxian version of meaning beyond the purely ideological' and negatively instrumental (Jameson 1981: 285).

> The concept of class is thus the space in which, if anywhere, a Marxian version of the hermeneutics of meaning [as opposed to 'suspicion'], of some noninstrumental conception of culture, may be tested, particularly insofar as it is from this same concept of social class that the strongest form of a Marxian 'negative hermeneutic' – of the class character and functionality of ideology as such – also derives.
>
> (Jameson 1981: 286).

As far as this bears on the business of criticism, then, we perhaps need to bear at least two considerations in mind: not only should the cultural text be 'negatively' released from the ownership of an originating individual 'genius', and so regarded as a particular inflection of its class voice, but also this social identification should be rendered capable of indicating its own utopian impulse in the text's own accents and emphases – what it apparently values and what it strives to ignore: see Jameson (1979) as well as the concluding pages of Jameson (1981).

The possibility of this 'positive' or 'utopian' hermeneutic arises from

> the proposition that *all* class consciousness – or in other words, all ideology in the strongest sense, including the most exclusive forms of ruling-class consciousness just as much as that of oppositional or oppressed classes – is in its very nature Utopian.
>
> (Jameson 1981: 289)

The paradoxical logic at work here – are not 'ideology' and 'utopia' contradictory conditions? – begins in locating the originary 'moment of class consciousness' in 'that of the oppressed classes'.

> On such a view, those who must work and produce surplus value for others will necessarily grasp their own solidarity – initially, in the unarticulated form of rage, helplessness, victimization, oppression by a common enemy – *before* the dominant or ruling class has any particular incentive for doing so. Indeed, it is the glimpse of such sullen resistance, and the sense of nascent political dangers . . ., which generates the mirror image of class solidarity among the ruling groups . . . The index of all class consciousness is to be found . . . first and foremost in the dawning sense of solidarity with other members of a particular group or class, whether the latter happen to be your fellow landowners, those who enjoy structural privileges linked to your own, or, on the contrary, fellow workers and producers, slaves, serfs, or peasants.
>
> (Jameson 1981: 289–90)

Prospero's vision of community, according to Jameson, should arise in response to the threat posed to it by that of Caliban.

Jameson (1981: 291–2) concludes:

> Such a view dictates an enlarged perspective for any Marxist analysis of culture, which can no longer be content with its demystifying vocation to unmask and to demonstrate the ways in which a cultural artifact fulfills a specific ideological mission, in legitimating a given power structure, in perpetuating and reproducing the latter, and in generating specific forms of false consciousness (or ideology in the narrower sense). [It] must also seek, through and beyond this demonstration of the instrumental function of a given cultural object, to project its simultaneously

Utopian power as the symbolic affirmation of a specific historical
and class form of collective unity.

It is time to test the validity and value of these propositions, revolutionary as they are in their departure from conventional Marxist
critique, against the historical and social dynamic represented by
The Tempest.

Practice: *The Tempest*

Jameson's attempt to discriminate and reclaim the 'utopian' dimension
of the cultural text from its 'ideological' and 'barbarous' shadow-side
begins in a question that remains deeply unsettling to the political
presuppositions of contemporary theory. So challenging is Jameson's
question, in fact, that it is not surprising it has gone virtually
unaddressed since it was first raised more than a decade ago in the final
chapter of *The Political Unconscious*. Jameson (1981: 288) asks:

> How is it possible for a cultural text which fulfills a demonstrably
> ideological function, as a hegemonic work whose formal cate-
> gories as well as its content secure the legitimation of this or that
> form of class domination – how is it possible for such a text to
> embody a properly Utopian impulse, or to resonate a universal
> value inconsistent with the narrower limits of class privilege
> which inform its more immediate ideological vocation?

Remote as *The Tempest* is from the critical context in which the
question arises, it might almost have been framed with *The Tempest* in
mind, so spectacularly has the long history of reception of Shakespeare's
final romance illustrated both the ideological and the utopian side of this
crucial formulation.

From the earliest years of its critical history, *The Tempest* has been
perceived and admired as what Coleridge termed an 'ideal drama' whose
powers of imaginative abstraction reach beyond historical contingencies
and point towards a more universal and utopian domain of human desire
and aspiration in their fulfilled form.[3] This 'idealist' dimension of
The Tempest found its most complete and detailed articulation in mid-
twentieth-century criticism, particularly in the enormously influential
readings by Kermode (1957) and Frye (1959; 1965). Kermode (1957:
xxxiv–lix) resituates the play within a renaissance humanist context,
within which Prospero's 'project' represents the triumph of 'art' and

'nurture' (broadly understood as 'education' and 'civilization') over 'nature' (conceived as 'unformed' at best and 'brutal' or 'debased' at worst). Frye identifies and foregrounds the play's mythic and archetypal vision, its encapsulation in terms at once Christian and secular, recurrent and universal, of 'the great rising rhythms of life: marriage, springtime, harvest, dawn, and rebirth'. For both critics, and for many others under their influence, *The Tempest* is 'a play not simply to be read or seen or even studied, but possessed' (Frye 1959: 26), a crystallization of the core values of western civilization.

Over the past two decades, however, the dominance of this 'idealist' reading of *The Tempest* has been contested and increasingly displaced by a political, that is 'materialist' or 'historicist' reading directed against precisely that 'core' of western civilization whose system of values the play was supposed to have so perfectly encapsulated. The thrust of this critique is not merely against the aesthetic dimension of the play as such – its 'masque'-like elements of magic, music, and spectacle – for offering an escape or distraction from social and political issues, but for its own negative and repressive politicality, its 'masking' in a classic ideological sense the vested interests of the dominant culture of the day, its own implicit politics of exploitation and oppression: that 'work of barbarism', in Benjamin's sense, which made this 'work of civilization' possible in the first place and has continued to make it so eminently reproducible ever since. This 'new-historicist' critique has attempted to bring to light the bad or uneasy conscience of *The Tempest*, its 'political unconscious' as it were, and has concentrated on its complicity in the discourses and practices of colonialism.[4]

While it has many variations and inflections, the political and ideological critique of *The Tempest* depends on an underlying parallel between the mysterious island setting of the play and the New World of sixteenth- and seventeenth-century colonization. Such an alignment – however unobvious it may be – has long been recognized; after all, Shakespeare was himself a shareholder in the Virginia Company, the play makes at least four more or less explicit references to the New World and its Amerindian inhabitants,[5] and an account of shipwreck and deliverance in Bermuda in 1609 was nominated as early as 1808 – by Malone (1808) – as the closest thing we have to a 'source' for the play as a whole. But it is only recently that these colonial connections have become the basis of a 'negative hermeneutic' or ideological critique. This is not in itself surprising. It is perfectly consistent with the theory of a political unconscious that the ideological structures of a text should become visible as such only when they have begun to break down in the ambient culture. In this case, the historical breakdown of colonial imperialism in this century seems to have been the precondition for its critique by those who were once unselfconsciously positioned within its ideological structure.

In any case, identification of the island with the New World and of the play with colonial discourse has issued in an ideological critique that has challenged an older humanist criticism at its strongest points. Perhaps the most important of these is the status of language in the play. The arts of language, crucial to the humanist project of education and civilization, have a central importance in *The Tempest*; it is his 'books', after all, that confer on Prospero his power over nature and his fellow human beings, and it was his exclusive absorption in them that set events in motion in the first place. Moreover, when Prospero and Miranda teach Caliban language in the effort to humanize or civilize him, the results are disastrous: 'You taught me language, and my profit on't/Is I know how to curse' (I.ii.362–3). 'Language', according to the Bishop of Avila, speaking on behalf of Antonio de Nebrija, in his presentation of the first grammar of a modern European vernacular to Queen Isabella of Castile in 1492, 'is the perfect instrument of empire'. This wonderful statement has become something of a *leitmotif* in post-colonial rereadings of *The Tempest*.[6]

It seems Isabella had expressed wonderment as to why a Spanish grammar was needed, and why anyone would undertake to produce one; after all, she and her subjects understood Spanish well enough already without benefit of a formalized grammar. But the acquisition of a language – as the inhabitants of the New World (who would doubtless have had an even more amazed reaction if they had been presented with grammars of their own Amerindian languages) were soon to learn – is also inescapably the internalization of a social order of vertical as well as horizontal differentiation, a system of hierarchical values and hegemonic relations as well as one of arbitrary naming and conventional communication. Queen Isabella, of all people, would have known this, if only in her bones. So the humanist mission that Prospero shares with the *conquistadores* and priests who came before him, while it doubtless has a certain benevolist dimension, cannot be prised altogether free of the larger imposition of hierarchy upon difference through superior power that has characterized colonial imperialism from the beginning.

That enterprise develops its own self-justifying 'discourse', its own highly ideological repertoire of linguistic devices and figures, through which the interests of greed and power are encoded in other, more apparently benign or altruistic, terms. The means by which Prospero defeats Sycorax and dispossesses and subordinates Caliban is represented in *The Tempest* not directly as superior military technology but through the metaphor of a virtuous 'white magic'; and its use justified in moral or theological terms. Caliban, after all, is repeatedly described by Prospero as not only different but demonic,

> A devil, a born devil, on whose nature
> Nurture can never stick; on whom my pains,
> Humanely taken, all, all lost, quite lost.
>
> (IV.i.188–90)

Characterizations of the native peoples of the Americas as somehow 'devilish', while not ubiquitous, are by no means uncommon in the early discourse of colonialism, which, like that of the play, was by no means unequivocal though generally condescending in its linguistic efforts to master the shock to its system posed by the strangeness of the beings of the New World.

But there is another discursive level; that of literary form itself, through which *The Tempest* has been held to reproduce and refigure its ties with colonialism, and the place where it operates most visibly – partly because its operations are disrupted – is in the betrothal masque. There, we are presented with a mythology and iconography in which pagan deities confer their blessings upon a human union and its dynastic succession. The imagery is drawn from the Roman epic narratives of Virgil and Ovid, and frequently adapted in the Renaissance to depict the union of the enterprising spirit of the Old World with the willing abundance of the New. The masque, in which this imagery is deployed, was also the form most favoured – and raised to its highest level of extravagant spectacle – by King James to legitimate his own claims to a divine right that was tantamount in its transformative power to 'magic'. So the betrothal masque works to assimilate the New World materials of the play to the culturally privileged forms of classical epic and Court masque, with all their associations of divine legitimation and royal authority. Or more accurately, the betrothal masque would do so, if it were not disastrously interrupted with 'a strange hollow and confused noise' (IV.i.138 s.d.).

For some of the critics with whose reading we are concerned, the breakdown of the masque figures the return of the repressed, of the political unconscious that Prospero's magic, music and spectacle were designed to keep at bay, to 'mask' as it were to consciousness. For it seems to be nothing other than the recollection of 'the beast Caliban,

and his conspiracy' of drunkards that disturbs the smooth progress of
Prospero's masque. Yet even this anxiety attack on Prospero's part,
while it may allow us to glimpse momentarily the guilty political
unconscious of the play – so the argument runs – does not ultimately
prevent the recontainment of that unconscious at the level of form.

> The shakiness of Prospero's position is indeed staged, but in the
> end his version of history remains *authoritative*, the larger play
> acceding as it were to the containment of the conspirators in the
> safely comic mode, Caliban allowed only his poignant and
> ultimately vain protests against the venality of his co-conspirators.
> (Francis Barker and Peter Hulme, 'Nymphs and reapers heavily
> vanish', in Drakakis 1985: 203)

This 'comic closure' is seen as 'symptomatic of the text's own anxiety
about the threat posed to its decorum by its New World materials' but
is at the same time 'necessary to enable the European "reconciliation"'
within a dynastic and providential design, the pseudo-epic form of
'Prospero's play' as a whole.

So the 'ideology of form' has worked its hierarchical, and repressive,
magic after all. Or has it? Not even the strongest of the post-colonial
readings claims to have exhausted the interpretive potential of the play's
historical contextuality:

> To identify dominant discursive networks and their mode of
> operation within particular texts should by no means be seen as
> the end of the story ... we have argued for the discourse of
> colonialism as the articulatory *principle* of *The Tempest*'s diversity
> but have touched only briefly on what other discourses are
> articulated and where such linkages can be seen at work in
> the play.
> (Barker and Hulme, in Drakakis 1985: 204)

While allowing for the multiplicity of discourses that reticulate the
text, however, Barker and Hulme are concerned to establish the
'ultimately hierarchical' relation among them, within which colonial
discourse is 'dominant'. It is in no way to deny the colonial dimension
of *The Tempest* to point out that such a project is highly precarious, not
only because of the sheer multiplicity of historical and literary-historical
discourses in play within this play, but because they are deployed in a
peculiarly provisional, elusive, and even self-denying way, including
the supposedly 'dominant' colonial discourse.

Consider, for example, the figure of Caliban, on whose status as an American indigene the colonial critique would seem to depend: his name, after all, seems to be a corruption of 'cannibal' or 'Caribbean', and his god 'Setebos' is of Patagonian origin. Yet Caliban's nature, like his name, is as discursively dubious, obscure and hybridized as it is genealogically. As one scholar writes:

> When we examine in detail the text surrounding Caliban, we are struck first of all by its contradictory nature; profusion of epithets side by side with scarcity of effective information about his physical presence ... As many as twenty-four epithets are applied seventy-one times by six characters to Caliban, but how much do we know for certain about his body? He is not naked, has long nails, and somehow induces an association with a fish.
>
> (Masaki 1991: 6)

His demonic and Mediterranean origins are firmly established in the discourse of Prospero and Miranda (Act I, scene ii) before New World images are attached to him by the clowns Stephano and Trinculo (Act II, scene ii).[7] The obscurity of Caliban's nature and origins only deepens as the play proceeds. It is almost as if the 'dead Indian' (II.ii.32) and 'men of Ind' (II.ii.57) to whom the clowns initially compare him, unleash the desire in Caliban to surround himself with his own discourse, which seems to relocate him from the Mediterranean to the Caribbean.

> But then the shift is cut short ... by another discourse – that of the clowns, which centres around the idea of a 'monster' – something Prospero never calls him; Prospero most frequently refers to him – seven times – as 'slave'. The ... linguistic violence inflicted on him throughout the play is certainly unparalleled in the whole of Shakespeare, and in this the clowns are no less coercive than Prospero, for they, as it were, give a cue to Caliban and then mercilessly suppress his attempt to re-establish himself in his own discourse as the native inhabitant of the island.
>
> (Masaki 1991: 7)

Even in the very last lines of the play, Caliban still hovers uncertainly between 'a plain fish' (Antonio's comment, V.i.266) and 'this thing of darkness' (Prospero's comment, V.i.275). Caliban seems to exist at the site of a conflict of discourses.

It would be tempting to write off this discursive disturbance surrounding Caliban as no more than the expression of different dramatic and ideological viewpoints – grounded in class difference – between

Prospero and the clowns. The ruling-class Prospero inserts Caliban within social, moral, and indeed theological systems – 'slave', 'demi-devil', 'beast' – that sanction and support his own hierarchical superiority in every conceivable respect, while the butler and clown tag him mainly as a commodity – 'Indian', 'monster', 'fish' – thereby asserting their own minimal leverage over him at the more basic and pragmatic level of the marketplace. The discourse of colonialism, after all, abounds in shifting conflations of the 'exotic', the 'demonic', the 'monstrous', the 'slavish' or 'subservient' under the master category of the radically and ineluctably 'other'. Clearly this explanation of the contradictory descriptions of Caliban in terms of the different social and ideological positionings of those who describe him has some claim to validity; yet it is limited by the fact that the discursive instability surrounding Caliban is by no means confined to Caliban. For the fact is that *all* the American allusions in *The Tempest* are singularly unstable, contradicted or denied in virtually the same, or the very next, breath in which they are made. Gonzalo's word 'plantation' applies to Ireland as well as Virginia, and the utopian daydream in which it occurs, derived from Montaigne's (1991: 228–41) second-hand account of life among the Indians of Brazil, is quickly deflated and dismissed by the sceptical dialogue that surrounds it. Ariel's reference to 'the still-vexed Bermudas' (I.ii.229) only makes clear a moment later that the play is *not* set there, but in 'the Mediterranean float' (I.ii.234). And Miranda's celebration of a 'brave new world' is immediately relativized and quali-fied to the point of dismissal by Prospero: ''Tis new to thee' (V.i.184). 'Shakespeare evokes a New World association', concludes the most rigorous textual examination to date of this dimension of the play, 'only to efface it almost immediately' (Masaki 1991: 7).

Having registered these doubts concerning the 'dominance' of colonial discourse in *The Tempest*, let me say straight away that it is not my intention to deny or dismiss either the colonial dimension of the play or the critique that has focused upon it to the virtual exclusion of everything else in it. In textual and theatrical matters – as could be illustrated by a thousand examples from Shakespeare – the smallest textual detail may speak volumes, fleeting theatrical moments may have momentous effect, and denial may constitute the surest form of affirmation. My point is not that recent colonial critique of *The Tempest* has misread its slight and fleeting, indeed almost subliminal, colonial evocations, but rather that it has overread them, and in so doing, has mistaken the part for the whole, has ignored or overlooked the much larger vision of history within which they are encapsulated. For within this play, the colonialism of the New World is merely an episode within a projection of nothing less than a historical totality that puts that episode into a much larger critical perspective.

The ideological critique of *The Tempest* as colonial discourse, that is to say, is not so much wrong or invalid as it is partial and local. It will find its completion only in a historical criticism that keeps in view the totality of the play, and the play of totality within it, a 'utopian hermeneutics' through which the political unconscious can be brought to light *in its entirety*, in its positive as well as negative aspect, in its fragmented utopian longings as well as its repressed class consciousness. Given the massive concentration of this text, such a historical criticism will have to pay attention to details as small but suggestive as those that in the critique of colonial discourse have all but eclipsed everything else. In the effort to construct that 'positive' and 'utopian' hermeneutic, let us start with one such tiny but telling detail, Ariel's casual reference to 'the Mediterranean float' (I.ii.234), on which the remainder of the wedding entourage are making their way back to Naples when the action of the play begins.

The phrase 'Mediterranean float' might well give us pause in its sheer strangeness to an Anglophone ear, albeit an appropriate strangeness coming as it does from the mouth of a 'spirit'. The effect is partly the result of the uncommon grammatical substitution, whereby the word 'float', more commonly a verb, is here used as a noun synonymous with 'sea'. Yet it is also a matter of the etymological dissonance that arises from the coupling of this Anglo-Saxon monosyllable with the Latinate, and still slightly exotic polysyllable, 'Mediterranean'. According to the *Oxford English Dictionary*, the word 'float' is of northern origin, deriving uncertainly through any of several linguistic stems ranging from Old Norse to Old High German as well as several other European vernaculars. Yet it is also the closest English counterpart in sense and sound to the Latin *fluctus*, one of Virgil's recurrent words not merely for the 'sea', but for the sea in its wave-like motions of the ebb and flow, rise and fall, of the 'tide', and is often used by Latin authors homologously with *tempestas*, in the sense of a turbulent build-up of weather, emotion, and circumstance, akin to the 'tide in the affairs of men' on which Shakespeare's Brutus imagines himself 'afloat' in *Julius Caesar* (IV.ii.268, 272).

Ariel's archaic diction draws attention to northern and to Latin derivations, and ultimately to their common origins in some remote Indo-European *Ursprache*, what in the Renaissance would have been regarded as the Adamic language before Babel, a 'natural' language endowed with the uncanny, almost magical, power of univocal and universal intelligibility. For this angelic sprite seems to speak a language that everyone in the play understands perfectly: Prospero in the instantaneous, almost telepathic, mode of 'thought' ('Come with a thought! – I think thee – Ariel, come!' (IV.i.164)); the guilty courtiers through the elemental sounds of 'nature' ('Methought the billows spoke . . ./The winds did sing it to me; and the thunder,/. . . pronounced/The name of Prosper' (III.iii.96–9)); and Caliban in a behaviourist language of bodily pain, the basically punitive discourse of pinches and cramps that regulates his conduct.[8] *The Tempest* does not tell us who taught Ariel to speak English, if it is indeed English that he speaks. But the language of this spirit, and the spirit of his language, I am suggesting, seem to draw us uncertainly into the pre-history of the play 'In the dark backward and abyss of time' (I.ii.50).

This resonant line, uttered by Prospero to Miranda in the effort to trigger her memory of events prior to their arrival on the island, is like a bell to toll us back at least as far as Milton, who rewrote it in *Paradise Lost* (see Book II. 405); and even further back to the epics of Virgil and Homer, which not only Milton but the Shakespeare of *The Tempest*, as we shall see, also rewrite. What with its own classicizing substitution ('dark *backward*') and diction ('abysme' in the Folio), the line insinuates itself within a context of memory, a shadowy discursive field constituted by poetic biography and cultural history and extending backwards from Shakespeare to Virgil to Homer and beyond, into the mythic and orphic origins of poetry, indeed of language itself. The all but magical line conjures up a receding perspective of epic vistas, a *mise en abîme* of infinite regress framed by the *Aeneid*, long recognized as an 'influence' on *The Tempest*, but one that is as elusive as it is pervasive; that has proved as difficult to pin down as that of colonial discourse; and that, as I shall contend, is no less crucial to the play's inscription of 'history'.

The importance of the *Aeneid* for *The Tempest*, while it can – and has – been misunderstood, cannot be overestimated. Not only was Virgil's epic viewed in the Renaissance as the greatest poem of classical antiquity[9] – in so far as its poet was supposed to have prophesied the coming of Christ and to have exemplified the 'career path' of all serious poets in his 'progression' from pastoral to epic – but it was also viewed as the matrix of all subsequent European history – in so far as it prefigures, in singing the founding of Rome out of the ashes of Troy, the founding of the modern European nations out of the ashes of Rome. In a fundamental sense, the *Aeneid*, linked through its poet to the birth of the Christian era, marks the birth of history itself out of the pre-history of Homeric epic and the myth-history of Homer's own pre-cursors stretching all the way back to Orpheus, the archetypal poet and, in Renaissance accounts, the bringer of civilization out of a barbaric state of nature.[10] Yet the Virgilian epic of the founding of Rome as the hard-won outcome of divine conflict and of human displacement, suffering, and sacrifice – for all its argument of celebration – is a vision of history as essentially tragic, as instinct with 'the tears of things' and pervaded by mortality and loss.

This tragic sense of history, quintessentially Virgilian, is never very far away in *The Tempest*, or in late Shakespeare generally. But it is central to Shakespeare's reinscription of Virgil's epic of Roman imperialism within his own final work that its tragic record of vindictiveness and oppression as the price of civilization – in Benjamin's terms, the seemingly unshakeable 'barbarism' of its shadow side – is recontained within a design larger and higher than that in which Virgil at once celebrates and unmasks the *pax Romana*. *The Tempest* projects an apocalyptic vision of history that promises more than another *translatio imperii*, in which the harsh impositions of civilization are only displacements of barbarism, and every 'new order' a repetition of the old. Shakespeare could rewrite the *Aeneid* as he does – and Prospero's fifth-act conversion at Ariel's prompting from an agent of 'vengeance' to one of 'virtue' (V.i.16–32) is its turning point – only if Virgil's epic did *not* have the status of a timeless and universal myth composed of unchanging archetypes – the status it has had for most modern critics who have seen its presence in *The Tempest* – but of a partial history of figures and prototypes whose completed form was unavailable to Virgil. *The Tempest* was produced, after all, in the same year that saw the publication of the King James version of the Bible.

For a Renaissance poet like Shakespeare – no less than, if differently from, Milton – the classical epics were fragments of a continuing historical revelation requiring supplementation in the light of one's own historical position; the very idea of a static realm of myths and archetypes is a much later, Romantic and modernist, construction. The Renaissance emphasis on 'imitation' of the classics was never meant to imply their mere repetition but their extension. As one influential study of this widespread practice puts it, the Renaissance imitator's dialogue with the past implies a heightened awareness of present difference that 'shook [the] absolute status' of the precursor text 'by calling attention to the altered circumstances of its production' (Greene 1982: 43). 'Imitation' is, by its very nature, an act of historical reflection. This valuable insight has led some recent critics to read the reinscription of Virgil in *The Tempest*, particularly in the masque, as Shakespeare's encoding of Jacobean political issues (Hamilton 1990; Schmidgall 1981: 70–84). The claims for a specifically Jacobean political commentary seem to me once again to have an undeniable validity, but like those made for colonial discourse, a validity that is local and limited rather than total and 'dominant', by virtue of their very historical specificity.

In making this qualification, my purpose is not to reinstate the play in a realm of 'high art' hermetically sealed off from history and politics in the splendid isolation either of an idealized 'epic tradition' or of an internalized psychomachia waged by strong poets with their precursors (though these latter stories, as told by some modern critics, also have their own partial and local validity). My point is rather that Shakespeare's rewriting of the *Aeneid* in *The Tempest* inscribes more than its own specific historicity through the discourses of early colonialism and of Jacobean absolutism it doubtless deploys – these belong to the limited domain of new historicist critique and ideological unmasking discussed earlier. But by putting these contemporary discourses of history and politics into place and into perspective within the much wider historical horizon provided by the *Aeneid*, *The Tempest* frames them, as it were, within a discourse of historical totality: this is the larger domain of a positive, and indeed utopian, hermeneutics of history in the full Jamesonian sense.

We have already seen how a single classicizing line within *The Tempest* begins to open a *mise en abîme*, a glimpse into a 'dark backward and abysme of time', from which we are invited to conjure up dim prototypes and prefigurations of characters and actions in the present. The pattern of Prospero's expulsion from Milan, his sojourn on the island and restoration to Milan re-enacts, with significant differences, the careers of Odysseus and Aeneas; his raising and calming of the storm, the actions of conflicting deities in Homeric and Virgilian epic; the betrothal of Ferdinand and Miranda, the unfulfilled 'marriage' of Aeneas and Dido; the 'monster' Caliban and 'spirit' Ariel, various non-human beings who block or help in Homer and Virgil; Prospero's intended vengeance but ultimate forgiveness towards his enemies, a revision of the conduct of Odysseus, Achilles and Aeneas. One could multiply examples of epic revision, and analyse each in turn, but my present purpose is rather to identify in all these examples a certain drive towards repetition of epic type and precedent, only for it to falter and change direction at certain crucial moments in the play, and issue in a new pattern or a new figure, a revised typology that completes the old.

The rarer action is in Virgil than in Homer; but the rarest action to date is in *The Tempest*.

Let us reconsider in this spirit of figural interpretation the more immediate history of the island. We are told by Prospero – and Caliban and Ariel corroborate this part of his narrative – that Sycorax, deriving her powers from a veritable coven of classical witches and herself exiled from 'Argier', had tyrannized over the island until Prospero's arrival. Prospero supplants Sycorax, frees Ariel from imprisonment, and institutes a kind of 'primitive communism'. When Caliban attempts to rape Miranda, Prospero punishes him with bondage and hard labour. The action of the play proper then begins with the storm, mobilizing Prospero's plan for revenge on the courtiers whose usurpation of his dukedom and expulsion of him from Milan had brought him and Miranda to the island in the first place. The local history of the island can be summed up as a recurrent cycle of dispossession, subjection and tyranny, a repetition in the fictional present of the record of conquest enacted in the historical past by ancient Greece, imperial Rome, and Renaissance Europe in concentric circles of expanding colonialism. At the time of *The Tempest*, both Milan and Naples were in fact tributaries of Spain, a domination made possible by the vast quantities of gold being extorted by Spain from the New World and used to pay her occupying armies![11]

It is worth noting at this point that the new historicist concentration on the parallelism between the 'history' of the island and that of the New World tends to leave much of the former out of account, in effect misrepresenting Prospero – and by analogy Renaissance Europe – as a *unique* agent of dispossession and tyranny, and repressing the larger vision of infinite regress within which Prospero's story unfolds, the vision of history as a cycle of repetition, a *recurrent* nightmare from which we are trying to awake. For the island, to which Caliban lays mock-dynastic claim as 'mine by Sycorax my mother' (I.ii.331) was never actually his mother's, any more than it is 'his' rather than Prospero's. The island had already been expropriated by Sycorax from its native inhabitants – the nymphs and nature-spirits of Ariel's *genus* – when Prospero expropriates it in turn from Sycorax. And its natives – at least one of them – were already in bondage before Prospero imposed it (or something similar but less harsh) upon her son. Here again, the parallelism with European colonization of the Americas, where slave societies at least as brutal as those of Rome or New Spain were already well established, holds true – somewhat too true for comfort on the part of new historicist critics. Their single-minded focus on one episode in a history of abysmal repetition, in which all its actors have been caught up, is not a historicism adequate to the text's impulse towards totalization.

Yet to project the action of *The Tempest* as merely a nested narrative receding from the present, a narrative in which a series of historical actors replay essentially the same functions of master and slave, victor and victim, in an eternal repetition of the same, is not adequate to the totality of the text either, and certainly not to its 'utopian' dimension. The utopian dimension to which I refer is not to be identified with those moments in the play when the fleeting promise of a new order, of an apocalyptic intervention in the cycle of history, is held out only to collapse back into the old almost immediately. Such moments as the 'primitive communism' of Prospero's early sojourn on the island, Gonzalo's daydream of an island 'commonwealth', Ferdinand's vision of an Edenic 'paradise' and Miranda's of a 'brave new world' – such utopian moments are merely wishful or nostalgic or escapist fantasies, themselves dialectically generated by the historical nightmare in which they are contained and back into which they quickly dissolve. The same might be said of the betrothal masque itself, a rewriting of the vision of harmony and abundance promised by Jupiter to Venus in Book I of the *Aeneid* as the compensation for Aeneas's suffering. For the masque occupies no clear position in relation to history, and in fact breaks down at the thought of history, of Caliban's conspiracy and the return of the political repressed.

The properly utopian dimension of *The Tempest* – 'properly' utopian because it lies beyond the toils of social and historical process, and hence beyond the explanatory reach of new historicist critique – emerges only *after* the breakdown of the masque; and it emerges in the mode and moment of what Jameson terms 'dialectical shock', in the positive potentiality nascent in the moment of negation. For the breakdown of the masque opens up another *mise en abîme*, this one stretching far into the future as opposed to the past, and seen by Prospero as the occasion to 'be cheerful' (IV.i.147) in the face of Ferdinand's alarmed consternation. For Prospero the ending of the revels prefigures the end of history itself as a cycle of repetition:

Our revels now are ended. These our actors,
As I foretold you were all spirits, and
Are melted into air, into thin air,
And, like the baseless fabric of this vision,
The cloud-capped towers, the gorgeous palaces,

The solemn temples, the great globe itself,
Yea, all which it inherit, shall dissolve,
And, like this insubstantial pageant faded,
Leave not a rack behind.

(IV.i.148–56)

The Renaissance commonplace of 'life is a dream' here turns into a totalizing and framing vision of history: as the masque has dissolved into the play now in performance at the 'Globe', so will the play soon disperse into the 'great globe' of the world, which will itself, with all that belongs to it and all to whom it belongs, dissolve into ... something else, invoked but unnamed by Prospero.

Before identifying overhastily that 'something else', let us consider its characteristics. All that is clear is that it will not be more of the same, history as usual and as we have come to know it, the recurrent nightmare. Prospero's invocation of last things, of an ultimate collective destiny, effectively brackets human history within a containing structure of radical indeterminacy and a containing discourse of radical unknowing. The language through which this wholesale dissolution of forms is envisioned is itself radically unfixed. Do the 'cloud-capped towers, the gorgeous palaces,/The solemn temples' refer to those of the masque or those of the world? They certainly recall the *alta moenia Romae* (walls of lofty Rome) invoked in the opening lines of the *Aeneid*. Do they stand for a history of glorious and significant accomplishment, or a narrative of vanity, oppression and mystification? What about 'the great globe itself,/Yea, *all which it inherit*'? Subject and object are here reversible; does the globe belong to all, or do all belong to the globe? What has happened to the dynastic relations of 'inheritance', the successions of property and power, on which the action of the play, and our readings of it, have so far focused and turned? Are these too now regarded as 'insubstantial'?

The great monologue seems to grasp that in some ultimate, profound, and prepotent sense *no one owns anything* and *never did own anything*: the condition of death or apocalypse or utopia. Indeed, the word 'inherit' – as editors often notice – resonates powerfully with its use in the prophetic context of the Sermon on the Mount, where it is 'the meek' who shall 'inherit the earth' (*Matthew* 5: 5). Yet it would be wilful to specify any further the content of Prospero's – and Shakespeare's – final discourse of last things, to name what exists at the vanishing point of this ultimate *mise en abîme*. The name we assign to it will be a function and projection of our own philosophy of history at any given moment. Is it the Christian apocalypse, an existentialist holocaust, a revolutionary utopia, a deconstructive aporia? All at once? Or something else? Whatever the destiny envisioned on the other side of this consuming dissolution of known forms and relations, it is clearly conceived as a collective destiny, one that throws into relief and into insignificance the clash of factional agendas that have held the stage up to now. Prospero's monologue projects a position and perspective from which the politics of the present – his and ours – can only seem petty and divisive in their insistent distinctions of 'mine' and 'thine'.

From this moment onwards, such distinctions prove increasingly difficult to maintain, as the systematic assertion of difference on which history – and the play – has so far moved, but moved in circles, suddenly seems arbitrary indeed. It is at this point that Ariel prompts Prospero, across the phylogenetic distinction between them, to 'become tender' towards the suffering courtiers – 'Mine [affections] would, sir, were I human' (V.i.20) – and Prospero responds in 'kind', affirming his bond of relatedness rather than avenging, like his epic precursors, its prior betrayal. This affirmation of community, it should be noted, extends not only horizontally to re-establish family and dynastic relations within his own social class but resonates vertically as well, across distinctions of class and perhaps even species: 'this thing of darkness I / Acknowledge mine' (V.i.275–6). Whatever else this 'mine' may mean, it suggests more than the relations of private ownership between master and slave. The play's final act of dissolution, it too a consequence of the changed perspective of the great monologue, signifies the breakdown of traditional relations of authority in all senses. Not only does Prospero regain his ducal power (one sense of his 'magic') only to anticipate its renunciation, but he also renounces once and for all his 'art' (his 'magic' in another sense) in which he had formerly insulated himself in the oxymoronic private utopia of his library. His epilogue, delivered on the egalitarian platform of the apron-stage, appeals to the audience in the closest thing to a utopian code to date: 'As you from crimes would pardoned be,/Let your indulgence set me free' (IV.i.337–8). The rewritten cadences of the Sermon on the Mount are once again hard to miss.

More than any other play of Shakespeare's, *The Tempest* has been the cynosure of a new historicist critique far less historically 'radical' than the play itself. This is not surprising when we recognize that *The Tempest* envisions the very opposite of the politics of cultural specificity and difference that underwrites that critical school. For of all Shakespeare's plays this is the one least vulnerable to ideological demystification in the name of 'difference', precisely because it knows what lies on the other side of 'difference' as its dialectical outcome, and does the full work of demystification – pre-eminently of 'difference' itself as only a displaced struggle for 'dominance' – by and on itself. A politics of cultural pluralism cannot be a politics of collective solidarity, but its opposite and obstacle. Yet the current logic of cultural pluralism – central to the new historicist critique of a universalist canon and a 'universal' Shakespeare – will, if carried far enough, lead forward to the reconstitution of a new historical metanarrative and a universal and 'utopian' Shakespeare always already at the end of it. After all, if Shakespeare – at least the Shakespeare of *The Tempest* – can be infinitely appropriated to every conceivable shade and position of 'difference', then the spectrum of difference begins to look, as it fills out, for all practical and indeed theoretical purposes like a rehabilitated universality. And some day *The Tempest* will begin to look to others, as it already does to me, like Shakespeare's greatest *history play*.

Theory in Practice

Our reading of *The Tempest* in the light of Fredric Jameson's theory of the 'political unconscious' has brought us to the point of openly engaging – and opposing – in the name of a more comprehensive historical criticism, the current politics of 'cultural pluralism' that underwrites the dominant new historicist readings of the play, their recourse to creative 'play' with history. This is only as it should be, if the claims of political criticism in general, and those of Jameson's 'enlarged' Marxism in particular, are to be taken seriously enough to be tested against the texts they purport to illuminate. The ultimate justification of theory, as Marx himself asserts, is practice,[12] and in the field of literary criticism, that must mean the reading of texts in terms of their political implications for the present and future, as well as for the past that produced them. From the viewpoint of a 'utopian hermeneutic', the 'negative critique' of the new historicism – in its fixation upon the strategies of containment enacted by the text within its early colonial context – seems itself unwittingly 'contained' within the currently dominant politics of 'divide and rule' that only increases the tensions but maintains the paralysis of our status quo.

But given its capacity to sublate this negative critique within an enlarged historical criticism, how well has Jameson's utopian hermeneutic served us as a theory of political reading? Does not its 'utopian' dimension, its reassertion of 'collective destiny', depend on a faith or credulousness towards grand historical metanarratives that most of us seem to have lost beyond retrieval? Is not its rehabilitation of the typological methods, if not the religious content, of medieval scriptural exegesis somewhat too redolent of the hermeneutic machinery – and the ghost within it – of an older idealist criticism, if not of an older religious ideology itself? Does Jameson's theory not return to contemporary criticism some of that mystification which made it for Northrop Frye, writing in the 1950s, 'a mystery-religion without a gospel' (Frye 1957: 14): precisely what critical theory in virtually all its forms has laboured so strenuously over the past two decades to expunge from it? Does it amount, after all, to one step forward and two steps back? Such nagging questions are only aggravated by the eloquent silence with which Jameson's 'utopian hermeneutic' has been received by left-wing critics in the decade since its publication.

Perhaps the culture of the 1980s, which witnessed on almost a daily and world-wide basis multiplying examples of unprecedented individual and corporate rapacity executed under the banner of a resurgent politics and economics of the Right, made this 'hermeneutics of faith' in a reinvented communal destiny seem 'utopian' indeed in the popular and pejorative, and indeed negatively Marxian, sense. Certainly the left-wing criticism that did become 'dominant' in that decade, at least within theoretical circles in the academy, was of a 'negative' rather than 'positive' valency, a 'hermeneutics of suspicion' towards all such metanarratives, the historicisms of Eagleton and Greenblatt rather than Jameson. Yet some unfashionable things prove to be only ahead of their time – just as some fashionable things are soon left behind for ever – and the value of Jameson's theory will be tested ultimately – and appropriately, only by history. By 'history', that is, not in the weak, conventionalist sense of its short-term *persuasiveness* to contemporary critical orthodoxies, but in the stronger, realist sense of its long-term *predictiveness* of the course of criticism and culture at large. The logic of Jameson's own criticism, after all, insists on no less; its sustained appeal is to a 'bottom line' that runs deeper than the ideological positionings that characterize criticism at the moment, to the 'absent cause' of the history that determines them, the ineluctable workings of which he compares to the 'invisible hand of the marketplace' in classical economics.

Yet 'history' – for reasons we have already explored – has always been hard to distinguish from 'ideology', particularly for a Marxism inclined to regard the latter as what is written by those in power and the former as precisely what shows its hand only after the fact and in the mode of 'shock', as 'what hurts'. My own lingering reservations over the theory I have here put to the test, concern precisely its own residual rhetoric of an older Marxist optimism that history is moving, invisibly yet inevitably, towards something better as well as larger than the particular and repeated nightmares of the past. Of course, without such optimism and its rhetoric there could be no Marxism. As a nineteenth-century – indeed a 'Victorian' – theory, Marxism carries with it a dual lineage: a 'scientific', or critical, side directed analytically against the capitalism out of which it was born; and a 'utopian' or residually religious side projected messianically or evangelically towards a socialist future. How the transition from one to the other is to come about in practice has always been a matter of contention.

Meanwhile, the · Marxist metanarrative of a nascent socialism struggling to emerge from its class struggle with a world capitalism on the verge of collapse under the weight of its contradictions remains open to suspicion and scepticism, as its antagonist continues to demonstrate amazing resiliency, while the 'progressive' forces of communist experiment in this century seem to be in a state of sweeping and accelerating collapse. Yet the Marxian *locus classicus* of this story – the great passage at the beginning of *The Manifesto of the Communist Party*, in which the history of all previous societies is characterized in its essence as that of class struggle – allows for another, less hopeful ending. Our story ends either with the 'revolutionary reconstitution of society at large', or – as has happened before in history – 'in the common ruin of the contending classes' (Marx and Engels 1959: 49). In either event, the metanarrative is preserved even if its antagonists are not.

Whatever the disasters of political practice in this century – and our premonitions of world historical catastrophe at the present moment – the Marxist theory of history lives on in Jameson's work in the form of a metanarrative driven by a materialist *logos* that shapes events in the world as their 'absent cause' and moves at least potentially towards a 'realm of freedom' as its collective outcome, despite all perverse efforts to repress and contain its working. This makes it sound, as has often been noted with reproach, a lot like the narratives of religion. But the comparison between Marxism and religion as rising narratives of collective destiny – explicitly drawn by Jameson himself – represents not a contradiction but

a two-way street, in which the former is not necessarily discredited by its association with the latter. On the contrary, such a comparison may also function to rewrite certain religious concepts – most notably Christian historicism and the 'concept' of providence, but also the pre-theological systems of primitive magic – as anticipatory foreshadowings of historical materialism within precapitalist social formations in which scientific thinking is unavailable as such.

(1981: 285)

The Tempest is not an explicitly Christian play, nor is its 'magic' the expression of a primitive pre-theological system; yet it is deeply compatible and consonant with both, as we have seen it to be with historical materialism as well. So much so, we might be justified in viewing the play's representation of history as a kind of 'missing link' between the historical schemes of Christianity and Marxism – or Hegelianism at the very least – in something of the way we, and many others, have viewed the *Aeneid* as just such a link between the proto-theology of Homeric epic and the Christian theology of the Bible and its exegesis. What else is it to regard Virgil, as he was regarded for more than a millennium, as a proto-Christian poet, an *anima naturaliter Christiana*? That history is a gigantic metanarrative of types and pre-figurations *under constant revision*, and, on its way to fulfilment, provides a strong textualism neither un-Shakespearian nor un-Marxist. Freud has been read repeatedly – initially by Freud himself – as transcribing the insights of the poets, pre-eminently Sophocles and Shakespeare, into the systematic discourse of a 'scientific' age. If something analogous can be said of Marx as well, then the current quarrel of materialist criticism with poetry – at least with Shakespeare – will have to take a different turn, if not be resolved altogether.

To read *The Tempest* along these lines, as I have attempted, with Jameson's powerful help, to do, is only to reinvent and extend an 'allegorical' mode of reading that was once the cultural norm – not only for medieval exegesis of the Bible but also for Renaissance interpretation of the pagan classics themselves – but a mode that has been fragmented and contained by the specialist, 'scientific' and professional vested interests within literary criticism, along with other forms of cultural activity, in its own historical development under capitalism. In the case of *The Tempest*, not even 'bourgeois criticism' at its most fragmented and contained has been able to resist the strong pull towards allegorization exerted by this text, albeit in the modes of fragmentation and recontainment: in the nineteenth century, the age of the 'author' and the flowering of 'bardolatry', the play was repeatedly allegorized as Shakespeare's autobiographical 'farewell to the stage'; and earlier in our own century, as a re-enactment of ancient mystery rites, of the triumph of Renaissance individualism, of the history of the Church, and so on.

Allegorizations of *The Tempest* had so proliferated by the middle of the twentieth century, in fact, that historical and formalist critics alike felt the need to put a lid on them. Kermode (1957: lxxxii–lxxxiii), for example, warned in his influential edition of the play against 'the wilderness of undisciplined allegory' and 'the vein of free allegory'. And Frye (1959: 19) himself claimed that '*The Tempest* is not an allegory, or a religious drama: if it were, Prospero's great "revels" speech would say, not merely that all earthly things will vanish, but that an eternal world will take their place'. To say the play is not an allegory of Christianity as such should not, however, mean it is not an allegory of history in a revised and secular sense – particularly for a critic who recognizes that all interpretation is essentially allegorical – what we have termed an act of 'transcoding' between literary text and discursive context. In this sense, the 'negative critique' of recent colonial interpretation is very much another allegorization. The problem with the multiplicity of allegories occasioned by *The Tempest*, including the most recent, is not that they are allegories, nor that they are 'undisciplined' or 'free', but that they are partial and exclusive allegories, tendentious appropriations of the text to the special interests, fragmented politics, and competing historical accounts of a culture no longer coherent enough to find the text legible in anything like its totality.

That *The Tempest* should again be legible to such an expanded transcoding may well be conditioned by the recent expansion of the political code in our own cultural discourse to include virtually everything from pronouns to prophylaxis, and certainly that domain of literary criticism which was formerly held to be 'above politics'. But the invitation for such a transcoding comes from the side of *The Tempest* as well, as its long history of repeated but partial attempts at allegorization attests. For, paradoxically, it is the powerful compression of its little world made cunningly, what can only be termed the 'radical formalism' of *The Tempest*, that enables so expansive a potential for representation and authorizes us to read nothing less than the great globe itself out of it. Shakespeare's all but shortest piece, a seamless and symmetrical – indeed neo-classical! – construct of 2000 lines, *The Tempest* spans the known world from the Old to the New, includes much of the phylogenetic scale or 'chain of being' in its cast, adumbrates the great cycles of human history in retrospect and prospect, subsumes the major genres of comedy, tragedy, pastoral, epic and romance within a single play, and enacts in the process the Virgilian progression of Shakespeare's own career as a poet. Never has a work of art done so much work in so little art; never has the allegorical power of that art been so inseparable from the art of power – that is, the politics – it allegorizes.

My own allegorical 'transcoding' of so economical a text is offered as only a preliminary and pedagogic contribution to a much larger project: a 'newer' and 'stronger' historicism that is simultaneously an intensive textualism more challenging to the heroic aspirations of contemporary critical theory than the decanonizing critique mounted by the new historicism under the banners of the various special interest groups within culture today. Such a project might help to return criticism from the cultural margins it currently occupies to the cultural centrality it once enjoyed. For the allegorical reinterpretation of the great texts of the past in the light of an unfolding collective destiny is the traditional role of criticism in all its major historical incarnations. Such an activity requires not the denial or repression of the ideological functions served by the texts of the past, but the fresh recognition and reinvention of that utopian perspective within which they always already exist, and, at their best, foreshadow with the power of prophecy. From the viewpoint of such a 'utopian historicism', the oppositions with which we began, between the formal and historical dimensions of literary texts and between the 'idealist' and 'materialist' traditions of their criticism, would dissolve into a genuinely *radical* humanism.

SUPPLEMENT

NIGEL WOOD: Your conclusion is 'utopian', as you suggest, wherein the oppositions with which you commence your essay are seen to dissolve (prospectively?) in a 'genuinely *radical* humanism'. This is a striking agenda for one reared on the axiom that Marxist thought is defiantly non-humanist. Is it as simple as that? Don't you have to deny the traditional humanist emphasis on individualism and a continuity with the traditionally derived canon to arrive at that point?

HOWARD FELPERIN: The difficulty you express may simply be a matter of terminology. My term 'radical humanism' may not be as oxymoronic as it might sound.

First, 'radical'. Many of those critics who label themselves 'radical' nowadays seem to me anything but. 'Radicalism' implies a going back to 'roots', to basic or first principles, in effect, to an irreducible or essential form of social organization. Such an 'essentialism', if that's what it is, is rejected out of hand by the various critical 'conventionalisms' dominant today, even those of a leftward or materialist cast. Such a rejection also seems to me inconsistent not only with *The Tempest* – the virtuoso example of imaginative 'radicalism' – but also with Marxism, which must presuppose a certain human essence, at least in a materialist sense, on which a more valid social reality than the ones we have could be constructed.

Which brings us to 'humanism'. This is a Renaissance term, after all, referring to an underlying compatibility between the most enlightened classical and Christian representations and explanations of human 'nature' – their 'canon', in fact. The 'humanists' were not only the intellectual but sometimes also the political avant-garde of their day, as attested by the example of More's *Utopia* (1516) – another indisputable 'source' for *The Tempest*. The 'liberal humanism' repeatedly vilified nowadays in left-wing criticism for its ideology of individualism is very much a later, post-Christian and post-industrial revolution idea. The humanism to which I refer has more to do with More's than with George Eliot's or George Orwell's, and does not seem incompatible, in its basics and concern with basics, with Marxism, if not with Althusser's version of Marxism. Hence, a 'radical humanism'. And one very much consistent with the style and substance of *The Tempest*, where such issues are inescapably in play and in question.

NW: I'm intrigued by your scepticism at the two new historicisms expressed most recently in your *The Uses of the Canon* (1990), where both cultural poetics and materialism (the latter unexpectedly) provide themselves with shaky theoretical foundations for historical analysis by denying history an extra-textual status, yet your '"newer" and "stronger" historicism' (this essay, p. 64) draws power from an unflinching textual emphasis. How, in short, do we relate the wider concerns of history to the needs of interpreting an individual text without resort to some generalized *Zeitgeist* or to more close reading?

HF: My scepticism is towards any criticism that tries to tell us what to think and do politically on the basis of historical interpretations that are ideological in the 'weak' sense – and that is all they can be when history becomes only another text. In such a situation – that of the textuality of history – our only recourse is to be very close and attentive readers rather than loose and tendentious ones. Cultural poeticians and materialists, in their zeal to get somehow 'beyond' or 'outside' a textuality they also claim is pervasive, have tended to be readers of the second rather than the first kind. I have always tried to acknowledge those who have seemed to me exceptions to this tendency, or who at least struggle with it. If reading is all there is – and the appeal to this or that *Zeitgeist* is also a function of 'reading' – let it be as close and complete as possible. Of course, this principle may work against political action or activism in the name of this or that interest group or movement. This is why left-wing academics felt such a strong need to oppose and, ultimately, to suppress deconstruction.

I myself believe that, as an 'absent cause', history has a non-textual form, but one that can be 'read' only after the fact and in its effects – that is to say, as the text it is not. It is apprehended, as distinct from 'read', largely in the mode of 'shock' or at least surprise. The idea of a *Zeitgeist* suggests too much in the way of purpose and predictability to historical process. It is a residually theological notion of history, but reflects a theology purged of its terror. My own view of history as 'what hurts' owes much more to Benjamin than to Hegel or Althusser, and so, too, I think, does Jameson's, who formulates it in this way.

NW: Does 'Shakespeare' as author matter much in your analysis?

HF: In a word, no. Criticism today is so concerned to deny 'bourgeois individualism' that it goes to absurd lengths to expunge such concepts as 'author', 'authorship' and especially 'authority' from its vocabulary – except, of course, to vilify them. When I refer to 'Shakespeare', I mean the text that bears this name on its spine rather than some biographical being who lived at a certain time and place. It is a metaphor and a metonymy of convenience we can hardly do without. I have even taken in recent years – in order to avoid the inevitable vilification – to naming graduate seminars of mine, not 'Shakespeare', but 'Shakespearian Textuality' or 'Shakespeare: the Text'.

But, to give my detractors their due, I do happen to believe that there was a man from Stratford who is distinctly and decisively responsible for these texts, if not exactly as they come down to us, at least for the fact that they come down to us, and that they carry with them a wisdom that merits their inclusion among the sacred texts of the world.

NW: Are political readings of *The Tempest* destined to be blind to certain textual features so that they can achieve shape and direction? If so, how do you counter those objections – I'm thinking especially of Rabkin's (1981) work on Shakespeare's 'meaning' – to myopic theme-hunters?

HF: I've partly addressed this question already, both in the essay itself and the above questions. In a word, yes, as long as the 'politics' and 'political readings' we are talking about are conceived as the unending clash of sectoral interest groups, such as feminist or gay or ethnic politics. Only what Jameson terms a 'utopian' politics and hermeneutics – and this means Marxism – can afford to take its shape and direction (to use your terms) from a social and textual totality, and its goal as the end of struggle. Very much an 'enlightenment' programme, and at the moment a politics out of time with an academy and culture dedicated to pluralist appeasement.

As for Shakespeare's 'meaning' – if we mean by that (as I do) the entirety of potential interpretations of his work – what is it but utopian, in the sense of affirmative, totalizing and prophetic?

CHAPTER 2

Embodying the Play

CHARLES H. FREY

[Charles Frey's approach to *The Tempest* may not seem like the application of a particular theory. Certainly, there is here a challenge to grand universalizing Theory, that is, the abstraction of principles of or reasons for aesthetic preferences. As he puts it, there is here an avoidance of *aesthetic* study: 'study through sense perception of the significant beauty in art' (p. 70). The objection that this is just subjective appreciation provokes the response that that verdict is indeed accurate but that this form of appreciation has often to be learnt, just as we must strive to be truly subjective. If this means letting go our hold of intellectuality, then so be it. This also entails a strengthened confidence in the reality of raw perception, that renews, as Clement Rosset stresses (in Kavanagh 1989: 86–7), the need to escape '"surreal" reality' (a thinking about it so as to preserve it) for the 'elusive' and 'immediate' reality that is actually as one experiences it.

One distinction must now be made: what Frey here illustrates is not one of those forms of criticism that stresses the subjective response and so makes a study of how various sets of readers actually make sense of and/or evaluate their literary understanding. This is but a sub-genre of 'analytical or social psychology' (p. 74) which usually at some point converts the immediate into the repeatable and standardized. For example, although David Bleich's *Subjective Criticism* (1978) has suggested the recognition of a 'subjective paradigm', this 'subjectivity' is not an aim in itself. This paradigm provides a framework for arriving at an understanding of just what *immediately* occurs when we perceive any exterior object that is not part of a transaction, that is, not one to which our attention is directed in advance by, say, a request or command in a 'situational' context. The object does not, however, remain very long in this autonomous state, for it is perceived, and so inevitably enters a sensory consciousness. The process entails the 'symbolization' of this object, whereby its 'real' existence is converted to its existence vis-à-vis the perceiving subject. It is only then that interpretation can proceed: 'the assumption of the subjective paradigm is that collective similarity of response can be determined only by each individual's announcement of his response and subsequent communally motivated negotiative comparison'. But why feel the need for such 'negotiation'? What would be achieved by it? While Bleich realizes that these 'announcements' would record no two identical responses, they would be 'the starting point for the study of aesthetic experience' (Bleich 1978: 97–8) – already a generalized destination.

In Frey's *Experiencing Shakespeare* (1988) there is no fully-fledged counter-theory (which would after all be Theory). On the contrary, there are several case studies where the immediacy of experience is dwelt on and, where possible, extended and enhanced. The aim of this is a form of self-knowledge rather than knowledge alone, an 'act-oriented' rather than an 'issue-oriented interpretation' (Frey 1988: 34). This still involves mental effort, the process of immediate 'analyzing, comparing, and generalizing' that constitutes a response of any kind and which is always bound up with the discovery of one's own subjectivity. The task is to 'make the analysis support the temporal encounter' with a particular play on a specific occasion, 'so that not all the reactive detail, the mix of sharp thoughts and keen feelings, seeps away through a sieve of generalization' (Frey: 1988: 38). It is not inevitable, there-fore, that this order of detail is destined to be ahistorical, for we are often quite aware of our history as we experience. For example, how else might we register the shock of anachronism or a revision of our views about a repre-sented past that we previously thought we understood? This accounts for Frey's approach to the play in his essay, '*The Tempest* and the New World' (Frey 1979; reproduced in Frey 1988: 48–62), where he resists 'colonialist' critical emphases to play off both historical and formalist readings to arrive at what the *effect* of formal experimentation and historical allusion might be.

Frey recognizes that theatre-going is always wedded to a discoverable context (Stratford-upon-Avon or Stratford, Ontario, fringe 'pub' performance or mainstream subsidized theatre, a play new to us or otherwise). We might predict a great deal from this about how it is likely that we would feel on such an occasion, but this would not give us access to how the evening was actually spent or what the process of watching the play was really like. In J.L. Styan's *Drama, Stage and Audience* (1975) we are reminded that live drama is not the sum of its theatrical conventions or textual meanings alone. The mediation of various choices, by actors almost performance by perfor-mance, engages an audience in subtly varied ways:

> The theatre reasserts that essentially primitive response to space and movement, colour and sound, the elements which literate man finds so alarming and perilous ... the picture must always anticipate the

words, and by generalized impressions the spectator is powerfully prepared for the specific and incisive focus of the words. The study of the drama is the study of how the stage compels its audience to be involved in its actual processes.

(Styan 1975: 4; see also McDonald 1991)

It could be the measure of Frey's challenge to Theory that this approach makes such a virtue out of its apparent hybridity and its refusal to provide materials towards a 'normal' or theorized response.]

NIGEL WOOD

Prolegomenon

Dear Student:

We haven't much time.

Sometimes more is less and less is more. You might think of Theory as agony at samsara, a necessary absorption into the external cycle of birth to death to rebirth, and as expressing desires to rise above this immersed, mundane, communal, body-soaked, unaware life, this quotidian, common-sensory *stuff*. Theory says that we tend to live in a blind, unrelative, shuffling round where we never know enough. Theory would wake us from dogmatic slumbers, out of our sleepy, childlike, sensational lives and our pleasure in accustomed rhythms. The Theorist persona, imagined from this particular practical perspective as minding everything, as needing desperately to abstract and generalize and control as it sidles toward our waiting ear, sharpens its tone to a hiss. Theory whispers: '*Carpe dais!*' (or *discum?*) 'You have so little time! Love is but love and touch but touch. Come up to the head, of your class, of your classic body, and look about you. Be aware. See the bigger pictures. Take time's survey. You can know so much more when flying with Theory's wings.'

Still, you may find enough time, or a truer, more resonant time, without Theory's domination. Sometimes more is less, less is more. Marx remarks (as engraved at his tomb) that philosophers have sought to interpret the world; the point, however, is to change it. Dear student, with and without the aid of Theory, you can question that gravely false polarity. For literature often beckons you neither to interpret nor to change the world. Literature often beckons you to find out where 'the world' is *and* to live there. Of course, you cannot live without interpreting or without changing things, yet these are neither polar nor all-inclusive categories. Theory, for instance, may help you see art as reflecting and setting social practice, as affirming and contesting economic/ethnic relations. But to *do* art, to practise it in any sort of emotion-involving or personally ruminative way, you may need sometimes to hold such sight quite quietly or even keep it momentarily at bay.

Theory watches the dance, the play, and notes how many ways there are to act. Practice slides out on the dance floor, the playing field, and does, ah yes, such a limited stepping, yet a stepping that can please in its very letting go of self-consciousness. Letting go of guilt, momentarily, over limitations in one's self- or social consciousness is not always a bad thing. Such letting go, momentarily, may free energy for going on with more, not less, responsible life beyond the dance floor.

Literature offers more and less than merely knowledge or power. Knowledge and power, however interanimating, may correspond roughly to two out of three ancient divisions of significant human activity as viewed philosophically: epistemology, or the theory of knowing; ethics, or the evaluation of doing (of exerting power or energy in relations); and ontology, or the study of being. Literature, here including drama, participates in knowledge and power, but it also functions importantly as access to being. The peculiar being of such art experience is more accessible through aesthetic (perceptual, sensory) study than it is through epistemological or ethical study, because aesthetic study (here defined, basically, as study through sense perception of the significant beauty in art) can help us experience its formal, playful quality, the way it seems to function in part as an end in itself, a way to let be.

In literary studies, in recent times, 'theory' has not looked, or often admitted that it looked, longingly at 'practice'. Theory has often assumed that practice is somehow fallen, that it takes place in a beneath world of unexamined assumptions, political unconsciousness, and hegemonic common sense, and that to experience or to appreciate a poem, play or novel is to wallow, without critical awareness, in unnamed and often objectionable ideological swamps. Since theory has tended towards the attitude that contexts and collectivities, seen from a generalizing height, have more significance than do individuated texts and persons, theory has also tended to discount uncategorizing differences among readers and their experiences. When you read *The Tempest*, in theory it either reinforces your social allegiances, class prejudices, historical identity, or it contests them, or it does both at once, but it does not function to help make your sensations, your breathing and pulse and other internal perception, more rhythmically alive, felt, yours. Such a claim for function would, in theory, be tantamount to endorsement of subjectivism or individualism. Even modest claims for only relatively local differences in response among individuals may offend dominant theoreticians who

> can write about reality as a social construct with almost no overt acknowledgment either that reality can set limits to the structures into which it can be built, or that individuals in a society may employ those structures in different ways. Oversimplification seems to be the theoretician's besetting sin.
>
> (Watt 1989: 195)

The idea behind theory goes back to ancient Greek accounts for an event or happening, public and official accounts submitted by persons constituting a *theōria*. 'Theory is the definitional opposite of *aesthesis* (or feeling) because it is characterized by a compelling, "jubilatory" sentiment forcing its expression beyond the sphere of individual, subjective perception and into the public realm' (Kavanagh 1989: 8). In the case of arts (such as painting, literature, drama, and the like), however, the reality of the art object can hardly be separated from aesthetic feeling and subjectivity since those are experiences designed to be stimulated by the art. To study the arts is to refine one's appreciation of pleasures and pains that can never be made wholly theoretical. When theoreticians herald a 'breakdown of the assumption that humanistic education is primarily aesthetic (has to do with pleasure)' J. Hillis Miller, 'The function of literary theory at the present time, in Cohen 1989: 110), they in effect deny the important reality of personal, immediate experience of the arts:

> This disqualification of the immediate real in favor of some more real or 'surreal' reality implies . . . a philosophical prejudice – a conviction about the insufficiency of immediate reality as something guilty of offering no firm hold either to reflection or to our hope for lasting happiness. To this philosophical prejudice we might well oppose another: a conviction about the intrinsic sufficiency of reality, and therefore about the futility of all those exterior illuminations called up in our failed attempts to elucidate its enigmatic singularity. Such a conviction about the sufficiency of the real is, of course, in no way tantamount to claiming that reality is self-explanatory, that it has no mysteries, that its existence is self-evident. Our position asks only that we consider this reality, as elusive and ephemeral as it may be, as, on the one hand, the only one there is and, on the other, as the only one capable

of making us happy. Yet even giving reality that status (one considerably reduced in terms of its philosophical pretensions) is generally rejected, because it frustrates all hope of rational explanation and all possibility of an alternative or a compromise. Hence the eternal taunts addressed by most philosophers to those thinkers who admit to being interested in immediate experience and even to being satisfied with it.

(Clément Rosset, 'Reality and the untheorizable',
in Kavanagh 1989: 86–7)

If significant aesthetic reality is elusive, ephemeral, and immediate, then no wonder it frustrates the generalizing drives of theory. A master-theoretician may attempt some sort of grudging compromise with demands of anti-theoretical experience and theoretical commentary:

> I am ready to concede that my text-dependence is a limitation. Yet I know what troubles me: I do not want to read in order to find illustrations for an argument or thesis, to appropriate texts that way. Reading literature is for me a deliberate *blinding*. I stumble about, sometimes hedonistically, in that word-world; I let myself be ambushed by sense or sensation and forget the drive toward a single, all-conquering truth; and I unravel the text only as it is simultaneously rethreaded on the spool of commentary.
>
> (Hartman 1991: 207)

Such compromise, notice, smacks of guilt, however, in the references to self-blinding, stumbling and being ambushed. How frightening it is to confront the reality of 'sense or sensation' within our own corporeal frames! Could that be a crucial component of reality?

> Theory's incapacity *really* to account for the real or, rather, its inadequation to the demands of the real – therein lies the source of the malaise evident among contemporary theorists who are hypersensitive to this question because, even though they do not attain the real through their theories, the real gets to them, like it or not.
>
> (Josué Harari, 'Nostalgia and critical theory',
in Kavanagh 1989: 193)

But what could such a reality be if not in part the elusive, ephemeral and immediate experience of aesthetic feeling personally and subjectively encountered within the human body? (In this essay, I am assuming, provisionally, that extra-brain, somatic messages are essential to emotional experience, 'that, in fact, emotion is, mainly, awareness of the disposition of the body' (Papanicolaou 1989: 129).) And if literature and drama deal in such seemingly private, subjective experience, then the question abides: can literary theory find means to accommodate itself to such reality?

Are there ways to do literary theory, to theorize about the practice of Shakespeare study, for instance, without oversimplifying or unduly stressing the degree to which we are socially determined in our responses or the degree to which our only significant responses may be those we can discursively share with interpreters sufficiently like-minded as to be able to comprehend us? Appealing to so-called personal 'experience' or to the immediate affective apprehension of literature has often seemed a tantalizing recourse for those who would avoid interpreting it in overtly ideological terms and avoid, particularly, the externalizing apprehensions of theory. In my book, *Experiencing Shakespeare* (1988), I attempt, with only partial success, to explore the attractions of 'experience' as very lightly burdened by overviews of theory. Let me share with you for a moment this book's attempts to press forward towards Shakesperience as a practice that could never quite shake the oversoul of theory.

Experiencing Shakespeare: Process-Oriented Theory

I begin, in *Experiencing Shakespeare*, by asking where Shakespeare is to be found. In old texts? In Elizabethan history? In ascriptions of authorial intent? In modern stagings and interpretations? Since all of these may be seen as versions of modern interpretation, as our own readings of texts, history, intent, and so on, then the issue of what particular methods we will use for our own reading, what assumptions and theories we will employ, comes to seem highly critical. The issue of choosing a method or theory should not become *too* critical, however, and I caution: 'Periodically taking stock of interpretive means and ends is one thing, but a wholesale flight to realms of methodological controversy is another. . . . I foresee . . . much fruitless bickering over which approaches are most valuable' (Frey 1988: 4). Such theory-obsessed bickering has, indeed, ensued, to the point that there now seems to be increasing interest among teachers and critics in favour of doing less theory and getting back, or on, to practice. Such practice, however, can never be as assured, or as relatively innocent, as it may once have been. In my opening chapter, I perhaps naively state as a goal

of Shakespearian interpretation the aim to help all playgoers and readers
'to see and to respond independently' (Frey 1988: 5). Theories of
response have helped to demonstrate the extent to which seeing and
responding to literature are rarely as 'independent' as we may wish to
believe but, instead, are dependent upon our social conditioning, our
group education, our membership in interpretative communities, and
our ideological orientation. Still, 'response' has always suggested a
species of interaction with literature much more immediate, emotional,
visceral, and, yes, relatively 'independent' of intellectual/social contexts
than other forms of interpretation or of criticism. (And nearly all forms
of 'reader-response' criticism remain mired in schemes of analytical or
social psychology that deny significance to literally immediate, direct,
or embodied response.) A little later in *Experiencing Shakespeare*, I come
at the difference partly in terms of the 'distinction between thinking
about a play and thinking the play directly' (Frey 1988: 31).

That distinction is a difficult one to maintain under some circumstances (as when Prospero refers to 'these our actors' or speaks his
Epilogue), but thinking about a play tends to summon up images of
post-play rumination, interpretation, criticism, whereas thinking a play
'directly' suggests experience opposed to more self-conscious kinds of
assessment. As I note:

> Though one can experience ideas, the term 'experience' in this
> kind of interpretation associates itself with the de-intellectualiza-
> tion of the theatrical encounter. A specially charged terminology
> of feeling and action tends to accompany appeals to 'experience':
> 'excitement,' 'gamut of emotion,' 'joyous re-vitalization.' Those
> who turn away from an issue-oriented interpretation of deeper
> meanings often gravitate toward an act-oriented interpretation of
> self-fulfillment and ritual release. 'Experience' begins to point
> toward synthetic temperaments as opposed to analytic ones,
> toward self-sufficient subjectivity of feeling as opposed to endless
> translations of thought.
>
> (Frey 1988: 34)

I proceed to outline problems of subjective impressionism associated
with appeals to experience and the counter-appeals by experiential
advocates to 'momentousness', 'wisdom', and 'significance' as integral
components of authentic aesthetic experience:

> At worst, experience shows itself to be a dangerous refuge,
> offering no real hospitality or warmth, only self-sufficiency, the
> opaque tautology of 'I am that I am.' In the essays of conceptualist
> interpreters, reference to 'experience' tends to appear, as shown,

at the moment in which the concept or deeper meaning being discussed manifests its remoteness and detachment from the reader's or watcher's encounter with the play. There follows the reasonable and natural attempt to absorb concept back into encounter. Deference to the superior revelations of experience then becomes a kind of verbal throwing up of hands, the Frenchman's *je ne sais quoi* – a simple admission that, after all, the play's the thing, there the action lies.

(Frey 1988: 36–7)

There is, in other words, a life in forms (conceived as stimuli for aesthetic taste or perception of art), a regenerative mystery of experience in Shakespeare's drama, that forever eludes the grasp of interpretation and criticism. That life or mystery, however, cannot be apprehended directly, without any thought whatsoever, and our grasp of such drama is always contextual:

Locus follows focus, that is, what one makes of the play depends on the purposive environment of one's study. There is no way to apprehend 'the play itself' freed from burdens of generic classification, historical origins, linguistic ambiguities, meanings as myth and ritual, psychoanalytic implications, vagaries of affective response, and the like.

(Frey 1988: 42)

Granted some truth in that statement, it must also be granted that not all experiences of a Shakespeare play will be equally 'burdened' by the factors enumerated therein. You, as a student of *The Tempest*, for example, may choose to apply a major portion of your energy spent in studying the play to considerations of its romance genre, historical origins, political functions and psychoanalytic implications, considerations perhaps prompted or furthered by essays in this present volume. You may also choose, of course, to emphasize one consideration more than others or even to neglect such considerations in favour of, say, giving yourself unrestrictedly to the sensory pleasures of Shakespeare's images and rhythms (a highly partial, if primal, method of reading). In *Experiencing Shakespeare*, I gropingly seek to assess some of these options, and I will proceed here briefly to outline my method and a view of certain results.

In Chapter IV of *Experiencing Shakespeare*, entitled '*The Tempest* and the New World' (Frey 1988: 48–62), I mediate between historicist and formalist readings of the play. I show that Elizabethan New World 'history' includes issues of race relations and of colonial politics but that

itself constructed in part out of recurring psychic tenden-
\[le, to fear and tame wilderness or strangers) and also out
...ic and literary traditions, traditions usefully viewed as less
... specific than commonly argued. My own argument favours a
flexible and historically aware blend of formal and content-based obser-
vations, observations rooted in long-term devices of poetic language and
theatrical art as well as in political history. I want to expose and contest
the myopic dominance of social constructions – such as the colonialist
Shakespeare – which fail to allow for ways in which the play's thick
texture and deep structure implicate many other significant issues.

While it is true that the text of *The Tempest* contains references to
the Bermuda islands, to the brave new world, to dead Indians, and
to a god 'Setebos' worshipped, in fact, by sixteenth-century natives
of South America, Prospero's island is narratively placed in the
Mediterranean. Caliban's mother was 'blue-eyed' and Caliban was a
'freckled' infant (I.ii.269, 283), so that any attempt to image Caliban
as a native American or as a black or negroid slave is distinctly
problematic. Shakespeare can, however, be shown to have been reading
in connection with *The Tempest* accounts of Jamestown settlers as well
as Montaigne's essay concerning Brazilian cannibals, and hence a
temptation to link Prospero and Caliban in some respects with inter-
actions in the New World between natives and Europeans may become
barely resistible.

What has happened among critics, as I show in '*The Tempest* and the
New World', is that one group attaches the play to class ideologies,
Eurocentric colonialism, and political debates that mainly postdate
the play. Another group attaches the play to its literary sources, to
partly fictionalized travel literature, and to widely collective models of
utopian and romance discourse, thus providing schemes of authorial
and readerly psychology or imagination that may seem less culturally
discrete or era-specific than the schemes provided by the first group.
I say 'may seem' because it should be questioned whether relatively
universalistic schemes of romance psychology can really be said in any
meaningful way to stand outside of 'history' as viewed through the
social practices and the hegemonic common sense specific to delimited
cultural bounds. For, 'indeed we have no other criteria of truth or
right-reason than the example and form of the opinions and customs of
our own country' (Montaigne 1991: 231). This is no modern or post-
modern doctrine, for the thought is Montaigne's in the same essay on
'Cannibals' that Shakespeare plagiarized in penning Gonzalo's speech on
the ideal commonwealth (II.i.141–62). In considering the idea quoted,

we need impute no universalizing intent or power to the Shakespeare who undoubtedly read Montaigne's culturally relativizing lines.

In the decade following my writing of 'The Tempest and the New World', any critics who have purported to find ageless wisdom and beauty in the play have been vigorously attacked by new historicist, cultural materialist, certain feminist and other critics who have argued, in a sense along with Montaigne, that all views of what may be ageless wisdom or beauty are views themselves quite historically conditioned and socially determined. Though such critics recognize in theory that there may be both 'the social dimension of an aesthetic strategy and the aesthetic dimension of a social strategy' (Greenblatt 1988: 147), the former has generally been vastly privileged over the latter. Thus, materialist critics have found, for example, 'that The Tempest is ultimately complicit with Prospero's play in treating Caliban's conspiracy in the fully comic mode' (Francis Barker and Peter Hulme, 'Nymphs and reapers heavily vanish', in Drakakis 1985: 203); and that

> Culture and Nature are not the simple opposites we tend to presuppose in our covert preference for one over the other, and convincing arguments exist to persuade us that what we call 'nature' is really just a special case, if not a deliberate invention, of what we term 'culture': that Prospero actively constructs Caliban as part of a complex self-establishing process.
>
> (Hawkes 1986: 23)

It is not difficult now to critique these materialist claims that The Tempest merely enacts imperialist discourse and promotes colonialist policies; nor is it difficult to reincorporate the 'colonialism' of the text into, say, the powerfully projective mechanisms of a psychological criticism stressing how Prospero learns to discover the Other within himself (Skura 1989). As the poet William Blake suggests (through the figure 'Los' in Jerusalem – Blake 1988: 153), we continually raise up our own systems of thought to escape containment in the systems of others. Theories that collapse art into politics will always be resisted by that part of us which suspects that personal imagination partly precedes and therefore shapes politics. Because The Tempest so palpably serves more than either social or private functions alone, it constitutes a special laboratory in which to study relations of art to social structures and individual freedoms:

> Shakespeare's play offers us a model of unresolved and unresolvable doubleness; the island in The Tempest seems to be an image of the

place of pure fantasy, set apart from surrounding discourses; and it seems to be an image of the place of power, the place in which all individual discourses are organized by the half-invisible ruler. By extension art is a well-demarcated, marginal, private sphere, the realm of insight, pleasure, and isolation; and art is a capacious, central, public sphere, the realm of proper political order made possible through mind control, coercion, discipline, anxiety, and pardon . . . The magic of art resides in the freedom of the imagination and hence in liberation from the constraints of the body . . . But . . . there is another version of mimetic economy, one in which aesthetic exchanges, like all other exchanges, always involve loss . . .

(Greenblatt 1988: 158–9)

The Tempest thus stands supremely now for 'the continued doubleness of Shakespeare in our culture: at once the embodiment of civilized recreation, freed from the anxiety of rule, and the instrument of empire' (Greenblatt 1988: 161).

In the chapters following 'The Tempest and the New World' in *Experiencing Shakespeare*, I trace a variety of responses to this doubleness, this reciprocating freedom and control, offered by *The Tempest* and, indeed, the rest of Shakespeare. I show how Shakespearian romance both attacks and preserves patriarchal power, turning from sons to daughters to extend the father's line (through sons-in-law) yet changing the nature and cultivation of love in the process. I outline ways in which Shakespeare's men, while in the tragic predicament of attacking women, force themselves and us to explore 'feminine' values of tears, milk and regenerative blood and their analogues in mood and meaning. And I argue that Shakespearian drama lends itself to authoritarian teaching of the moral high ground yet also waits patiently for teacherly recognition of its dramatic potential for radically corporeal and freely expressive learning, for student-centred and culturally creative study.

My experiential or process-oriented approach is thus designed to admit, on the one hand, the often repressive constraints of ideological Shakespeare as generally produced in the books, school and theatres that mainly reflect dominant cross-currents of cultural or collective energies. This dares to suggest, on the other hand, that the body is much, much larger than culture, that 'much of the mind works in the body', that 'corporeal and medical issues are invoked' in the study of Shakespeare (Frey 1988: 164–5), so that we may reverse the suggestion in the extended quotation above that *The Tempest* as 'art' pleases our imaginations because it liberates us from 'constraints of the body': we may assert, on the contrary, that our imaginative pleasure in *The Tempest* centres and grounds itself in the very closest attention possible to our immediate temporal-affective experience of the play's line-by-line unfolding. Such experience registers itself somatically, and, though 'culture' influences our interpretations of that registry, the somatic registry is far more complex than and more influential upon culture than the other way around.

To illustrate this emphasis of the experiential approach upon 'acknowledging the body' (Skura 1989: 67n. 107) as both one subject of *The Tempest* and one subject of our responses to the play, I will outline in the next section of this essay certain visceral interchanges between macrocosm and microcosm in the play and how those interchanges may connect with readers' own somatic registers.

Application of Frey's Experiential Approach to *The Tempest*

Having discussed relations between theory and experience, and having defended a space for a less theory-burdened approach to experience than may be apprehended commonly in criticism, I want now to dwell on one particular emphasis upon a reader's experience of *The Tempest*, the emphasis that such reading experience may be appropriately aesthetic or artistic and yet still attend to visceral, kinesthetic and proprioceptive sensations within the reader. In the two sections of this middle portion of my essay, I first briefly defend the argument that a student's experience of *The Tempest* may rightly include such somatic awarenesses as mentioned in the preceding sentence. I next outline certain relations of external and internal 'worlds' in the play (macrocosm and microcosm) and show how a reader may register such relations somatically.

First, to foreground an embodied version of appropriate student response, I must concede that, for a long time, it has been common among persons (mostly white, male academics) writing on the kind of experience most suited to artworks such as *The Tempest* to identify an 'aesthetic attitude' of enjoying merely perceiving the artwork without attempting to use it for any external purpose. Thus John Hospers, a philosophy professor writing in *The Encyclopedia of Philosophy* ('Problems of aesthetics', in Edwards 1967) defines the aesthetic attitude as one of 'savoring the perceptual experience itself', and he notes how different this is from applying a 'cognitive attitude' to increase one's knowledge rather than to enhance perceptual experience:

> Students who are familiar with the history of architecture are able to identify quickly a building or a ruin, in regard to its time and place of construction, by means of its style and other visual aspects. They look at the building primarily to increase their knowledge and not to enrich their perceptual experience. This kind of ability may be important and helpful (in passing examinations, for example), but it is not necessarily correlated with the ability to enjoy the experience of simply viewing the building itself. The analytical ability may eventually enhance the aesthetic experience, but it may also stifle it. People who are interested in the arts from a professional or technical aspect are particularly liable to be diverted from the aesthetic way of looking to the cognitive.
>
> (Edwards 1967: 36–7)

From such a statement, you might think Hospers was advocating a full, mind-and-body sort of enjoyment through 'aesthetic experience', but Hospers is quite typical of modern aestheticians in stopping short of any such recommendation:

> When we are viewing a work of art or nature aesthetically, we concentrate on internal relations only, that is, on the aesthetic object and its properties, and not on its relation to ourselves or even its relation to the artist who created it or to our knowledge of the culture from which it sprang.
>
> (Edwards 1967: 37)

Such an attempt to project attention out into a supposed aesthetic object and its internal relations, leads, of course, to great difficulty in the case of literature. Hospers writes:

> No one would wish to say that our appreciation of literature is nonaesthetic, and yet the 'aesthetic object' in the case of literature does not consist of visual or auditory percepts. It is not sounds or marks on paper, but their *meanings* that constitute the medium of literature, and meanings are not concrete objects or percepts.
>
> (Edwards 1967: 38–9)

A better, more workable truth is that, in the cases both of visual or auditory arts and of literature (which can usually be made auditory), the aesthetic 'object' consists of signs which we apprehend and process with our various senses. Seeing or hearing such signs leads, for example, to manifold responses within our bodies, responses which may weakly be termed 'images' or 'percepts' for some limited purposes but which actually include all the complex sensations that may produce thoughts, feelings, and even externally observable behaviour such as laughter, crying, changes in heartbeat and breath rates, muscle tension or relaxation, postural shifts, exclamations, and so on.

Aestheticians often argue, however, that art need not make us actually feel the emotions with which the art is concerned; such art can give us knowledge of an emotion without making us feel it. Thus another philosophy professor, Curt John Ducasse, has opined: 'listening with aesthetic interest to sad music *acquaints* the listener with the taste of sadness, but does not ordinarily make him sad' (Ducasse, 'Art and the Language of the Emotions', in Rader 1979: 69). Here, what is more likely to be a question of degree is converted to a question of quality. Sad music and literature may well make us sad, indeed, though often not sad enough to cry or sad about any particular existential problem. Still, our sadness is far from a disembodied thought. When we read or hear, similarly, in *The Tempest*, the Boatswain shout 'Hey, my hearts!' (I.i.5) or Prospero shout to the spirit-dog, 'Hey, Mountain, hey!' (IV.i.256), we 'know' what these exclamations 'mean' and what they 'signify' in the text not because of any visual image of them in our minds or auditory capture of them as sheer sound but rather because we can consult, through memory or recall, experiences of being roused in our attention and readiness for action by 'Hey!' We have learned to respond to this particular sound to alert ourselves and others to demands of effort, and such alertness only has meaning because we have felt and can still consult or recall the physiological coordinates of tensing muscles, straightening posture, widening eyes, and the like that tell us what an arousing 'Hey!' is for.

Literary *study* may thus properly enrich literary *experience* when such study helps or trains the student to read responsively (and responsibly) with growing awareness of the extent to which literary or dramatic intake is not disembodied, mental, of the mind only, but is instead embodied, attuned to, and exercising many registers of distinctly somatic feeling. It is not particularly difficult for a clinical psychologist to prove that readers can attend not merely to what an image looks like in detail as a mental picture (the 'stimulus proposition') but also to what physiological activity the image might appropriately arouse (the 'response proposition'). Such readers themselves exhibit measurably greater physiological activity during imagining than that exhibited by readers who restrict attention to the stimulus (Peter J. Long, 'Language, image, and emotion', in Pliner 1979: 113; Miller *et al.* 1987: 387–8). You might, for example, read the following lines from *The Tempest* so as merely to picture in your mind a body under water: 'would thou mightst lie drowning/The washing of ten tides!' (I.i.56–7). Or, you might read the lines so as imaginatively to perceive yourself drowning impossibly slowly, your lungs gradually filling with water, as you lie on the sandy shore-bottom feeling the water wash around you, rolling restlessly day after day, night after night, the length of ten long tides. The second style of reading is almost certain to produce more feeling and emotion within you in most senses of those terms – somato-visceral, cerebral, commonsensical. Yet the contexts of study and discussion traditionally provided for students of Shakespeare (and other artists) rarely encourage such a style of reading and response. It is not improbable, in fact, that many students who read those lines of Antonio's in the text do not even bother to 'see' a drowning man but merely note the fact that Antonio is cursing the Boatswain, thus converting Shakespeare's sensuously evocative image to a moral or social judgement: Antonio in effect calls the Boatswain a pirate; or Antonio wishes the Boatswain harm; or Antonio is angry and vaguely rails at the Boatswain.

What is at stake here is an argument over the main social and political functions of art and study of art. Will our culture see and teach art (including Shakespeare) mainly to express in us a disembodied sense of difference and alienation from the world and each other? Or will we reach through art our connections and sameness with world and others? If your study of *The Tempest*, of literature, in English courses teaches you further to objectify and distance your experience of the world as 'out there', as a threatening, inconsonant reality of external culture and nature, then you will further lose your own personal 'touch' with the world and probably with much that your inner physiology contributes to your feelings, thoughts and judgements. If you learn and give your energy, on the other hand (or in addition), to the myriad ways in which Shakespeare encourages you to enact and embody within yourself forms and pressures of the wider world and to project on to that world forms and pressures of your inner working, then you will find his plays such as *The Tempest* wonderfully challenging laboratories, or playgrounds, for your self-discovery and growth.

I will now mention a few of the devices through which Shakespeare draws the reader (or spectator) into styles and rhythms of attention to the blended energies of outer and inner worlds. Attending with perhaps unaccustomed care to what Shakespeare says and how he says it promotes the conversion of ordinary, objectifying experience into lively, subjective or inwardly responsive 'Shakesperience'.

The first scene of *The Tempest* presents an apparent storm and shipwreck, one that later turns out to have been largely in the minds of those aboard the ship, of Miranda who saw the vessel sink (I.ii.32), and of those aboard the other vessels 'Supposing that they saw the King's ship wrecked,/And his great person perish' (I.ii.236-7). What appeared to be 'reality' was but a play, such stuff as dreams are made on, yet it was real enough in the minds and bodies of the courtiers that they leaped overboard, 'Plunged in the foaming brine and quit the vessel' (I.ii.211). The magician's art has, in this instance, gathered or conflated outer and inner worlds, touching off the 'very virtue of compassion' in the spectator, Miranda (I.ii.27) and 'a fever of the mad' (I.ii.209) in those on board. Surely, all this is hint enough that we spectators and readers who inherit this seemingly insubstantial pageant of the play are enough 'like' (IV.i.155) its actors that we, too, may experience their passions, be 'moved' as Ferdinand is later said to be upon viewing the masque of Ceres, Juno, and the Nymphs and Reapers (IV.i.146), and even cast our own 'spell' out over the actors as Prospero alleges in his Epilogue (V.i.326). Such is Shakespeare's vision of an inter-animating relation between beholders and what they behold.

In the first scene, we find considerable talk of the court party seeming to 'assist the storm' (I.i.14) and exhibiting 'a mind to sink' (I.i.39). Though the Boatswain asks specifically, 'What cares these roarers for the name of king?' (I.i.16-17), it turns out that the winds and waves were but the sideshow agents of a providential overseer who cared very much for the name of king. Once more, the gap between man and matter closes. And, even, as the 'wide-chopped' Boatswain (I.i.56) guzzles down his liquor, so the sea seems to imitate him, making 'every drop of water .../... gape at wid'st to glut him' (I.i.58-9). Sea and seaman gape at each other, as if made of consubstantial stuff.

Again and again in the play, we will find this blending or interchange of outer and inner natures. The howling court party is 'louder than the weather' (I.i.37-8); the Boatswain can only be as 'patient' *as* the sea (I.ii.15); the old councillor, Gonzalo, is specifically invited to 'command these elements' (I.i.21); the Boatswain addresses himself in the same breath to what the Master may blow on his whistle and what the nearly bursting winds may blow (I.i.6-7). Though the sea is verbally personified as an impatient, roaring, gaping blusterer, it is the human actors on the ship who most concretely and evidently embody that tempestuous energy. That is, the world is like us; it can be apprehended in terms of our own being. The ship is 'leaky as an unstanched wench' (I.i.47–8), an image of both taking on and giving out fluids of various kinds (drinking, being inseminated, urinating, menstruating). Miranda imagines both the sea 'sunk' within the earth and the ship 'swallowed' by the sea (I.ii.11–12). Shakespeare creates a fluid, interappetitive, intestinal world where 'things' behave like people, where what we see can be no other than what we feel ourselves internally to be.

Shakespeare's relentlessly somatic imagination constantly urges our own conversion of external sights to inward feelings. Prospero describes his evil brother, Antonio, as 'The ivy which had hid my princely trunk,/And sucked my verdure out on't' (I.ii.86–7). The verb 'sucked' refers less to visual than to tactile or proprioceptive memory; we don't *see* ivy suck up moisture, but we have all experienced our own activity of sucking up fluids and feeling the pressure of a sucking mouth. We need to 'see' Shakespeare's image with our feelings. In Shakespeare's great tragedy, *King Lear*, the blind character, Gloucester, speaks of the man 'that will not see/Because he does not feel' (IV.i.63–4), and Gloucester later declares that he can 'see' how the world goes: 'I see it feelingly' (IV.v.143). When we work towards seeing Shakespeare's images (and the world we live in) less 'object-ively', we, too, are learning to see feelingly.

Shakespeare's depiction of Antonio as sucking ivy blends into the later reference to Antonio as thirsty for power, 'So dry he was for sway' (I.ii.112). Antonio says he will teach Sebastian 'how to flow' (II.i.220); he and the others in the court party have been 'sea-swallowed' and 'cast again' (II.i.249); he can make his conscience 'melt' like candy (II.i.278); and he believes he can make the other courtiers 'take suggestion as a cat laps milk' (II.i.286). Incessantly, almost obsessively, Shakespeare suggests the many ways in which our own consumptions and eliminations of fluids interact with analogous flowings in the 'outer' world. Set adrift with Miranda, Prospero 'decked the sea with drops full salt' (I.ii.155), an imitative action that provided him with 'An undergoing stomach' (I.ii.157). When editors and their readers 'translate' that phrase into 'courage to endure' (Orgel, 1987: 109n) or the like, they desomaticize the image of much more literally intestinal fortitude; they disembody the image, and literally cut off feeling. Prospero is carefully imaged by Shakespeare as one who can 'cry to th' sea' (I.ii.149) and sigh to the winds who in their turn return the imitated actions. Standing beside the 'holy Gonzalo' (V.i.62), whose tears are 'like winter's drops' (V.i.16), Prospero feels his eyes 'Fall fellowly drops'

(V.i.64). Through his agent, Ariel, moreover, Prospero rea
merely towards fire and air but also towards water and
world's digestive body. Ariel can swim, perform a tempest, make wav
shake, fetch dew from the Bermudas, do business 'in the veins o'th'
earth' (I.ii.255), risk confinement in the 'knotty entrails' of an oak
(I.ii.295), and image the underwater interchange of coral for bones,
pearls for eyes (I.ii.398–9). Through his intense imaginative power in
Ariel, Prospero connects the rhythms of his own blood and appetite to
the world's grand, intestinal power. When Ariel sets off on an errand
for Prospero, Ariel says (V.i.102–3): 'I drink the air before me,
and return/Or ere your pulse twice beat.' Ariel half resides within
Prospero's pulse and thirst; for the 'three men of sin' (III.iii.53),
Prospero/Ariel punningly imagines an instrumental Destiny who
caused an oceanic swallowing of the men and who 'the never-surfeited
sea/Hath caused to belch up you' (III.iii.55–6). On Shakespeare's
stunningly projective island, people see beyond themselves to what they
are within.

Prospero's other agent, Caliban, is also imaged in appetitive terms.
His very name suggests 'cannibal', and when he first appears he com-
plains 'I must eat my dinner' (I.ii.330). Prospero calls him 'poisonous'
(I.ii.319), yet he is the one who knows the 'fresh springs' of the island
(I.ii.338) and offers to show Stephano 'the best springs' (II.ii.154).
Ironically, this master of fresh water gets drunk on Stephano's wine
which Caliban takes to be 'celestial liquor', 'the liquor is not earthly'
(II.ii.112, 120). Caliban enters in the scene (II.ii) cursing upon Prospero
all the watery, boggy infections 'that the sun sucks up' (II.ii.1) while
Trinculo sees in the same moment a storm 'brewing': 'Yon same black
cloud, yon huge one, looks like a foul bombard the would shed his
liquor' (II.ii.20–1). Trinculo calls Caliban a 'fish' (II.ii.25). These 'low'
characters are, of course, mired in a tempestuous world of strong
waters; even as they inebriate themselves they are led by Ariel into a
'filthy-mantled pool', a 'foul lake', a horse-pond which makes them
'smell all horse-piss' (IV.i.182, 183, 198). Their inner and outer conditions match. Caliban, in a special mix of satire and poignancy, thinks
to imbibe divine wine even as he dreams of clouds dropping riches upon
him (III.ii.140), but his 'god', Stephano, who asks him to 'kiss' and
'swear' upon the 'book' of the bottle (II.ii.119, 124, 136, 137) in parody
of missionaries giving biblical instruction to natives, can help Caliban
to imbibe (imbible?) only a like drunkenness until he has 'drowned his
tongue in sack' (III.ii.11–12).

Of Caliban, Prospero says, 'This thing of darkness I/Acknowledge mine' (V.i.275–6) as if Caliban, like Ariel, enacts or extends a portion of Prospero's full psychosomatic being, embodying in the outside world what Prospero feels inside. The operative terms for this full range of being experienced in and through *The Tempest* are 'monster', 'man' and 'master'. Those who are monstrous, like Caliban, mis-take their appetites for drink, food, and power; they try to imitate the usurping sea. Not only Caliban, Stephano and Trinculo (Drink-you-low?) but also Antonio and Alonso participate in a 'monstrous', tempestous world of insubordinate attack upon the 'master' Prospero and his agents. As Antonio and Sebastian are about to murder the sleeping king, Ariel enters (II.i.295), declaring 'My master through his art foresees the danger' and singing his song to wake the sleepers. The murderous Antonio says the song was 'a din to fright a monster's ear,/To make an earthquake' (II.i.312–13). In his turn, the guilty king, Alonso, who helped Antonio suck up Prospero's 'sway' in Milan, thinks to 'stand to, and feed' (III.iii.49) with undeserving appetite upon Prospero/Ariel's 'banquet' which vanishes (III.iii.95–102):

> O, it is monstrous, monstrous!
> Methought the billows spoke and told me of it,
> The winds did sing it to me; and the thunder,
> That deep and dreadful organ-pipe, pronounced
> The name of Prosper: it did bass my trespass.
> Therefore my son i' th' ooze is bedded; and
> I'll seek him deeper than e'er plummet sounded,
> And with him there lie mudded.

In this play, as in life, to be in touch with the monstrous is to acknowledge the 'deep', 'bass' organ-pipes, without and within, that register our rage and low despair.

Such inter-expressiveness of inner and outer worlds may approach sentimentality or fallacious pathos at times, as when Miranda asserts that Ferdinand's logs, when they burn, 'will weep' (figuratively with bubbling sap) because they wearied him (III.i.19) or when Gonzalo thinks he spies in Antonio and Sebastian, as well as Alonso, a kind of appetitive guilt which 'like poison' can 'bite' their spirits (III.iii.105–6). Still, the vast, overarching metaphor of 'tempest' in the play as the all-dissolving storm of time and sea-change works well with the much more close, familiar range of embodied analogues employing shifting, swirling, vexed fluids within our mortal bodies.

Though Ferdinand is certain his honour will not 'melt' into promiscuous lust (IV.i.27), Prospero warns him against 'th' fire i' th' blood'

(IV.i.53), and Prospero soon confronts the hypnotized court party 'Brimful of sorrow' (V.i.14), running over with tears, afflicted with brains that 'boil', (V.i.60), and in need of water-clear reason:

> The charm dissolves apace,
> And as the morning steals upon the night,
> Melting the darkness, so their rising senses
> Begin to chase the ignorant fumes that mantle
> Their clearer reason.
> . . .
>   Their understanding
> Begins to swell, and the approaching tide
> Will shortly fill the reasonable shore,
> That now lies foul and muddy.
>
> (V.i.64–8, 79–82)

Insistently Shakespeare images the dark charms of entrancement and despair as melting, dissolving in clear tidal waters. Each of Prospero's three masques or shows (for the court party, for Ferdinand and Miranda, and for Caliban and company) acknowledges and abruptly interrupts ephemeral appetites for food, procreation and things (gowns, jerkins, luggage). Purgation and renewal of such earthly appetite tends to the pattern of clarifying, melting and dissolving. Thus the dance of 'temperate nymphs' (IV.i.132) and 'sunburned sickle-men' (IV.i.134) who sensually 'encounter' one another in 'country footing' (IV.i.137–8, with possibly bawdy punning) is dismissed and followed by Prospero's famous description of how the actors are 'melted into air' and how even the great globe 'shall dissolve' (IV.i.150, 154). Internally, the rhythm of the play is to instil and still the 'beating' pulse and mind (I.ii.176; IV.i.163; V.i.103; V.i.246) and so perhaps to urge reader and spectator towards a similar rhythm and release. Though you may by the tempest-charms of the play be 'jostled from your senses' (V.i.158), still, at the end, you have the ultimate command to release the magician and magic through the rhythmic motions of your 'good hands' and 'gentle breath' (V.i.328–9). Always the 'spirit' spell may be dissolved in the somatic cell, the book of magic drowned in the watery workings of bodily life – ever renewed, ever free.

The experiential, affective, enactive, embodied, process-oriented readings of *The Tempest* recommended here are not so much interpretations or theories as they are invitations to you, the student, to let the play help you get in touch with rhythms of feeling, waves of excitation, inside your own body. For many decades, interpreters have been recognizing or acknowledging in Shakespeare image clusters of the sorts adduced above, but those interpreters have suggested no way to 'see feelingly' (in Gloucester's terms). Such feeling response is far from automatic or easy. Though it requires little overt behaviour in terms of speech, gesture, or other movement, it does require patient, almost meditative, attention to the interior, below-the-neck reality or massaging of one's own body.

Conclusion

The particular kinds of significance ascribed here to *The Tempest* are obviously limited in depth and scope. No one theory or application of theory can hope to provide more than a partial reading or use of the text. Not even the most eclectic approaches can foster much sense of wholeness in treating Shakespeare's inter-tensional, ambivalent, ever unfamiliar plays. Theories and specific applications of theories are likely, in particular, to seem crass *usings* of their chosen texts. Instead of 'giving in' to the text in its 'plain' meanings, they appear to wish the text would give in to them and become but an example of their metastatements, one more specific to fill out their generalization. While I, therefore, have attempted to move in this essay so 'close' to the immediate, word-by-word language, texture, working of the play that my 'theory' might seem experientially, inductively verified, I must acknowledge that, of course, my induction only dances with a mated deduction, and I can find only what I am looking for. There is no blank access.

You as student must decide, ultimately, if you choose to look for the same features in or about *The Tempest* that any of the contributors to this volume recommend. In debating this choice, I suggest you consult your senses both of politics and of pleasure (terms which divide and join in various ways). You might, for instance, consider whether Howard Felperin and I somewhat conservatively treat *The Tempest* as if it were capable of reaching beyond or beneath ordinary confines of historical and cultural definition and limitation such as class affinity. My argument seems to assume, in particular, that 'the body' might provide some sort of innocent, privileged, apolitical ground for experience and that political and therefore wearisome and suspect 'mind' is to 'body' as political and therefore wearisome and suspect 'theory' is to 'practice'. To be clear and fair, however, you as student might need to review the first pages of this essay to review my questions as to whether mind and theory, like culture, not only define and shape body, practice and nature but also are defined and shaped in their turn by those forces. Unless you think you can solve that issue completely in one direction or the other, you need to be extremely careful in judging what you take to be either political or apolitical criticism.

Possibly unlike Howard Felperin or John Turner, I seem to seek, in an almost reactionary mode, to reauthenticate a species of non-social or individual experience of art and to connect theory and criticism to that experience. Most theory and criticism of recent years assumes the primary meanings and significance of Shakespeare, and all art, are social, communal, collective, and that truly individual (or personal or subjective) experience can hardly have communicable significance except on the unprovable assumption of an essential subject similar to others in an inter-subjective reality. That which is truly individual is private and must remain so. Notice, however, that I do not equate individual bodily experience with privatizing subjectivity. Though individual bodies are separate and distinct in many ways and to many degrees, their equally prevalent similarities in form and function reassure us that our 'own' experiences can be shared in some significant measure. When, indeed, we find in artworks such as *The Tempest* means to register the confluence, as shown above, between outer and inner bodies or worlds, or between other and self, then we can be happier knowing, or feeling, that what we see of outer world and other persons is in large part what we are within.

Felperin's defence of *The Tempest* as utopian historicist romance, Turner's insistence upon the play as historicist 'ironic' romance, and Wheeler's problematization of individual and social 'history' seen through the romance fantasy of the play all brilliantly exemplify the theory that art, or at least this artwork, exists importantly for criticism to think about in social terms, in terms of how the play connects to the historical societies in which it emerged. I maintain that these critics assume such social relations and functions of the artwork to be of highest concern when, in truth, the capacity of the artwork to employ its particular sign system so as to help us know and acknowledge that our relatively ahistorical bodily (internal, below-the-eyes, fluid-shifting, tempestuous, intestinal, organ-soaked, biological) life deserves, at this particular historical moment, equal if not paramount attention. What is each of us four critics seeing or showing in *The Tempest* to register its historical importance in this era as world cultures shift, paradigmatically, from opposing mind and body to joining them, thus welcoming the bodymind? If Prospero (and Shakespeare) could acknowledge the body as a thing of darkness, a tempestuous tumult of fluids, and a return home from drowned books, may we not aspire to like acknowledgment? I say yes.

Lastly, I have written in letter form to address the individual student as a person considering literary theory within the specific practice of performing *The Tempest* (whether through reading, seeing or acting). To me, 'theory in practice' implies not practising theory of the play but theorizing practice of the play. Such practice implicates individual performance. I do not see the other essayists as addressing practice in this sense. To my way of thinking, Howard Felperin provides a magisterial defence of possible utopian political functions for artworks such as *The Tempest*; John Turner lyrically urges us to doubt such romance-ic consolation or harmony; and Richard Wheeler brilliantly mediates between common and distinctive, universal and historical, features of authorial, characterological and readerly psychology in relation to ideas gleaned from the play. None of them, I would argue, goes beyond practice of theory to a genuine theory of student readerly practice. They all address *The Tempest* as a form of abstraction, a set of ideas without much concrete embodiment. For their purposes, it matters little whether the play be written in English or another language, whether it be in prose or poetry, whether the lines should be spoken in one tone or another, or whether readers vary in reading habits and capacities. They ignore, in other words, most of the concreteness – the material, sensuous, time-bound reality – of any specific practice of the play.

Notice, to give a final example, how Prospero's 'revels' speech has been interpreted and evaluated in the three other essays. Felperin sees Prospero addressing a 'collective destiny' but one attracting contradictory 'projections' (p. 58); Turner insists that Prospero's fantasy 'fails to soothe his beating mind' (p. 119); and Wheeler finds Prospero wishing beyond his vision of universal emptiness for a 'world of oneness with maternal bounty' (p. 157). What disturbs me in all of these treatments is not their variety but their apparent lack of interest in detailed, experiential, evidentiary, concrete registers of text. Application of theory to practice here seems to require not only little concern for implication, of key *Tempest* imagery such as actors liquidly melting and clouds and population dissolving (into metaphoric union with the fluid, tempest world) but also little concern for implications of common Shakespearian associations among 'round' bellies, breasts and wombs. I would argue that, for example, Turner's notion of failed soothing might acknowledge the amazing and arguably soothing echoes of vowel and consonant patterns in the corresponding feet of Prospero's two lines (IV.i.161–2):

Ĭf yō͞u | bĕ pleā͞sed, | rĕ tīre | ĭn̄ t͞o | m̆y cēll,
Ăn̄d there | rĕ pō͞se. | Ă tūrn | ŏr t͞wo | I'll wa͞lk.

The Theoreticians' cursory or cancelled interest in a concretely imaged and sounded life of the text promotes a dispirited subjectivism and relativism in contemporary criticism. It may be time to rethink an assumed alliance of idealism and formalism. A freshly careful formalism might discover shared embodiments of sensory reality deeply resistant to authoritarian or other manipulation.

Beyond such notice of the Theoreticians' inadequate appeal to the text's sensoria, however, extends my reiterated objection that art exists for more than historical, political, generic, or psychological evaluation. Prospero's 'revels' speech works to persuade us that, like fluid 'spirits', we living things will melt in air and dissolve as earth dissolves in water. What we may *do* about our intimations of that condition depends mightily upon the depth and breadth of our participation in its reality or being. Know that you breathe before you breathe what you know. 'A turn or two I'll walk/To still my beating mind': instead of merely doubting whether Prospero's political or sexual guilt permits such relief, we can apprehend, even absorb, the six-syllabled parallels here enacting physical rhythms through which bodily walking may still the pulsing material blood that we aggregate to immaterial 'mind'. Whether or not the character we summon up as Prospero deserves spiritual calm, the verse proclaims in formal proof that walking bodily turns may still our mental beats. That formal proof constitutes one crucial dimension of perceiving this text.

To rediscover through art that we live like winds and waters of the earth (melting to thin air, dissolving, minding our coursing blood) is to gain access to sensory being and beauty. Such being and beauty can never be wholly subsumed into categories of pernicious political quietude or rapt maternal longing. Shakespeare's art escapes, works below, the pasts and futures of political or familial wishing and regret. Such art subjects itself, of course, to social meaning and significance, contributes to communal shaping or decay, but its formal immediacy, like the formal immediacy of painting, sculpture, architecture, music, and sport evades discursive capture solely for the ends of truth or goodness. That evasive supplement or end in itself or immersion in *now* is what I mean by 'experience'. It is reached by 'practice'. May you come to it, dear student, always in your own sweet time and place.

SUPPLEMENT

NIGEL WOOD: I'm wondering how relevant your general critical propositions might be for the reading of non-Shakespearian texts, that is to say, those that might lie outside 'Shakesperience'. Are you asserting that Shakespeare's texts provide a distinct form of inwardness with such artefacts, distinct from those ascribed to Middleton or Marlowe?

CHARLES H. FREY: While I believe that Shakespeare does display a uniquely 'materializing imagination', one that relentlessly connects abstractions, ideas, and ideals to material and bodily worlds, I also believe that my call for embodied, experiential, process-oriented reading applies to other Elizabethan dramatists and, indeed, all art. Were students, teachers and the general public to resuscitate their imaginations through attention to somatic imageries and response propositions as outlined in my essay, they could enter a new reality of perception, sensation, feeling and thought. Typically, theory-driven criticism of, say, Ben Jonson or Christopher Marlowe will attend to ideological implications of authority, power, gender, class or morality in their works. This is what might be called 'Drum a drama' to make it march in one's political parade. Yet, truly, only the thinnest slice of a working brain will want to reduce drama – a material, sensory, corporeal activity – to discursive tics of hegemony or subversion. We may thus be told, of Jonson's *Bartholomew Fair*: 'Its renewed popularity, particularly with younger audiences, rests in its relevance to our concerns with class and with morality' (Teague 1985: 138). Class, however, cannot be apprehended directly; only playgoers and readers who really immerse themselves in, for instance, the sound and style and feel of Jonson's game of 'vapours' (IV.iv), testing the expressions of partly class-based language and behaviour on their own pulses, can begin to apprehend some of the refractory, trapped, yet comically liberating energies of Jonson's rakes, rangers, roarers, bawds, puritans, and the like:

Wasp.   'Slid, but I have sense, now I think on't better, and I will grant him anything, do you see?

Knockem. He is i'the right, and does utter a sufficient vapour.

Cutting.   Nay, it is no sufficient vapour neither, I deny that.

Knockem. Then it is a sweet vapour.

Cutting.   It may be a sweet vapour.

Wasp.   Nay, it is no sweet vapour, neither, sir, it stinks, and I'll stand to't.

Whit.   Yes, I tink it dosh shtink, Captain. All vapour dosh shtink.

Wasp.   Nay, then it does not stink, sir, and it shall not stink.

Cutting.   By your leave, it may, sir.

Wasp.   Aye, by my leave, it may stink, I know that.

Whit.   Pardon me, thou knowesht nothing, it cannot by thy leave, angry man.

Wasp.	How can it not?
Knockem.	Nay, never question him, for he is i'the right.
Whit.	Yesh, I am i'de right, I confesh it, so ish de little man too.
Wasp.	I'll have nothing confessed, that concerns me. I am not i'the right, nor never was i'the right, nor never will be i'the right, while I am in my right mind.
Cutting.	Mind? Why, here's no man minds you, sir nor anything else.

(Jonson 1981-2, 4: 84-5)

The energy of performance that Jonson requires inheres mainly in styles of enacting contradiction and quarrel, and the energy of apprehension that Jonson rewards inheres mainly in feeling the sound and motion and reach of the argument, the explosive scoff at puritanical Wasp who robotically distances himself from all 'confession', the soundplay and the dizzying punning on 'think', 'stink', 'right' and 'mind'. Do drink and vapour, as experienced here, etch out significances of class distinction, or elide them, or both? Jonson, like Shakespeare, is not so much to be figured out as to be figured forth. Imagination means as it moves, for we can only apprehend 'class and morality' as they emerge from the sensations of bodily life.

NW: In your essay, 'The Tempest and the New World' (Frey 1988: 52), you tussle with the central realization that 'when works of art are asked to generate their own meanings, they and culture generally suffer. For language is never autonomous'. Given the emphasis of this essay, how should we consider all the contextual information given us almost yearly, and how can we sift it and so develop a technique/method accordingly?

CHF: Ask yourself: does this information enhance my experience or re-experience of Shakespeare (or other author or work)? Am I being helped to see it feelingly? Are the terms of this information so remote from the terms of the text they treat that I have to do double and triple translation to make the indicated connections? How much of the full experience of the work in question does the contextual information point towards? Does the information help me respond to the actual words of the text and to the full range of its perceptions, actions, characters and ideas? In varying eras, varying kinds of information may come into greater relevance. Right now, I can envisage a whole generation or two of students interesting themselves anew in historical lexicography, pointing out that many editors don't seem to know very much about what individual words and phrases in Shakespeare (and elsewhere) signified in context. How could the large number of references in Shakespeare to homosexual behaviour, for example, have been missed or suppressed for all these years? Instead of working away from linguistic surfaces towards ungrounded abstractions concerning gender, sexuality, and the like, why not work, for a time, on the very materials, the words and phrases and images, that should ground the abstractions concretely?

NW: If I've read your essay correctly, then you seem to endorse a process of 'unlearning', where the intellectual responses kept at bay to allow more basic ones to take root. How have you tried to carry this out in your teaching?

CHF: I do not believe that my suggestions really keep genuine intellectual responses at bay. I am opposed to what I see as a kind of false intellectualism that employs only the thinnest slice imaginable of cerebral cortex to abstract from a fully resonant text one or two exemplifications of ideological or other theory. The unlearning I recommend takes place in the context of post-secondary education in English where students often learn to produce verbal abstractions concerning texts studied without learning to observe or respond to more concrete dimensions of the texts. An example of 'unlearning' I typically propose in class is the following exercise:

> In *Measure for Measure*, I.i, certain of Shakespeare's words are 'glossed' (annotated, translated, synonymed) by Bevington (1980) as follows:
>
> | Shakespeare | Bevington |
> | --- | --- |
> | 15 warp | deviate |
> | 21 organs | instruments |
> | 36 touched | endowed |
> | 37 issues | purposes |
> | 41 bend | direct |
> | 49 mettle | substance |
> | 52 leavened | considered |
> | 79 bottom | extent |
>
> How would you compare Shakespeare's words to Bevington's in terms of Latinate versus non-Latinate etymologies, levels of diction, specific versus general, concrete versus abstract, invitations to respond with somatic awareness, invitations to read emotionally?

This is a wonderful exercise to show students how editors typically gloss Shakespeare's sensuous language into non-sensuous channels, and it allows for very immediate, direct and sustained engagement of students with Shakespeare's language at primary levels of explication.

In class, I ask students to read aloud *with no observable emotion in their voices*. The results are often hilarious. We then discuss the sorts of emotion appropriate to the passage and work with all the defences that student readers, teachers as readers, and even actors might employ against deeply felt rendition. As the discussions of Shakespeare's use of sound, rhythm, tone, attitude, and the like all deepen, then students often begin to read aloud with considerable sensitivity. I may occasionally read aloud, too, say from the blinding of Gloucester or the first meeting of Caliban with Trinculo and Stephano, so as to model one species of emotional engagement with Shakespeare's language. I may ask a class to interpret and evaluate a claim such as the following by Linklater (1992: 31, 195):

The *way* you speak Shakespeare's words will determine the *depth* at which you plumb his meaning . . . Time and again I have seen, heard, and felt Shakespeare's words enter and restore power to a boy or a girl, a woman or a man, whose sense of worth has been obliterated by childhood abuse, social inequality or racial bigotry. This happens *not when they read Shakespeare, not when they hear Shakespeare, but when they speak the words themselves.*

I use myriad methods to encourage students' engaged reading and speaking of Shakespeare. Students sit in circles and read aloud, first making individual words their unit of responsibility, passing the speech around the circle. Successive students then speak in phrases (working from any punctuation mark to the next); then they share the speech by each speaking a full sentence, and so on to passages and scenic units. This method asks for no 'acting', dims the fear of the text, promotes full, democratic sharing, and leads to intense observation of how Shakespeare sounds, how he constructs his phrases and sentences and speeches, varying *kinds* and *lengths* and *structures* of all the speech units.

I ask students to write parodies and sincere imitations and to perform whole scenes in groups given plenty of time to memorize lines, work out stage movements, and shape a particular mood and purpose in their production. I ask students to write daily on study questions of their own and my devising, questions covering a very broad range of traditional and non-traditional topics (concerning performance, explication, interpretation, evaluation, backgrounds, sources, pedagogy, the institutional productions of Shakespeare, ideological and other approaches, social and personal functions of drama in past, present and future, and many other topics). Sometimes I summon a panel of four or five students who sit in the front of the class, sort out the students' writings for the day, and conduct the ensuing class discussion; the method allows for peer-speech discussion, swerve of topics toward genuine student interest, very full engagement of large percentages of students, and much humour, emotion, wit and mutuality. Always my emphasis is to connect feeling and thought, body and mind, to keep overly intellectualized responses at bay, when necessary, to allow more basic ones to activate themselves. Beginner's mind.

NW: You make the case of a play having a rhythm, from which we can release ourselves at the end of the play. Does that mean that our experience of a play always dissolves and cannot therefore be recaptured by criticism?

CHF: If the polar terms shift from 'theory' versus 'practice' to 'criticism' versus 'experience' then I would argue that the second set of terms may be conceived and employed in less strictly dichotomous ways than seems likely with the first set. That is, while criticism is often opposed to experience (see Frey 1988: 31–2, on Northrop Frye), there are obvious degrees of more and less practical criticism. Criticism, in my view, can quite directly assist in enhancing a reader's or spectator's *experience* of varied rhythms in Shakespeare's plays, and such assistance may be thought of as preparation for re-encounter with text or production or as meditation upon past encounter. Reading criticism, to me, is not the same thing as reading the play, but reading the play involves 'critical' kinds of responses. The question for me is when some kinds of critical thinking (employed while performing, reading or spectating) might abstract from and whiten out the full sensory, sonorous, colourful, synthesizing, ritualizing, whole-life-sensing attributes or functions of the play. I come back to the difference between playing and thinking about playing. Acting Shakespeare is performative. Reading Shakespeare is also performative. Reading Shakespeare is not the same as 'thinking about playing'. Doing theory or criticism – reading, writing or thinking about it – is different from performing Shakespeare in any direct sense, but it should contribute, in some significant way, to such performance. In educational settings, these distinctions are most apt to blur, and rightly so, as we move back and forth between concrete and abstract responses to Shakespeare, but that fact provides little excuse, it seems to me, for ever attenuating the more concrete kinds of response in favour of the more abstract.

CHAPTER 3

Reading by Contraries:
The Tempest as Romance

JOHN TURNER

[Psychoanalytic criticism of literature forms no consistent pattern. In broad outline it concerns itself with the origin of desires and even self-identity: the unconscious. Freud's essays on art and literature relate art to the dream, where the artist is kin to the neurotic, 'oppressed by excessively powerful instinctual needs', but without the 'means of achieving these satisfactions' (Freud 1953–74, 16: 376). Art, therefore, is an activity to 'allay ungratified wishes', both in the artist and also in his/her audience or readers (Freud 1953–74, 13: 187). Strategies of creation (*and* of reading) may be studied for their attempt to resist full acknowledgement of the unconscious. Primitive wishes have to be transformed into the culturally palatable or 'traditional'.

Analysis of art has therefore to scrutinize the text of the 'dream'. It appears rather as an archaeological site, with significant layers that need to be unearthed and reconstructed. The goal is to re-form, out of these fragments, an intelligible order. Freud's case histories usually result in 'cure', whereby the patient can be reabsorbed into 'normal' life, *but* the process of analysis is hardly a simple process of re-construction. The analyst's imposition of order involves an imaginative linkage between dislocated items. Just as a text can never be exhaustively (and thus totally accurately) interpreted, the analysand does not return to the past through analysis, but rather achieves a new understanding of it in the *present*. Far from recovering the past, it is reassessed according to a current perspective. Freud (1953–74, 10: 120–1) describes this goal of analysis in his case study of 'Little Hans':

> Therapeutic success . . . is not our primary aim; we endeavour rather to enable the patient to obtain a conscious grasp of his unconscious

wishes. And this we achieve by working on the basis of the hints he throws out, and so, with the help of our interpretative technique, presenting the unconscious complex to his unconsciousness *in our own words*. There will be a certain degree of similarity between that which he hears from us and that which he is looking for, and which, in spite of all resistances, is trying to force its way through to consciousness; and it is this similarity that will enable him to discover the unconscious material.

Just as the analyst involves him/herself in the process, we should not keep ourselves fenced off from the creative potentialities for association and even 'play' in our reading of the text. If the psyche is radically divided by the need for self-protection or self-delusion, the view of reality will be a *constructed* one and related to hidden wishes or fears – in short, the unconscious. The 'past' is always revised by a present-day need to colonize it, and this process addresses the need to 'tell stories' about ourselves (to ourselves) in order that we attain a shape or 'character' (in time and space) when we are confronted by the alien mystery of formlessness and the unknowable.

For Carl Gustav Jung, the emphasis for this analysis fell on how the self sought to express itself in recurrent myths or 'archetypes', not just through grammar or semantics. The struggle between the demands of self and the control exercised by social norms is evidenced in certain communal patterns of representation which are derived from some primordial store of images, that is, myths from the 'collective unconscious'. Jungian interpretation of literary texts aims to restore a harmony in the psyche that is attained by a focus on the particular form of these myths in the dreams or recurrent fantasies of the patient.

Both Freud and Jung held that the unconscious has a structure. Repression tussles with the unconscious, the id (the body's instinctual drives) with the ego (the body's defensive check on these drives) and so with the superego (the internal recognition of strong external prohibitions, such as parental or social authority), yet both believe that analysis can bring this conflict to moments of definition and so balance.

John Turner's interest in *The Tempest* as a romance stems from its attempt to synthesize divisive social forces. In so doing, it taps some of the mythic power that Bruno Bettelheim found in the simplest narrative: the fairy tale. In his *The Uses of Enchantment* (1978) Bettelheim understood that apparently sophisticated ideologies or philosophies could mask quite basic and primitive desires. Principally a child psychologist, he derived much of his wider social comment from the close observation of how early development structured apparently unrelated later behaviour. In work such as *Love Is Not Enough* (1950) he illustrated how emotional disturbances in the developing mind grew not only from repression but also from a lack of organization in the personality: where 'their living experiences have failed to coalesce and stayed fragmentary to such a degree that no more than the rudiments of personalities have developed' (Bettelheim 1950: 27). One of the most effective methods of integration was by way of allowing the child to grasp a totality or purpose to experience by way of fictional and imaginative explanation. In *Freud and Man's Soul* (1982) he emphasized not only Freud's explicit but also implicit reference to several sustaining myths (Bettelheim 1982: 10–15, 20–36).

Fairy tales expose the imagination both to dark and often otherwise inexpressible fears and anxieties. The threat of the unbridled 'id' is usually averted by eventually beneficent 'ego/superego' drives, but they at least avoid a one-sided 'sunny' world-view that the child will at some point find is palpably false to 'real' experience. Coping with the conscious understanding (defining it or fostering confidence in the growing self) often can only be fully embraced when the unconscious is channelled and given form:

> by becoming familiar with it through spinning out daydreams – ruminating, rearranging, and fantasizing about suitable story elements in response to unconscious pressures ... the form and structure of fairy tales suggest images to the child by which he can structure his daydreams ...
>
> (Bettelheim 1978: 7)

Given this almost therapeutic value, it is perhaps ironic to note in relation to *The Tempest* how Bettelheim also regarded fairy-tale heroes as possible role models in their typical progression from isolation to association. Starting from a usually non-social position (exile or a planned time of test), the hero 'is helped by being in touch with primitive things – a tree, an animal, nature' (Bettelheim 1978: 11). Not only does Prospero eschew any such contact, it could be argued that his alienation is deepened by his reliance on magic, in contrast to Caliban and Ariel's intimacy with the island's natural elements and their servitude.

In contrast to Bettelheim's concentration on psychological matters, Bronislaw Malinowski approached the necessity of myth in his 1926 essay, 'Myth in Primitive Psychology' from an anthropological or sociological perspective. Far from being an 'aimless outpouring of vain imaginings', myth was 'a hard-working, extremely important cultural force' (Malinowski 1954: 97). Its form may be fictional, but it has the force in savage society of a 'reality lived' whereby it 'expresses, enhances, and codifies belief' (Malinowski 1954: 100–1). Much like the cured patient's arrival at a viable image of his/her past, myth does not re-*construct* the past so much as *use* it in the service of the present: it is a 'retrospective, ever-present live actuality ... the statement of a bigger reality still partially alive' which also explains the complexities of social organization in a consoling or, at least, acceptable manner (Malinowski 1954: 126). From this viewpoint, *The Tempest* can cast light on Jacobean society by its very attempts at Romantic evasion.]

NIGEL WOOD

There is something of an old wives' tale in fine literature.

When Yeats wrote these words in 1906, he was struggling to define his dissatisfaction with a contemporary drama preoccupied with the dilemmas of 'modern educated people'. What it lacked, he said, was passion, characters of genius whose poetry had the power to enkindle their audience. Its meagre successes derived only from its 'being able to *suggest* fundamental contrasts and passions which romantic and poetical literature have *shown* to be beautiful' (Yeats 1961: 274–6; emphasis added). For Yeats, that is, modern naturalistic drama was parasitical upon the heroic drama of an earlier age; hence 'the stale odour of spilt poetry' (Yeats 1955: 280) that he smelt in Ibsen's plays. Hence, too, his disgust with the recent obituarist of Ibsen who had written: 'Let nobody again go back to the old ballad material of Shakespeare, to murders, and ghosts, for what interests us on the stage is modern experience and the discussion of our interests' (quoted in Yeats 1961: 283). It was, however, precisely Shakespeare's use of old ballad material that fascinated Yeats. Struggling to ground a new Irish theatre in Irish legend, he admired Shakespeare for his use of the passionate archetypes of popular imagination – archetypes which, in Yeats's view, gave Shakespearian drama its depth, its power, its inexhaustibility in the face of interpretation.

It was in his late plays that, as Leo Salingar has shown, Shakespeare most obviously set himself to make theatre out of popular tales and stage romances, 'grounded in folk-tales' (Salingar 1974: 30): tales whose narratives courted such deliberate implausibility that, in Paulina's words from *The Winter's Tale*, if their events were to be heard and not seen, they 'should be hooted at/Like an old tale' (V.iii.116–17.) These teasing lines, it seems to me, induce a momentary hesitation in an audience, akin to that which Tzvetan Todorov has identified as a characteristic response to the fantastical event in Romantic and post-Romantic prose fiction. To believe or not to believe? Todorov (1973: 157) argues:

> This hesitation may be resolved so that the event is acknowledged as reality, or so that the event is identified as the fruit of imagination or the result of an illusion; in other words, we may decide that the event *is* or *is not*.

For Todorov, the reader's choice is simple: a fantastical event is either real, imaginary or illusory. Yet perhaps Paulina's words open up a different range of possibility, more in keeping with the inherent illusoriness of stage performance. Perhaps the force of the metadramatic perspective that she introduces is not to clarify but to confuse choice. Do not her words tease the audience out of thought, mixing those categories that seem so separate to Todorov? Is not Shakespeare staking out for his audience the space in which his last plays exist – a space *between* the familiarity of the real and the ideal wonder of romance, a paradoxical space where, in Yeats's words again, 'things both can and cannot be' ('The Curse of Cromwell' (1937), l. 19, in Yeats 1950: 351)?

Traditionally, literary critics have followed Coleridge (1960, 2: 130) in approaching *The Tempest* as 'one of those plays in which the ideal is most predominant'. In his introduction to the Arden edition, Kermode (1957: lv) argues that the play celebrates ideal moral laws which can only operate imperfectly 'in the world of actuality', while Frye (1957: 286) honours this same idealism as a conscious abstention from irony on Shakespeare's part: 'The further comedy moves from irony, the more it becomes what we here call ideal comedy, the vision not of the way of the world, but of what you will, life as you like it'. Such an approach values the play as what we now call – although a word little used by the Elizabethan and 'never used to describe a play' (Stanley Wells, 'Shakespeare and Romance', in Brown and Harris 1966: 49) – romance: a fictive mode devoted to the idealization of human feelings and conduct. Humanists such as Sir Philip Sidney had praised poetry because it could bring forth a golden world out of a world that was all too palpably brass (Sidney 1973: 24); and the poet's labour thus stood for Sidney as a type of the moral duty of man to improve upon a fallen nature. From this point of view, Hermione's resurrection at the end of *The Winter's Tale*, implausible as it may seem, is an image of the precious triumph of patience and forgiveness over injustice in human affairs; and so too, of course, is Prospero's forgiveness of his enemies at the end of *The Tempest*.

Recently, however, critics have become more sensitive to what they take to be the ironies of Shakespeare's last plays; and, in particular, they have set out to challenge Prospero's power in *The Tempest*, seeing him not as a magus intent upon 'the restoration of harmony at the human and political levels' (Kermode 1957: xlviii) but as a colonialist bent upon the presumptuous imposition of his own will. They have concentrated upon the multivocal nature of a text which gives voice not only to Prospero but also to those whom he subjects; and they have emphasized what Patterson (1989: 156) calls 'the incompleteness of his reconciliatory and regenerative plan'. It is the openness of the play's conclusion that they most admire, since here they find an acknowledgement of the intractability of those real-life political conflicts that lie beyond the power of art to resolve. In a similar vein, we might read the deliberately improbable ending of *The Winter's Tale* as an exposure of the brazen realities of patriarchal power in Jacobean Britain, and of the impotence of human art even to gild them over. The weakness of such criticism, of course, lies in its insensitivity to the plays as romance. It is a radical criticism, the work of 'modern educated people' concerned to disarm and deconstruct those romance archetypes out of which these late plays have been shaped; and its scepticism may come too easily. Does not the theatrical power of *The Tempest* or *The Winter's Tale* depend upon an ability to reawaken ancient habits of response deep within the childhood of each individual, deep within the history of our culture? Only by first acknowledging these ancient habits of response, I think, can we begin to understand the sophisticated games that Shakespeare plays with them.

Yeats (1961: 524) wrote of Milton's verse:

> If I repeat the first line of *Paradise Lost* so as to emphasise its five feet I am among the folk singers – 'Of mán's first dísobédience ánd the frúit,' but speak it as I should I cross it with another emphasis, that of passionate prose – 'Of mán's first disobédience and the frúit,' or 'Of mán's fírst dísobedience and the frúit'; the folk song is still there, but a ghostly voice, an unvariable possibility, an unconscious norm. What moves me and my hearer is a vivid speech that has no laws except that it must not exorcise the ghostly voice.

It is the ghostly voice of the old wives' tale behind *The Tempest* that I should first like to invoke in this essay; and so I shall begin with a book in praise of the romance elements of an oral tradition still very much alive today, Bruno Bettelheim's *The Uses of Enchantment: The Meaning and Importance of Fairy Tales* (1978).

I

Bettelheim's beliefs about the fairy tale may be summarized in three main propositions. First, its origins are essentially endopsychic: that is, like those 'endopsychic myths' of which Freud (1954: 237–8) wrote to Fliess on 12 December 1897 (see also the reference in *The Psychopathology of Everyday Life*, Freud 1953–74, VI: 258) – it is shaped chiefly by the inner desires and fears of its tellers – of tellers, however, who are disciplined by the needs of a listening child whose own desires and fears help to shape their own. Second, its materials originate in the 'existential predicaments'[1] that characterize childhood and that continue to haunt the immature child within the adult narrator. And third, its purpose, its social function, is to provide the listening child with hope through the consolation of its happy endings. I want to examine each of these propositions in turn.

First, let us consider the origins of the fairy tale. Bettelheim wrote his book in the early 1970s in order to point out the limitations of those sanitized stories for children that had recently become popular in a newly liberal United States: stories full of good intentions and progressive sentiments but empty of imaginative depth. His book thus takes its place in a tradition dating back to Romantic times, praising the imaginativeness of popular culture over the sterile texts of bourgeois self-improvement. Wordsworth, for example, in a famous passage from the 1805 *Prelude*, had satirized the child who was a prodigy 'in learning and in books' (V: 319) but knew nothing of 'the wishing-cap/ Of Fortunatus, and the invisible coat/Of Jack the Giant-killer Robin Hood,/And Sabra in the forest with St. George!' (V: 364-7; Wordsworth 1979: 170). In emphasizing the endopsychic origins of such tales, Bettelheim traces their imaginative depth to the unconscious elements which they engage. Hence, he argues, the symbolic meanings that gather round their unrealistic characters and miraculous events; and hence, too, their sense of inexhaustibility, before all attempts at interpretation – an inexhaustibility, he believes, upon which the experience of enchantment depends.

Bettelheim is writing within the tradition of Freudian psychoanalysis, and discussing material already familiar to that tradition. Both Freud and Jung had discussed the importance of the unconscious elements in fairy tales:[2] Freud had treated them as evidence of universal psychic conflicts, while Jung had seen them as evidence of the integrative power of the creative imagination. Bettelheim utilizes both these positions but also has something new to add, which belongs to his appreciation of the experience of the tale as a story told by an adult to a child within the context of an already existing relationship. It is crucial to Bettelheim that these tales be told, that their experience is a shared one, that there be what Winnicott liked to call a 'holding environment' during their narration.[3] The telling of the tale is work done within a relationship. Bettelheim (1978: 150–1) sees the folk fairy tale as

> the result of a story being shaped and reshaped by being told millions of times, by different adults to all kinds of other adults and children. Each narrator, as he told the story, dropped and added elements to make it more meaningful to himself and to the listeners, whom he knew well. When talking to a child, the adult

responded to what he surmised from the child's reactions. Thus the narrator let his unconscious understanding of what the story told be influenced by that of the child.

The unconscious and conscious mind of the teller cooperate in producing a work which, by appealing to the child's unconscious, may also help to structure and enrich the daydreams that occupy its conscious mind.

Second, Bettelheim finds the characteristic materials of fairy tale in those quests, ordeals, rites of passage and initiatory moments that make up the existential predicaments of a child's life. Young children consumed by feelings of impotence, worthlessness or sibling rivalry, by anger towards or hatred of their parents, by guilty desires to usurp their father, by the dangerous pleasures of orality and greed, older children knowing that one day they must leave home to make their own way in life, win their own love, find their own path, make their own success – it is precisely the difficulty of these predicaments, Bettelheim believes, universal to the process of growing up, that prompts the spinning of fantasy around them. It has been the proven use of the fairy tale that its heroes or heroines – whether by strength of mind or body, by cunning, or by enlisting the help of others – may console the child with pictures of such predicaments met and overcome.

The crucial feature of the fairy story here from Bettelheim's point of view is that, in comparison with the sanitized children's literature of a newly liberal America, it does not lie about the violence of the feelings involved in these predicaments. The witches, ogres and giants that throng the pages of fairy tales embody accurately the hatred, anger and jealousy alive and active within the child. All the fantastic actions and characters of fairy tales are ways of being true to the inner realities of the child's psychological life; and the stories are of such value because they provide an imagery that prevents those realities, in all their violence, from being denied. The parent playfully dramatizing the desires of a wicked witch during the telling of a tale both allows that there are such desires in the world and provides the child with a framework within which they may begin to be managed.

Third, this emphasis upon the valuable purposes of the fairy tale makes clear that Bettelheim's approach is a functionalist one. As his title suggests, he is interested in the *uses* of enchantment to provide a child with hope that the most severe tests imposed by life may be met and overcome. This hope is invested in the figure of the hero or heroine, an everyman figure designed to encourage the child's projective identification. All the characters of fairy tales 'are typical rather than unique',

Bettelheim (1978: 8) says; and should the hero be of high birth, or the heroine marry into royalty, this is important only in so far as it provides the child with symbolic assurance of his/her own inner worth. It is the fact of the hero that matters, and the promise of his eventual triumph, not his birth, his strength, his cunning or virtue; such qualities, important as they are, are no more than the outer garments of his heroism.

Yet, once the crisis has been faced and overcome, the hero and heroine abandon the miraculous world of their adventures and live happily ever after. Such an ending, narrated within the holding environment of good-enough parental care, celebrates the power of love over separation, and encourages the child in its acceptance of inner reality – a reality enriched and made more resourceful by the reparative fantasy of the story itself. So, gradually, the child's sense of self is built up; and it is this facilitation of ego-integration that Bettelheim finds the greatest 'love-gift' of the fairy tale (Bettelheim 1978: 26–7n, quoting Lewis Carroll). It is an integration which allows id and superego their respective satisfactions but subordinates them to the claims of the emergent ego – an ego increasingly at home in a world which, to quote The Prelude once again, is 'the world/Of all of us, the place in which, in the end,/We find our happiness, or not at all' (1805, x: 725–7; Wordsworth 1979: 398). By regenerating our subjectivity, romance is able to corroborate our faith in that world.[4]

II

Bettelheim's approach to the predicaments which prompt the reparative fantasies of fairy tales was an intrapsychic one: he was interested in them only in so far as they exist within the individual mind at the level of fantasy. It was the approach of a practising psychoanalyst whose business lay with the understanding and helping of disturbed children; and it helped him to elucidate a genre which had evolved in part to appease children's anxieties. But there are other ways of considering the predicaments of such tales – predicaments which, in so far as they belong to family life, have social origins and need sociological analysis. In order to discuss this sociological dimension, I want to turn now from Bettelheim's work on fairy tales to Malinowski's treatment of myth in his essay of 1926, 'Myth in primitive psychology' (Malinowski 1954).

Malinowski's argument, although sociological rather than psychological in cast, is in fact similar to Bettelheim's. The origins of myth, he says, lie among the deepest fears and desires of a society; its materials are formed out of its most explosive situations – 'where there is a sociological strain, such as in matters of great difference in rank and power, matters of precedence and subordination, and unquestionably where profound historical changes have taken place' (Malinowski 1954: 126); and its purpose, in these situations, is to provide an imagery of hope and right conduct, 'a pragmatic charter of primitive faith and moral wisdom' (Malinowski 1954: 101). Put simply, the function of the mythical charter of a society is to soothe and heal its areas of greatest strain, to protect its weak points, its fault-lines, its *Bruchstellen*. Myth must legitimate power and justify inequality; and if its consolations seem less innocent than those of the fairy tale, they are no less important for the acceptance of reality.

Malinowski's project is primarily to demystify the ideologies of power, to demythologize myth by making it yield its secret histories of usurpation and subordination. But towards the end of his essay, in likening the characteristic themes of myth to those of tragedy and romantic narrative, he suggests a further project too: the reading of literary forms in order to decode the typical tensions and power struggles of the societies to which they belong. If we are by nature story-telling animals, the stories that interest us most are likely to be those that express the most recurrent anxieties of our social experience. Tragedy and romance, we might say, show fiction blossoming along the fault-lines of their societies, the former enacting disaster and the latter – our subject here – bringing consolation. Its business is to avert danger, to appease discontent and to contain those powerful, contaminating forces that always threaten to erupt in violence.

Malinowski's approach is essentially a historical one, as Bettelheim's is essentially universalist; and I wish to pursue them both together here, compatible and incompatible as they will seem at different moments of my enquiry. For in this way we may outline the two different but related areas in which the romance of *The Tempest* performs its healing work – within the individual and within society – and at the same time suggest how the historically specific form of Shakespearian drama brings history itself into play, offering us provisional readings of our common human destiny in no matter what society we find ourselves.

III

The Tempest is unique among Shakespeare's plays for the prominence and power given to its hero, the magus-king Prospero; by his side the other characters always threaten to dwindle into stereotype. It is this fact that has led critics to discuss the play as an offshoot of the new cultural form of the masque – a form designed to legitimate the authority of the new Renaissance monarchs often by depicting them as magi triumphing over their supernatural enemies in the antimasque (see the summary on pp. 15–20). However, the masque itself was only a reworking of earlier cultural forms, its magus-king a reincarnation of the countless wizards and sorcerers of romance and popular lore; and *The Tempest*, I think, represents the start of the next stage in this long history of reappropriation, replaying popular and aristocratic forms within the arena of the new bourgeois theatre. Certainly the play is more than the 'essay on the power and art of the royal imagination' that Orgel (1975: 45) makes it. It is an essay, too, upon the earlier genre of popular romance, drawing upon romance stereotypes, with their roots in general existential predicaments, quite as much as upon the historically specific stereotypes that belong to courtly life. Both forms are invoked, and a fascinating tension is set up between the different expectations they raise; and all this, as we shall see, is done with a consciousness which is also self-consciousness about the marginality of the new public theatres to the supposedly mercenary and denatured society of Jacobean London.

Clearly the play does revolve around Prospero, his power and the four sets of potentially explosive power relationships in which he is involved. These are relationships that suggest both general human predicaments, such as romance might soothe, and also the particular *Bruchstellen* of Jacobean Britain, such as the patriarchal dreams of masque address. There is his relationship with his brother and with the courtiers stranded after the shipwreck; his relationship with his daughter, Miranda; his relationship with his 'servants', Ariel and Caliban; and finally his relationship with Stephano and Trinculo in their drunken spree with Caliban. These four areas cover between them the main dramatic action of the play, and I want to look at each in turn.

Let us begin with Prospero's relationship with his brother and his fellow courtiers. *The Tempest* is a revenge play which enacts a common – maybe a universal – fantasy of retribution: a fantasy originating in an experience of humiliation and the subsequent inner violence caused by harbouring vindictive feelings. Revenge and the intolerable psychological burden of the avenger's role had long been staple themes of Elizabethan and Jacobean tragedy; but here in *The Tempest*, through the magic of Prospero, the play brings a romance solution to a potentially tragic situation.

After long years of waiting, an elder brother avenges himself upon a younger sibling who had usurped his inheritance; and the play shows, in typical romance fashion, how the studiousness that had initially undone him becomes the very quality finally to save him, through the magical control that it gains for him over man and nature. Weakness is converted into omnipotence, and Prospero brings all his enemies under absolute control. 'At this hour/Lies at my mercy all mine enemies', he says at the end of Act IV (IV.i.263-4), and goes off to put on his magic robes. Revenge seems to be inevitable; but then the play takes another direction. There is a moment in Act V, well rendered in Derek Jarman's 1980 film version, that discloses perfectly the fantasy structuring the play: Prospero confronts his enemies entranced before him and – with great difficulty – converts the violence of his revenge into forgiveness. 'I do forgive thee,/Unnatural though thou art', he says to his brother (V.i.78-9). It is a tense moment charged with ambivalence, suggesting the psychological proximity of the moral opposites of revenge and forgiveness; and Jarman has Prospero say these words while pressing the point of his sword into the skin of Antonio's lower eyelid. Such forgiveness, heavy with an elder brother's authority, comes perilously close to the discomfiture of a rival which is the aim of revenge; and it is, of course, a familiar strategy of royal power, incurring a debt that demands repayment.

Yet Prospero, though feeling revenge, promises forgiveness; the omnipotence that he has established allows him to take the nobler course – to prefer 'nobler reason' to brutish 'fury' (V.i.26). In Bettelheim's terms, the pleasure principle yields to the reality principle: the lower pleasure of revenge is sublimated into the higher pleasure of forgiveness.

But there is another way to consider the end of the play; for the theme of revenge, although of universal interest, has a particular relevance to Elizabethan and Jacobean society. Even if we restrict its scope to family jealousies and the question of sibling rivalry, its relevance was sharper within a society whose laws of primogeniture advantaged the first-born son at the expense of his younger brothers. But considered more broadly in relation to the fault-lines of sixteenth and seventeenth-century society, the play shows us the right to private revenge, so dear to the Elizabethan and Jacobean aristocracy, being forfeited in favour of a higher state ethic: a Christian ethic endorsed by Renaissance monarchs in order to subjugate their rebellious aristocracy and maintain their own power.

Thus the forgiveness that Prospero enforces upon Antonio and his fellow courtiers at the end of *The Tempest*, while creating the happy moral ending appropriate to romance, also confirms the inequitable political structure that had initially led to his usurpation. In a play hauntingly full of utopian images, Prospero's final state is no different from his first: the transformative power of forgiveness within his soul does not transform the political structure of the world in which he lives but rather, as he resumes his dukedom, reinforces it. The romance idiom of the play may imply that forgiveness is a universal moral virtue. But its masque elements, in appropriating that sense of universality, suggest that forgiveness is a virtue with very real practical advantages for the monarch; and it is in the tension between these two possibilities of interpretation that so much of the vitality of the play resides.

I want to turn now to Prospero's relationship with his daughter. There are two personal dilemmas here: the father's acceptance of his daughter's sexuality and his own old age; and the daughter's willingness to submit desire to the patriarchal structures of her society. Prospero's predicament arouses a deep ambivalence in him, and characteristically he responds with a power whose omnipotence is the stuff of fantasy. He uses two strategies to quieten Miranda's anxiety about the ship, and the 'noble creature' it no doubt carried (I.ii.7). First, in a series of long expository speeches, he exercises his paternal right to be in charge of the story of her life; and second, when her anxiety reawakens, he sends her into a sleep akin to the long prepubertal sleep of the Sleeping Beauty. He defers what D.H. Lawrence (1971: 108) called 'the hour of the stranger' until he can direct it towards his own ends. Then, when Ferdinand finally enters, sword in hand, Prospero sends him into a trance and makes him submit to one of those love tests so beloved of romance. The reason for this, he says, is 'lest too light winning/Make the prize light' (I.ii.452–3). But perhaps, too, he wishes to possess his daughter as long as possible and to assert dominance over his rival – to get his retaliation in first, as it were, in pursuit of his ultimate aim, a 'political marriage' that will successfully unite the kingdoms of Naples and Milan.[5]

It is a dangerous game he plays, as his irritable anxiety at Miranda's supposed inattentiveness in Act I, scene ii shows. But it is a game that many parents do play, protecting not only their children but also themselves, fighting to keep the developing sexuality of the younger generation within the limits of what they themselves want and are able to tolerate. Often in real life they long for a power that is likely to frustrate the end they desire; but in *The Tempest* this familiar parental dilemma is resolved through an omnipotence which brings the lower pleasures of both parental jealousy and filial desire to a mutual acknowledgement of the real demands of others. Ferdinand and Miranda submit to Prospero, and he in turn accepts their desire; the romance pattern is complete.

But if the romance elements of the play celebrate chastity as a type of the restraint universally necessary within human relationships, its masque elements remind us of the political necessity of such chastity.[6] Prospero's insistence that Miranda preserve her 'virgin-knot' until her marriage (IV.i.15), though appropriating the language of religious virtue, is expedient, too. Virginity is a question not only of personal virtue but also of social taboo – a taboo weighing heavily on marriageable daughters of royal blood, upheld by all the 'sanctimonious ceremonies' of marriage (IV.i.16) and, like all such taboos, designed to avert an outbreak of violence dangerous to the body politic. No doubt it is the purity of virginity that Prospero would stress; but, if we are tracing the characteristic fault-lines within patriarchal society, it is its dangerousness that matters.

For the concept of virginity signals both purity and danger. A virgin, in its usual meaning of a young woman who has reached the age of puberty but who remains chaste, may be thought of as someone who lives in a state of innocence, complete and sufficient to herself; or she may be thought of as someone who, being unmarried, inhabits a marginal state outside the central family structures of her society, awaiting full integration but capable of resisting or subverting it. Virginity in this latter sense is a something-about-to-be, a potency as yet untapped; and hence its dangerousness. For, as Prospero knows, virginity may not only be forcibly usurped by undesirables such as Caliban; it may also be freely bestowed by the woman herself, in ways that depreciate her value upon the marriage market and excite violence both against herself and her family. From this point of view, the apparently powerless and marginal virgin finds herself in possession of great power – the power to breach taboo and subvert patriarchy. It is this power that D.H. Lawrence hoped to liberate in his modern romance 'The Virgin and the Gipsy' (1930), by having his virginal heroine consort with a gipsy;[7] and it is this same power that *The Tempest* discloses in the pastoral figure of Miranda, the curiosity of whose desire is only just held in check by wonder and modesty. Jarman's casting of the rebellious pop-star Toyah Willcox as his Miranda catches something of the waywardness of this curiosity, something of the potential for disobedience inspired by her desire for Ferdinand. She dare not offer, she says, 'What I desire to give', nor take 'What I shall die to want' (III.i.78–9); and for a moment we wonder just what she has in mind. 'Speak not you for him', commands her father (I.ii.461); yet speak she does. Her vitality as a heroine depends upon our sense that, outsider as she is, she is always about to dispense with convention and expose the arbitrariness of the virtues upon which the patriarchal system rests.

A similar ambivalence about patriarchal power may be felt in Prospero's relationships with his two 'servants', or 'slaves', as they are also called in the text (see I.ii.270, 308, 313, 319), the two original inhabitants of the island, Ariel and Caliban: in the Folio 'Names of the Actors', the one described as 'an airy spirit', to be freed at the end of the play, and the other as 'a salvage and deformed slave', whose final destiny remains unknown. If we take these relationships in Bettelheim's manner, intrapsychically, the play becomes an integration myth, an adult fairy story with Ariel as the spirit of fantasy and Caliban as the spirit of bodily desire. Ariel is Puck on a tight rein, a wayward moody spirit whose obedience and gratitude are compelled by threats of punishment. It is this spirit of fantasy, once released from its perverse bondage to Sycorax, that empowers Prospero in pursuit of his enemies; and it is this same spirit, so obsessively controlled, that must finally enjoy its freedom if Prospero is to return to the exchanges of civilized life. Caliban, on the other hand, embodies those physical desires upon whose restraint all civilized life depends – desires which Prospero, preoccupied by his revenge, violently repudiates as distractions hostile to his purposes. But finally, when revenge is refined into forgiveness, he acknowledges 'this thing of darkness' as his own (V.i. 275); and in so doing, he admits his own appetitive nature and prepares himself for the everyday self-restraint to which he will have to return, now that his grievances are removed.

But *The Tempest* is more than the anatomy of a brother's studied revenge and its subsequent relaxation; it casts light, too, upon the troubled conscience of a Jacobean Britain alert to the many ways in which revenge sprang from inequalities of wealth and power, not only within the family but within society at large. Christopher Caudwell noticed in 1937 how the play was preoccupied with class relations and utopian images of classlessness, and he assimilated this interest to current class tensions within Jacobean society. Prospero's noble dream of an educated retreat, he said, was based upon exploitation: for clearly 'there is an exploited class – Caliban, the bestial serf – and a "free" spirit who serves only for a time – Ariel, apotheosis of the free wage-labourer' (Caudwell 1946: 91). Thirteen years later in 1950, Mannoni discussed the play as a colonial parable, with Ariel and Caliban condemned to act out the roles prescribed for them by Prospero's imperialistic imagination – Ariel as a depersonalized compliant native whose service is rewarded in the end by the 'gift' of freedom, Caliban as the sullen resisting native whose defiance is demonized and savagely punished (Mannoni 1964: 105–8).

Such readings insist that the true subject of *The Tempest* is not psychological but political, depicting the basis of Prospero's power in the labour of others, and showing how mutual fantasies of revenge characterize the unequal relationships of master and man, both at home in Jacobean Britain and abroad in its colonies. Prospero's controlling static presence at the heart of the play, while others busy themselves about him, makes the point for us. For here is an emblem of ducal power which the end of the play will do nothing to change. The freedom conferred upon Ariel, and the pardon held out to Caliban, may humanize these two particular relationships; but structurally nothing will change.

Popular romance sets out to make us feel in harmony with the mysteries of nature, whether of our own nature, after the fashion of an integration myth, or of a natural world containing strange beings like Ariel and Caliban; and masque tried to appropriate and politicize this vision by the most fantastic celebrations of 'the indivisible integrity of the laws of nature and government'.[8] We see something of this in Prospero's betrothal masque for Miranda and Ferdinand in Act IV. Yet Prospero's masque is interrupted by a servants' rebellion, and in this we see the failure of his whole ideological enterprise. Service is not harmonious on the island and it will not be harmonious in Milan; the happy ending to the play only serves to disclose the unhappy continuance of injustice in the greater world outside.

Prospero's relationship with Stephano and Trinculo reinforces the same point; for in their drunken spree with Caliban, Stephano and Trinculo also confront him with the structural injustices of Jacobean Britain, bear witness to the exciting vengeful desires that it bred to breach taboo and overturn the status quo. Offering him his bottle, Stephano says to Caliban: 'Kiss the book. I will furnish it anon with new contents'

(II.ii.136–7). He escaped from the shipwreck astraddle a butt of sack, and sack continues to buoy him up on the island. 'Thought is free' (III.ii.121), he sings, and his freedom is devoted to the drunken pleasures of sacrilege, turning the familiar pieties of his world upside down, seeking to usurp the power and dress of his superiors, staking his own claim upon those good things of life from which he is commonly debarred.

Viewed from Bettelheim's psychoanalytic perspective, the sub-plot explores the pleasures and temptations of intoxication, whose restraint is necessary to personal maturity and political order. But considered sociologically, the 'comic' rebellion lays bare the dangerous pleasures attendant upon carnival. From time to time, in drink and festivity, the tensions created within the psyche and within society by inequalities of wealth and power break out beyond what is customarily permitted. Desire reaches out for that which has been denied, often with a wild ambition like that of Stephano and Trinculo, determined to satisfy long-starved bodily appetites. Such appetites, of course, are matters of short-term gratification only; undisciplined by a political programme, they constitute no more than oppositional opportunism. To reduce the complex duties and reciprocities of civil society to the demands of the individual body is to display the same hubris as Macbeth's 'for mine own good,/All causes shall give way' (III.iv.136–7). There is relish here, and enormous desire; but it is a desire which can never enjoy a commensurate pleasure. Its greatest satisfactions are transient and unstable. Dramatically, however, such desire serves to disclose tensions deep within the society that Shakespeare has imagined for the play, contradictions between its official and unofficial ideologies. The desire to share in the good things of life was as powerful in the inns and market places of Jacobean England as in its ducal palaces; and the drunken aspirations of Stephano and Trinculo, no less than the repeated treacheries of Sebastian and Antonio, are too powerful a force to be contained within the cultural form of the antimasque. The inequalities of the patriarchal hierarchies of Renaissance Europe are not so easily justified.

It is here, in the tensions belonging to these four sets of power relationships, that all the conflicts of the play arise. Even the sub-plot, in which Antonio and Sebastian plan the murder of Alonso, is modelled consciously upon the earlier displacement of Prospero. From the most personal of relationships within the family to the most impersonal within society at large, the play deals with some of the conflicts most significant for Jacobean Britain. Prospero is brother to Antonio, father to Miranda, master to Caliban and Ariel, class superior to Stephano and Trinculo; and in each case he finds his position under threat. Only magic can save him, conferring an omnipotence sufficient to disarm threat and confirm patriarchy in a power equal to its desire. In each case Prospero is able to ensure that all the alliances forming around him – among the shipwrecked nobility, between Ferdinand and Miranda, between Caliban and the ship's crew – are either broken up or else brought in under his control, negotiated through him. By the end of the play, in the dream scenario of every patriarchal ruler, he has placed himself where he can be seen to be the necessary channel through whom the future must flow.

A tempest is pacified, it seems; and of course the tempest is Shakespeare's metaphor for what we have been discussing here: the unruliness of desire, as it flares out from those existential predicaments that each of us may face, along those fault-lines that define our own particular society. From the very first lines of the play, when we see the boatswain mutinously angry with his noble passengers for endangering the ship during the storm, to Prospero's last words when Ariel is dispatched to ensure 'calm seas' and 'auspicious gales' (V.i.314), we are made aware of the recurrent threat of tempest, of mutinous impulses breaking out in rebellion against the conventional hierarchies of society. 'What cares these roarers for the name of king?' asks the Boatswain of Gonzalo: 'You are a councillor; if you can command these elements to silence, and work the peace of the present, we will not hand a rope more' (I.i.16–23). He is right to rebuff the courtiers on both counts; for in the eye of the storm, as it were, there is no difference between king and sailor, save that the sailor is the more useful of the two. As the wrecked colonists found in the real-life events that provided the source for *The Tempest*,[9] in times of privation the official ideology of Jacobean society was vulnerable to those traditional alternative ideologies that the Boatswain draws upon here: belief in the equality of all men in the face of disaster and death, and belief in the superiority of those with the more useful skills.

Suffering and inequality breed oppositional ideologies; and nowhere is this more evident than in the famous political utopia dreamed up by Gonzalo in Act II (II.i.145–54, 157–62):

I'th' commonwealth I would by contraries
Execute all things, for no kind of traffic
Would I admit; no name of magistrate;
Letters should not be known; riches, poverty,

And use of service, none; contract, succession,
Bourn, bound of land, tilth, vineyard, none;
No use of metal, corn, or wine, or oil;
No occupation, all men idle, all,
And women too, but innocent and pure;
No sovereignty –
. . .
All things in common nature should produce
Without sweat or endeavour. Treason, felony,
Sword, pike, knife, gun, or need of any engine
Would I not have, but nature should bring forth
Of it own kind all foison, all abundance
To feed my innocent people.

These lines may serve as a paradigm for my argument here; for they set out a little romance designed both to cheer the king in his existential predicament (he has lost his son and been shipwrecked on an apparently deserted island) and also to pacify a bickering court whose competitiveness is about to erupt into open rebellion. Yet at the same time, their gentle primitivist satire – inspired by Montaigne (1991: 228–41) – invites a very different kind of reading, a reading by 'contraries', which discloses the society of the play in a very different light. For Gonzalo's anathematizations reel off like a check-list of all the troubles felt not only in Milan and Naples but also on Prospero's island. Trade, law, learning, economic and political inequality, service, inheritance, private property, labour, all kinds of civilized art and produce, all kinds of violence, personal, political and international: each of these 'evils' finds an echo in the events of the play, each of them discloses a site of contestation in its society, and each of them is banished by Gonzalo in favour of a Golden Age where the natural equality between men is sustained by a profusion of freely available natural resources. So powerful is this pastoral vision of Nature that Caudwell (1946: 91) was led to read the play as 'a bizarre forecast of communism'.

It is left to the unscrupulous and cynical Sebastian, however, to point out the fundamental contradiction of Gonzalo's vision: namely, that he reserves for himself the position of king within his imagined commonwealth. The natural utopia of which he dreams can only be brought about by means of the civilized arts which he despises – arts which would corrupt his vision even in the process of realizing it. Sebastian's barb is a sharp one, puncturing Gonzalo's little romance and unravelling the seemingly seamless romance of the play as a whole; for if Gonzalo's vision of a general equality rests upon his own particular power as king, the patriarchy re-established at the end of *The Tempest* rests similarly upon the impossible omnipotence of Prospero's magic. Each vision of power is born out of its own despair, and is haunted by the trace of its own impotence. The reparative fantasies of romance and masque, if read by the logic of contraries invoked by Gonzalo (and by Bettelheim and Malinowski after him), cannot but suggest those existential predicaments and sociological fault-lines that originally nurtured them. If the romance elements in the play tempt us to universalize its values, its masque elements – by the transparency with which they appropriate those same values for political ends – bring us back to the *realpolitik* of a particular historical period. *The Tempest* does not aspire to the innocence of romance. It is romance grown self-conscious, self-critical, in today's jargon self-deconstructive; and it is in this tension between the healing power of romance and its political expediency that, like Gonzalo's soliloquy, the play finds its deepest life.

IV

Prospero's irascibility with Miranda in Act I, scene ii is more than a psychological quirk, more than a stroke of characterization designed to make a long passage of exposition theatrically palatable. It is more, too, than a father's anxiety in the face of his daughter's sexuality and the dangerous power of her virginity. It betrays, even in this tiny island community, the suspicious watchfulness that was so characteristic of Renaissance Court life, the sense of fearful impotence that lay at the heart of its royal power. Prospero's ambition in Act II, scene i is to make Miranda – and the other 'subjects' on 'his' island – submit to his own reading of history. He wants to establish himself as the controlling power over all the narratives of his society, to be seen as the author of all its goings-on – and hence the familiar temptation (justified, I think) to see in him Shakespeare's self-conscious meditation upon his own role as artist, as author of romance.

Prospero maintains his monopoly of history as long as he may. Repeatedly in Act V, he withholds the narrative which he promises to the wondering courtiers around him. 'For 'tis a chronicle of day by day,/Not a relation for a breakfast' (V.i.163–4), he says; and in so saying he marks out an important difference between *The Tempest* and a play like *Cymbeline*, whose dénouement consists of elaborate tellings and retellings of a story with which the audience is already deeply familiar. Romance in *Cymbeline* is a ritualistic form whose purpose is to reinforce social cohesion. But *The Tempest* is different. Here our attention is directed not so much towards the community as towards its ruler, towards the facts and fantasies of his patriarchal empire. Prospero's history – and the mystery in which initially he shrouds it – may help to confirm his authority; it may help to occlude the awkward hiatus in which he will abjure his magic. 'I'll deliver all', he says to Alonso (V.i.313); 'I will tell no tales' (V.i.128), he says to Sebastian and Antonio. Both the texts and silences of history are power; and it is power that Prospero seeks.

The Tempest, however, remains sceptical about such power to the very end. Both plot and poetry encourage an ironic scrutiny of Prospero's dream as it moves towards its fulfilment. Each of the four main strands of the plot eludes his narrative control, each resists the closure expected of romance and masque. The relationship between Prospero and his brother is not mended; neither Antonio nor Sebastian offers the apology to be expected from romance. Abashed they may be, but only by the same superior power and knowledge that, so many years ago, made Antonio usurp his brother. Also, the future relationship between Prospero and his daughter appears to be problematical. The last image that we have of Ferdinand and Miranda seems to be of his cheating her at chess and then lying about it. 'Sweet lord, you play me false', she says. 'No, my dearest love', he protests (V.i.172). This is not the only place in Jacobean literature where chess is used as an image of sexual manoeuvring (see especially Middleton's *Women Beware Women* (*c*.1622; pub. 1657), II.ii) and the accusation of cheating serves to remind us of the likeliest fate, despite all Prospero's paternal vigilance, that will await their marriage in Milan. The relationship between Prospero and his social inferiors, too, remains unresolved. Ariel is freed, Caliban cringes, Stephano and Trinculo play the fool and deflect aggression by the show of humour: 'touch me not; I am not Stephano, but a cramp' (V.i.286). But the fundamental problem created by the power of one man over another still remains. With the exception of Alonso, each of the characters stays in character, we might say. In each case, the brightness of the romance ending casts a shadow in which the familiar outlines of the real world may be descried. The logic of contraries discloses a patriarchal world whose existential predicaments and sociological flashpoints remain obstinately troublesome.

The quality of the poetry, too, like the dénouement of the plot, shows us a Shakespeare 'to double business bound' (*Hamlet*, III.iii.41), both dignifying and deconstructing the romantic fantasies that sustain

Prospero in his patriarchal power. The poetry of romance is acknowledged but submitted to a rigorous test.

> You do look, my son, in a moved sort,
> As if you were dismayed. Be cheerful, sir;
> Our revels now are ended. These our actors,
> As I foretold you, were all spirits, and
> Are melted into air, into thin air,
> And, like the baseless fabric of this vision,
> The cloud-capped towers, the gorgeous palaces,
> The solemn temples, the great globe itself,
> Yea, all which it inherit, shall dissolve,
> And, like this insubstantial pageant faded,
> Leave not a rack behind. We are such stuff
> As dreams are made on, and our little life
> Is rounded with a sleep. Sir, I am vexed.
> Bear with my weakness, my old brain is troubled.
> Be not disturbed with my infirmity.
> If you be pleased, retire into my cell,
> And there repose. A turn or two I'll walk
> To still my beating mind.
>
> (IV.i.146–63)

These famous lines originate in Prospero's anger, not only against his
enemies but also against himself. Absorbed by his masque for Miranda
and Ferdinand, he quite forgot the conspiracy against him; and the
roughness of his outburst on remembering indicates an incompatibility
between the languages of romance and *realpolitik* that lies at the heart
of the play. Poetry must yield to political necessity, it seems; and the
'strange hollow and confused noise' (IV.i.138 s.d.) with which he
interrupts his masque acts as a satire upon it, ridiculing a literary
form whose vision of harmony cannot contain either the desires of the
conspirators or his own rage against them. Now, however, seeing the
effect of his outburst upon Miranda and Ferdinand, Prospero rouses
himself to protect them against the knowledge of such desire, such
rage; and he does so, characteristically, by turning back to the poetry
of romance once more.

   The moods between which he is oscillating here are psychic opposites
which structure the whole of the play: the desire for power over the
outside world, seen at its most extreme in Antonio, and wonder at its
otherness, seen at its most extreme in Miranda. His words thus express
the play's deepest contradictions: struggling against a tempest of rage,

he cultivates a romantic vision which derealizes those very towers, palaces and temples that he is so anxious to regain. Romance and expediency exert opposite attractions upon him, and the result is a curiously rambling speech whose inconsequentiality only gradually dawns upon him towards its end when he apologizes for his weakness and his troubled brain. It is, after all, unusual to comfort those whom you have upset with your anger by reminding them of the transience of all things earthly. Nor is he himself comforted. His fantasy fails to soothe his beating mind, as fail it must, because of the imminence of 'that foul conspiracy/Of the beast Caliban and his confederates/Against my life' (IV.i.139–41), and because this conspiracy in turn jeopardizes his successful return to Milan. The business of power must be attended to, in a real world which may always make romance appear irrelevant, especially where (as here) that romance is haunted by so powerful a sense of mutability.

Such melancholy, of course, is a characteristic note of romance, a self-confession of its frailty, an acknowledgement of its cultural marginality in a world of competitive self-seeking. Hence the plangency of Prospero's tone when, for one brief moment, he dissolves his ambitions into an 'insubstantial pageant', turns them into the stuff of dream. For he of all men cannot but be aware of the gulf between *realpolitik* and romance. Has he not just used his secret power to create the illusion of romance in the masque? Again and again, his experienced voice is set over and above the voices of Miranda and Ferdinand, reminding us that none of the virtues celebrated in the play – innocence, forgiveness, pity, chastity, fidelity – is to be easily won into the real world. 'O brave new world . . .!' Miranda exclaims. ''Tis new to thee', her father replies (V.i.183–4). His irresistible impulse to qualify her idealism epitomizes the way that, throughout the play, romance inevitably calls up its opposite – the world of 'beating minds' struggling in perpetual competition for power. Jacobean Britain was haunted by this sense of competition; and nowhere was it more fiercely felt than at Court.

It is the particular job of romance to map the world along the contours of our idealism – either to glamorize the status quo, to satirize it or perhaps to do both things together – and it is most active at times when such competition occurs under conditions of special insecurity. The Court of James I was just such a place. He refused to distance himself from his courtiers as Elizabeth had done; and by opening up access to his private apartments, he turned his Court into what one historian has called 'a hotbed of factional intrigue',[10] riddled with favouritism, loose in manners, and at odds with both city and

Parliament. It was the job of the royal masque to assimilate this highly competitive, insecure world to its romantic self-image. But *The Tempest*, in adapting the masque for the public theatre, draws out the wishful thinking of the whole enterprise;[11] its logic of contraries insists upon the fundamental irreconcilability between romance and real. Prospero's magic, although hoping to transform the world according to the demands of patriarchal fantasy, can only flourish in the marginal condition of his desert island. Obscurely he knows – though the reason is never spelt out – that he must drown his books before returning to Milan.

Even upon his desert island, indeed, the opposition between romance and real makes itself sharply felt. As the colonists of Jacobean Britain discovered, such contradictions are found at the margins of a society as often as at its centre; it was at the frontiers of empire that the need to subjugate Indian life came into conflict with wonder at its otherness. *The Tempest* raises again the theme that had lain at the heart of *Othello*: the theme of the fatal split within the ruling class of a society between its romantic self-image and its daily connivance in the unromantic demands of imperial self-interest. Othello's tragedy was rooted in his position as an outsider, susceptible to the romance of Venice but unable to negotiate the contradictions between its glamorous self-image and the pragmatism of its daily life. Prospero is less naive: he knows Antonio, he knows Alonso, and he knows that he must dispense with magic when he returns to Italy. The baseless fabric of his 'so potent art' (V.i.50) will not stand in Milan. It will survive only as a memory, a dream of power upon the margins of life. Yet it is a dream that saddens him as now he turns to contemplate a world drained of its romance. The melancholy in Prospero's voice in Act V is that of a man who has accepted the fatal split responsible for Othello's tragedy, but has been unable to heal it.

The Epilogue to the play, formally identifying the theatre with the magical island, suggests that the conflict between *realpolitik* and romance was not confined to Court and colonies but that it ran throughout Jacobean society. It suggests that, despite the current theatrical fashion for romance, prompted perhaps by those strains within contemporary patriarchy that we have already noticed, such romance was always fated to identify itself as marginal. No doubt Shakespeare himself knew well the self-division that made Prospero so melancholy. His job as dramatist must have entailed it upon him; for despite the beauty of its patriarchal utopia, the 'project' of *The Tempest* – like that of the colonists within the play – was to win wealth and honour. Hence perhaps the curious turn that the Epilogue takes, as the applause that Prospero invites brings his hands together in a gesture that reminds him of prayer. Both the duke intent upon his succession, and the actor and author upon their success, must live in a state of guilty despair unless their audience pray for them. For one last time, it seems, romance, newly sacralized, offers to dissolve all earthly ambitions into a bygone dream; and yet those ambitions survive. Perhaps Shakespeare's sense of himself was like that of Wycherley some seventy years later in the court of Charles II, when in his Epistle Dedicatory to *The Plain Dealer* (1676) he confessed that his satire against the world was tainted with the same mercenary aims that he himself was satirizing.[12] Be that as it may, *The Tempest* – like much of Shakespeare's drama – confesses a dual allegiance to the theatre, both as a place of romance and of competition, self-seeking. Its poetry cannot help but wonder at the value of its own illusions, questioning romance in the very act and place of its creation.

V

Bettelheim and Malinowski were primarily interested in stories whose continuing vitality depended upon oral tradition: stories which imaged the integration of mind and community, and symbolized that integration in the perpetually renewed relationship between storyteller and audience. The security confirmed in the narrative act epitomized the safety of the world which, through their accounts of conflict, it was the function of these stories to guarantee. Both fairy tale and myth aspire to an unchallengeable authority. Their rights and wrongs are beyond question, and their psychological and social functions confer powerful unconscious satisfactions. Paradoxically, by virtue of their professions as psychoanalyst and anthropologist, both Bettelheim and Malinowski set out to analyse these narratives so that their unconscious elements might be raised to consciousness and understood; but, equally by virtue of these professions, each was bound to honour what remained unconscious in the original relationships between parent and child, between storyteller and tribal audience.

Shakespearian romance, however, like the rest of his drama – and like much of the rest of the drama of his age – lifts taboo; it raises unconscious desires into consciousness and makes them an object of scrutiny. The single voice of oral tradition, addressing a known and intimate audience, contains and controls the voices of dissent; but Jacobean drama is multivocal, the work of individual authors who voiced dissent and breached taboo in order to trade upon the ambivalence of an unknown public in a commercial theatre. *The Tempest*, like the rest of Shakespeare's plays, is dangerous because it neither completely controls desire nor fully anathematizes dissent. Despite Prospero's power – which in any case does not extend over the minds and wills of other people – the play refuses to integrate Sebastian or Antonio, Caliban, Stephano or Trinculo into its happy ending; and in so doing it challenges the sufficiency of the patriarchal and imperial dream that it creates. Perhaps, the play allows us to think, Jacobean colonialism, for all its self-righteousness, was no more than usurpation by another name; and yet, in measuring the distance between Prospero's magic island and Milan, Shakespeare shows himself aware of the marginality of such a theatrical judgement to an imperial age. This is newly sophisticated romance: in Yeats's phrase, 'beauty born out of its own despair' ('Among School Children' (1928), l. 59; Yeats 1950: 245), alert to its own illusoriness amidst the general delusions of society, and sceptically analysing its own dream as it goes.

The play is both dream and dream interpretation. As a dream, it shares the healing power of fairy tale and myth which Renaissance rulers sought to colonize in the masque. Its pictures of human kindness arm the imagination against 'the desolation of reality' ('Meru' (1935), l. 7; Yeats 1950: 333) and give us heart to live in an imperfect world. Prospero's pardon of his enemies, for example, justifies our faith in that world by the pattern of virtue which it sets. Like a dream still, the play baffles our sense of time, bringing the particularities of history into play and offering us provisional images of the universality of virtue.

Yet dreams may be poor guides to the real world; as Reginald Scot wrote in *The Discoverie of Witchcraft* (1584), 'here in *England*, this proverbe hath beene current; to wit, Dreames proove contrarie' (Scot 1964: 163). As dream interpretation, *The Tempest* lacks the healing power of fairy tale and myth. Heliodorus said that comic writers have always 'made very contrary things agree, and joined sorrow and mirth, tears and laughter, together, and turned fearful and terrible things into a joyful banquet in the end' (*Aethiopica*; Heliodorus 1895: 288).[13] But here is a comedy that directs our attention towards the disagreement of contraries; and in this way it shares something of the power that Sidney ascribed to tragedy. It 'openeth the greatest wounds, and showeth forth the ulcers that are covered with tissue' (Sidney 1973: 45). The intractability of the real-life conflicts inspiring its plot, and the implausibility of its conclusion, suggest existential predicaments and sociological fault-lines far too troublesome for romance to mend. Its dreams of happiness disclose the discontents of the civilization that produced them; and its virtues, universal though they seem, serve only to sustain that civilization in an unjust status quo.

Dream or dream interpretation? Old wives' tale or sophisticated deconstruction? *The Tempest*, I think, is both together; and hence its peculiar poignancy, with its profound moral evocativeness haunted by an evanescence whose roots lie in the conditions of its own production. For the *embourgeoisement* of popular romance, and of the aristocratic masque that had already begun to usurp it, was financed by an audience whose assembly was as transient and occasional as the performance they witnessed. It is no accident that Shakespeare used metaphors of magic, dream and madness to explore this new romance; such metaphors suggest perfectly the beauty and transience of theatrical illusion, the marginal condition and denatured community of its audience. Two centuries later, inspired in part by the platonism of aristocratic romances written on the margins of Elizabethan Court life, the Romantic poets evolved a language to explore the interplay between dream and reality; but for Shakespeare, selling dreams in the market place of Jacobean London, they were contraries whose irreconcilability epitomized the fundamental paradox of theatre as a place where things both can and cannot be.

SUPPLEMENT

NIGEL WOOD: Have you ever used Bettelheim's book or other psychoanalytic writings in your teaching of pre-Freudian literature? Have you found that difficulties arise when you include theoretical texts in the consideration of literary history?

JOHN TURNER: I've never been very interested in psychoanalytic criticism that aims to 'see through' texts or to analyse an author. That seems to me to be for those people who believe that psychoanalysis is a science; but for me psychoanalysis is an exercise in hermeneutics, a search for provisionally adequate meanings that you may or may not find during the course of a shared relationship – even of a shared relationship with a text, although, of course, you can't share a relationship with a text in the same way that you can with a person. If you do approach psychoanalysis as a branch of hermeneutics – as, for instance, Charles Rycroft does – you can at least hope to avoid the ahistorical, essentialist method of those writers who use, let's say, the same Oedipal model to see through texts as historically different as *Hamlet* and *Sons and Lovers*. I think it's a matter of tact, of respect, to play along with the text without drowning its own distinctive voice, 'full fadom five' beneath your own. All I've used Bettelheim for here is, in quite a traditional way, to cooperate with the 'self-consciousness' of *The Tempest*: to illustrate its 'talefulness', if you like, to trace its deliberate connections with recurrent motifs in folk tales and fairy tales – motifs that interest us because they belong to recurrent existential predicaments but that nevertheless manifest themselves quite differently at different periods of our history.

NW: Don't you think, though, that these two different kinds of reading that go on in tandem throughout your essay – exploring both the recurrent existential predicaments *and* the particular fault-lines of Jacobean patriarchy – are in contradiction with one another?

JT: No; they're different kinds of reading, I agree, but not contradictory. To me they seem complementary. I've always been much impressed by Wordsworth's words in his Preface to *Lyrical Ballads* (1800), where he wrote that 'upon the accuracy with which similitude in dissimilitude, and dissimilitude in similitude are perceived, depend our taste and moral feelings' (Wordsworth 1988: 297). I'd go further and say that all our thinking depends upon such accuracy – that the complex shuttling back and forth between now and then, between self and other, between particular observation and general rule, is no more than the ordinary everyday activity of our understanding. But I also think that there's something particular to literature which encourages such shuttling back and forth. When Ibsen wrote that all art was symbolic, he meant that its vision was never simply local – that, for example, the Norway of *Ghosts* (1881) offers itself as the provisional site of our common human destiny in this world. Of course, we need to understand Ibsen's tragedy in terms of the cul-de-sac of nineteenth-century bourgeois liberalism, with its incapacity to imagine the regeneration of the individual self; but the play has more to offer us than that. We are not only historians or antiquarians in the theatre; and as we try to understand a play in its own particular history, we may also find it understanding us in ours. *Ghosts*, or *The Tempest*, may help us to articulate our own world to ourselves, in all its similarities, continuities and differences. This to me is the playfulness of literature, that it can bring history into play.

NW: A lot has been written in recent years about the ludic in literature. How would you relate your own interest in the playfulness of literature to that?

JT: Most of the work on the ludic has fallen into one of two camps. First of all, there has been the interest in carnival, originating in the work of Bakhtin. This has contributed much to our understanding of Elizabethan and Jacobean theatre, both in referring its materials to social traditions of carnival and in relating its comic practice to the kind of communal release of desire that we see in carnival. Michael Bristol's book *Carnival and*

Theater (1985) is a lovely example of both these things. Second, there has been the interest in deconstruction, originating in the work of Derrida. He has developed a particular brand of philosophical scepticism which, by weakening the bonds between words and things, has encouraged readers to take greater freedoms in the hermeneutical act. Both traditions have been liberating; and yet both have lacked something that seems to me essential – namely, an account of the nature and origins of the individual capacity to play.

To go back now to your first question about psychoanalysis, I should say that it is in the British school of object-relations psychoanalysis, and particularly in the work of D.W. Winnicott, that I have found much of what I wanted – a theoretical account of the development of play from infancy onwards. Winnicott's account, in his book *Playing and Reality* (1974), does not describe play as predominantly passional in character, as it so often seems to be in discussions of carnival; it is, as a matter of fact, the eruption of passion into play that spoils it, for Winnicott. Neither does he present play as solipsistic, as it so often is in deconstruction. He sees play rather as relationship, a privileged mingling of subjective fantasy with objective reality that begins in relationship with the mother and eventually spreads out across the face of the world. If Derrida is interested in playing with the world, Winnicott is interested in playing within it. Winnicott's emphasis, like Bettelheim's in his book on fairy tales, falls upon the value of the frame within which we play – be it the nursery, the playground, the analytic hour, the theatre, the tutorial, the seminar – and in this way his ideas constitute a fruitful way of approaching the experience of the literary text: not indeed as something that can be fully known, but as something that in its otherness can exert a discipline upon us, so that it might make sense to say that we have come to know it better.

NW: You dissociate play from desire; and yet your reading of *The Tempest* is one that attends closely to its accents of desire. Are these not the accents that characterize all the drama of the Elizabethan and Jacobean period? Is there not a contradiction in your argument here?

JT: Certainly Elizabethan and Jacobean theatre is the arena of desire, as you'd expect within a hierarchical society whose social bonds were under great strain. Let's take an example: Viola's entrance in *Twelfth Night*. She laments the loss of her twin brother, asks which country she's in, and then asks after its ruler: 'Orsino! I have heard my father name him./He was a bachelor then' (I.ii.28–9). A pause by a skilled actress after the first line, and the second line brings the house down. Why? Because we recognize the accent of desire, and because as an audience we warm to it. Then she says she will dress up as a man, and our interest is roused still further; something dangerous is in the air, and that's more exciting still.

But if Viola is experiencing desire, we are only witnessing it; and this distinction is a crucial one. Our position as an audience is a privileged one;

we are free to entertain the desire without committing the deed – and the same is true in tragedy. Macbeth carries the dagger for us. It is the presence of desire that excites us, but it is its containment that makes our excitement enjoyable. The fashion of today is for Lacanian psychoanalysis, with its bleak picture of an ex-centric self and a desire doomed forever to endless deferral. But for Winnicott, play is an act of concentration in which the relationship between the self and the world may gradually be realized. Like dreaming, or the work of the analytic hour, it can begin to do what I have claimed in this essay that Shakespearian drama can also do: it can begin to raise unconscious desire into consciousness for our scrutiny.

CHAPTER 4

Fantasy and History
in *The Tempest*

RICHARD P. WHEELER

[Richard Wheeler's understanding of *The Tempest* is in terms of the repeated psychological patterns that can be traced through from Shakespeare's 'crucial past' (p. 129), not his actual autobiography. For more of the more general underpinning of this approach, see the headnote to John Turner's essay.

The utility of Hans Loewald's *Psychoanalysis and the History of the Individual* (1978) lies in its focus on the interrelatedness of images of past and future in the present grasp of the self. This is traceable in the repetition (with variation) of certain key concerns which are not pathological or compulsive but rather exploratory and salutary. This is a necessary confrontation with the past:

> to be responsible for our unconscious . . . means, to bring unconscious forms of experiencing into the context and onto the level of the more mature, more lucid life of the adult mind . . . They are part of the stuff our lives are made of.
>
> (Loewald 1978: 21)

Such early and particularly deep memories recur as dreams or even aesthetic preferences in a process almost of (inter)play called 'transference'. This is no mindless circularity, as Freud himself pointed out in *The Interpretation of Dreams* (1900), as the investment of external events or persons with one's projected inner life is a return with interest (Freud 1953–74, 5: 562–4) and may be the means of perceiving a historical thread or continuity in our own myth of the self. To proceed with such psychoanalysis is to find some genetic 'symbol-forming libidinal spark' in the subject under review (Loewald 1978: 50) – as here with Wheeler's movement away from and back to *The*

Tempest: to relate the play to recurrent patterns of symbols in the whole oeuvre.

Freud pointed out in his essay on 'Creative writers and day-dreaming' (1908) that 'past, present and future are strung together, as it were, on the thread of the wish that runs through them' (Freud 1953–74, 9: 148). This wishfulness is constantly moulding images of the future from a past store of half-examined memories and 'selves' while remaining distracted from the present moment of remembering and reflection. Nothing is seen either as clearly prior to anything else or, therefore, as basic to it (see Bowie 1993: 12–21). Prospero, Caliban and Ariel are therefore *all* facets of Shakespeare, none more clearly alien or familiar than the other. The drama and 'play' between them are a sophisticated and yet oddly truthful rendition of personal history.]

NIGEL WOOD

Prospero's tense account to Miranda of his brother's past treachery and of his own expulsion, with her, from Milan, is history in the making – a rendering of the past by one who has a compelling interest in telling it as he does, as if recounting its only possible truth. It is not difficult to imagine alternative versions, which would instead emphasize Prospero's responsibility for the events culminating in his overthrow. I am less concerned with how Prospero remembers his past, however, than with how the play remembers its past, with how *The Tempest* looks back on, and takes its place within, Shakespearian history. I am concerned with how *The Tempest* recalls and retells some motifs central to the development of Shakespeare's drama, with how it acts upon a history that is internal to that body of work.

I

Hans Loewald (1978: 29) writes: 'In the process of individuation, the human being becomes historical'. Loewald's characteristic concerns in his *Psychoanalysis and the History of the Individual* are with the ways in which our respective individualities emerge from and perpetuate a past that is alive in our present and indispensable to our future. The three chapters in Loewald's short volume were first given as the Freud Lectures at Yale University, where Loewald was clinical professor emeritus of psychiatry. These chapters, grounded in his life's work as a practising analyst and as a psychoanalytic theorist of exceptional sophistication, reflect the depth and complexity of that work in ways that far exceed the reach of the short commentary that follows. But I have used Loewald's little book as the theoretical text to accompany my commentary on *The Tempest* because of what I find to be his apt and eloquent emphasis on a historical dimension fundamental to psycho-analytic enquiry since Freud started tracking down links between the symptoms of his earliest adult patients and events that had occurred early in their childhoods. Loewald's chapters are designed to identify what psychoanalysis shares with the disciplines of the humanities: 'It is the scope of psychoanalysis to consider human nature in the fullness of the individual's concrete existence and covering the full range of human potentialities, with special attention given – for a variety of reasons – to its historicity' (Loewald 1978: 6).

The part of individual history that psychoanalysis deals with most distinctively is infantile and childhood history – the development of the individual subject as separate from maternal environment, the history of the formation of the unconscious, the sequence of psychosexual developmental stages culminating in the Oedipus complex and its dissolution, and the development within that subject of id, ego and superego from an undifferentiated matrix. Tracing the deep psycho-logical structure of a human subject or the work of a writer is to recover the durable and dynamic outcome of that childhood history. To identify the individual's historicity is to recover what can be inferred about how an individual has emerged from a past shaped by the interrelations of the individual's constitutional or genetic endowment, the social world in which the individual has matured, and what psychoanalysis speculates about unconscious mental processes.

In this project, all recovery is necessarily inferential, speculative, interpretative. The nature/nurture relationship – with which *The Tempest* is itself quite preoccupied – has been a subject of fierce and unresolved dispute in our own century as well as in Shakespeare's. Even if we had a complete history of every familial and social interaction Shakespeare experienced in growing up, and knew as much as could be known about qualities associated with his family (and, in fact, we know relatively little along either of these lines), we could not produce a factually verifiable account of the effect of his infantile and childhood experience on the shape of his later development. Reaching to the actually lived past of Shakespeare the person is not my goal in this essay, nor is it ordinarily the goal of psychoanalytically informed criticism. The crucial past in Shakespeare is what is carried forward from play to play and reconstructed throughout his career as a dramatist. The psychoanalytic understanding of human development can help identify and illuminate psychological patterns that emerge in such repetitions and reconstructions.

Loewald is sensitive to how that past shapes the individual, and to how the individual shapes a future through a confrontation with the past:

> The past comprises the inherited, innate potential of our genes, the historical, cultural, moral tradition transmitted to us by our elders, and finally that primordial form of mentation, called unconscious or id, and the 'contents' of our lives that are experienced in this primordial form at the earliest level. The past is to be acquired, appropriated, made ours, in the creative development of the future.
>
> (Loewald 1978: 24–5)

The past, in psychoanalytic thought, is never left behind. Highly sophisticated forms of thinking emerge from what Loewald calls the 'primordial form of mentation' associated with the unconscious, but they do not replace the unconscious. According to Loewald (1978: 30) 'In its fundamental meaning, unconscious is the name for a mode of experiencing or mentation that continually, throughout life, constitutes the active base and source of more differentiated and more complexly organized modes of mentation'.

Loewald's statement of the enduring coexistence and interaction of unconscious and 'more complexly organized modes of mentation' is a characteristic claim for the psychoanalytic model of infantile and later human development. Psychoanalysis posits a series of phases of infantile development, out of which a mature social identity ultimately emerges, but the experience of those early phases remains active in the psyche. The past, as it exists for psychoanalysis, is not something that is left behind, but that endures as 'an earlier, archaic, form or level of mentation, an undifferentiated form or experiencing, that characterizes early developmental stages but is operative as well at chronologically later stages' (Loewald 1978: 12).

The psychoanalytic theory of development from the psyche of the newborn baby to the psyche of adulthood is complex and incomplete. But the process just enumerated is basic to many aspects of it. The individual gradually emerges as a separate being from an undifferentiated matrix of experience fusing infant and maternal care-giver. In the 'primordial infant–mother psychic unit', Loewald (1978: 13) writes, the mother functions 'as a living mirror in which the infant gradually begins to recognize, to know himself, by being recognized by the mother'. But the achievement of separation through self-recognition, upon which all subsequent development of the individual is based, is also an estrangement, a loss of a primary unity with the world. The wish to be absorbed back into that primordial unity, and, alternatively, the fear that this wish is dangerous and will lead to a destructive loss of self, remains in the psyche through life. Similarly, in later phases of development, as a complex inner self is constructed from identifications with crucial others in the child's world, a higher level of organization is achieved, which enables the self to function as an individual in a complex social world. As Loewald (1978: 14) observes:

> But this internal other is only the end product of a complex differentiating – from another viewpoint, self-alienating – process that takes its start in the primary unity of the infant–mother psychic relationship. This development constitutes the individuation of the individual.

In psychoanalytic thought, the initial, tentative emergence of the individual as separate from a maternal care-giver involves an estrangement from a primary oneness with the world. The later emergence of the fully differentiated psyche rests on an estrangement from what has become that individual's primary desire – for the mother. To this latter estrangement Freud gave the name 'repression'.[1] He saw in repression the constitutive gesture of the unconscious as a mental realm unaccessible to consciousness, and hence of ordinary human, Oedipal subjectivity. In repression, the boundary hardens between a crucial arena of desire and aggression in the dynamic unconscious and what is available to the self as conscious thought. The differentiated psyche is formed by its alienation from the desire that has been at the centre of its developing existence and is now relegated to the unconscious. But this unconscious remains the 'enduring origin and source for those more developed processes. What is repressed is drawn back into the archaic sphere of mentation, whence it stems' (Loewald 1978: 18). And this archaic sphere continues to exert its force over the whole psyche.

The model of development so constructed is not a linear progression through time: 'Human time consists in an interpenetration and reciprocal relatedness of past, present, and future' (Loewald 1978: 23). Repetition is as basic to this model as is change. 'Individual development' could be described as an ascending spiral in which the same basic themes are re-experienced and enacted on different levels of mentation and action. The transference relationship at the heart of psychoanalysis brings expectations initially structured by infantile and childhood experience into the analysand's ongoing relationship to the analyst, submerging the present in the patterned desires, fears, and frustrations of the past.

But if repetition is basic to the process of development as conceived by psychoanalysis, not all repetition is the same. 'Repetition may be a reiteration of the same, an automatic, driven reenactment of early relationships. This is neurotic or pathological transference', the usurpation of present and future possibilities by the imposition of past patterns of relating. 'But repetition also may be a re-creation, an imaginative reorganization and elaboration of the early, life-giving love experiences – troublesome, frustrating, and full of conflict as most of them have been' (Loewald 1978: 48). Such repetition, Loewald (1978: 49) writes, 'reveals transference in its nonpathological meaning, as the dynamic of psychological growth and development'.

The development of Shakespeare's art is repetitive in this latter sense. There is nothing like a clear, linear progression from one work to another or from early work to late. As in the development of the human psyche, nothing is ever just left behind in Shakespeare's art. From the *Comedy of Errors* and the early history plays to *The Tempest* and beyond, characteristic themes, conflicts, relationships, configurations of desire and frustration and fear, are repeated over and over again. But nothing is ever just repeated either. Instead we can watch his art finding new possibilities in old configurations, and renewing the basis on which the old configurations exist. If the Sonnets poet frets over making 'old offences of affections new' (Sonnet 110, 1.4), the drama is always making new explorations of affections old. *The Tempest*, a very late play, apparently written with a keen self-consciousness of coming near the end of a long and extraordinary career, is, for all its brevity, remarkably comprehensive in its reworking of major Shakespearian preoccupations. I hope the pages that follow can suggest how psychoanalytic thought can shed light on some of them.

II

The story Prospero tells Miranda about their past, whatever its claim to historical veracity, contains a simple and important truth at the heart of his post-Milan life. Once when he gave his brother his trust he lost his inherited political power; now that he has found another source of power he will trust no one. Prospero's power over the action of *The Tempest* is unparalleled in Shakespeare's drama – control by physical coercion over the worker Caliban; control by contractual agreement backed by physical threat over Ariel; control through Ariel over the men who took away his dukedom and over all the other visitors Prospero brings to his island; control over every condition of his daughter's courtship by and marriage to Ferdinand.

As Prospero tells of Antonio's treachery, a rather startling metaphor stands out. Antonio transformed the loyalties of the Milanese subjects, turning their hearts where he pleased, creating a situation in which, Prospero says, 'now he was/The ivy which had hid my princely trunk,/And sucked my verdure out on't' (I.ii.85–7). Antonio was the parasitical ivy wrapped around and sucking the living substance out of Prospero the ducal tree.

Perhaps the vine/tree metaphor seems startling here because it links two brothers in a figure often gendered female and male. In benign forms, the vine is a grapevine associated with fruitfulness and nurture. An apparent biblical source – 'Thy wife shall be as a fruitful vine by the sides of thy house' (Psalms 128: 3) – links wife/vine/fruitfulness, though without situating the husband as tree. In proverbial uses, vine and the tree unite in harmony: 'The Vine and Elme, converse well together', or 'As we may see of the Vine, who imbraceth the Elme, ioying and reioycing much at his presence' (Tilley 1950, V: 61). In Ovid, the female vine and the male tree are joined to mutual benefit in a story used in an attempt to seduce Pomona, a garden-tending nymph who has spurned many suitors. Pointing to an elm supporting vines loaded with grapes, the satyr Vertumnus (disguised as an old woman promoting his own cause) observes that if the vine did not grow round it the beautiful tree would be barren of fruit, and that if 'the vyne which ronnes uppon the Elme had nat/The tree too leane untoo, it should uppon the ground ly flat' (Ovid 1961: 183). Here form, strength and uprightness gendered male and fruitfulness gendered female combine in an image of two joined in one to mutual benefit and to the benefit of others. In Prospero's image, the male ivy hides the male tree and drains its strength to the detriment of a dukedom thus bent 'To most ignoble stooping' (I.ii.116).

Shakespeare uses the vine/tree metaphor in two earlier comedies in which magic is a preoccupation. In *Comedy of Errors*, benign and parasitical forms indicate alternative fates for the man Adriana thinks is her husband.

Thou art an elm, my husband, I a vine,
Whose weakness, married to thy stronger state,

Makes me with thy strength to communicate.
If aught possess thee from me, it is dross,
Usurping ivy, briar, or idle moss,
Who, all for want of pruning, with intrusion
Infect thy sap, and live on thy confusion.

(II.ii.165–72)

Adriana, as a vine who shares in and is strengthened by her husband's
strength, does not offer her own fruitfulness in the metaphor, but
neither does her sharing of the husband's strength diminish its source.
She is pleading her need, flatteringly, not her bounty. The invasive ivy
(or briar or moss) alternative – the other woman Adriana suspects – is
parasitical growth out of control, which contaminates the man/tree's
strength and thrives on the destruction resulting from her 'intrusion'.
The ivy/sap/intrusion link here closely parallels the ivy/verdure/
extrusion link in *The Tempest*; the breakdown of the parallel – female
ivy that invasively corrupts the manly substance rather than sucks
it out – adds to the interest. 'Usurping ivy' certainly would seem to
connect with the usurpation of Prospero's place and power by his
ivy-like brother. But the female ivy Adriana refers to suggests a sexual
threat to her husband. Is there any relation here to Prospero's meta-
phorical rendering of his brother's past crime?

Titania speaks the most eloquent and moving instance of the ivy/tree
metaphor in *A Midsummer Night's Dream*:

Sleep thou, and I will wind thee in my arms.

. . .

So doth the woodbine the sweet honeysuckle
Gently entwist; the female ivy so
Enrings the barky fingers of the elm.
O, how I love thee! How I dote on thee!

(IV.i.37–42)

Here what is expressed is not the woman's bounty nor her need but her
satisfaction. Enchanted Titania finds the fulfilment of her desire in her
embrace of ass-headed Bottom.

Although Bottom is powerless to escape Titania's attentions – 'Out
of this wood do not desire to go:/Thou shalt remain here, whether thou
wilt or no' (III.i.126–7) – her power over him hardly seems to be the
contaminating power Adriana imagines for 'usurping ivy', much less
the eviscerating power Prospero claims his brother exercised over him.
And as the object of her desire, Bottom does not seem to figure male

strength either as complemented or diminished by female ivy. As with an infant, Bottom's dependence creates a situation in which he seems to be magically empowered; he will come to experience omnipotence of mind, a magical responsiveness of the world to wish, defined for him by Titania's bounty:

> I'll give thee fairies to attend on thee,
> And they shall fetch thee jewels from the deep,
> And sing, while thou on pressèd flowers dost sleep;
> And I will purge thy mortal grossness so
> That thou shalt like an airy spirit go.
>
> (III.i.131–5)

For Bottom the demands of maintaining a masculine identity in opposition to the otherness of female sexuality – the demands that structure Oberon's world – are suspended. Without ever ceasing to be 'bully Bottom', the centre of his experience is 'translated' back into the realm of infantile at-oneness with comfort, pleasure, fantasy, and conflict-free sensuality. The sight of the sleeping pair appears pitiful and hateful to Oberon, but Bottom awakens to recall 'a most rare vision', a 'dream, past the wit of man to say what dream it was', indeed, a dream that 'shall be called "Bottom's Dream", because it hath no bottom' (IV.i.200–9).

Bottom's dream can point us back to *The Tempest*, but not directly to Prospero's curious use of the ivy/elm figure. Titania promises to purge Bottom's 'mortal grossness', letting him 'like an airy spirit go', but the figure in *The Tempest* who recalls Bottom's experience is not the airy spirit Ariel but the unpurged monster Caliban. As with Bottom, Caliban's monstrousness is clearly connected to sexuality and taboo. But whereas Bottom is for a brief time transported into a magical realm defined in part by a temporary suspension of taboo, for Caliban, a past, failed effort to break taboo has radically and permanently altered the world he inhabits. Bottom, ass-headed only for the night he spends in Titania's arms, regains his non-monster status as soon as Oberon reclaims his sexual partner. Caliban's irredeemable monstrousness, 'Which any print of goodness wilt not take' (I.ii.351), is represented most vividly by his early effort to rape Miranda. Bottom's night of pleasure is licensed by Oberon, who uses the occasion to recover his status as Titania's lover. Caliban has failed to overcome the taboo on Miranda's sexuality enforced by her father, who is also subject to it.

Caliban's account of his island's magical bounty, however, provides a curious parallel to the enchanting presence Bottom recalls. 'Be not afeard', Caliban comforts the frightened Stephano and Trinculo:

> the isle is full of noises,
> Sounds, and sweet airs, that give delight and hurt not.
> Sometimes a thousand twangling instruments
> Will hum about mine ears; and sometime voices,
> That, if I then had waked after long sleep,
> Will make me sleep again, and then in dreaming
> The clouds methought would open and show riches
> Ready to drop upon me, that when I waked
> I cried to dream again.
>
> (III.ii.133–41)

Caliban, too, has had a most rare vision, one of sublime, passive fulfilment – though with Caliban it seems to be fulfilment always just out of reach, something lost to the new order Prospero has brought to the island, particularly since the failed rape of Miranda. Bottom awakens to recall, as if in a dream, a world in which wish and reality corresponded, where one's complete dependence on the other was experienced as magical omnipotence. His emergence from this dreamlike world is experienced as a gain – it has given him something he can bring into the world he re-enters upon awakening, his characteristic zest for life renewed and enriched. For Caliban, by contrast, the sounds and sweet airs, the twangling instruments, the lulling voices, the riches poised to drop from the clouds of his dream, all are experienced as utterly alien to his everyday life of subjection.

The pleasures Caliban knows through a dreamlike rapport with the island's mysterious musical and sensual abundance have no place in his present reality. Something of the tenderness of the experience he describes to Stephano and Trinculo seems to have had a place in social reality in the distant past of his earliest relationship to Prospero:

> When thou cam'st first,
> Thou strok'st me and made much of me; wouldst give me
> Water with berries in't, and teach me how
> To name the bigger light and how the less,
> That burn by day and night; and then I loved thee,
> And showed thee all the qualities o'th' isle,
> The fresh springs, brine pits, barren place and fertile
>
> (I.ii.332–8)

Something of this readiness for adoring submission emerges again in Caliban's response to Stephano and the fantasy he brings of a future released from subjection to Prospero. But in his ongoing reality, there is no place for the responsiveness he brings to the island's bounty, or which that bounty elicits in him. Bottom wakes to bring a sense of dreamlike wonder back into his world, but Caliban cries to dream again.

I have moved from Prospero's ivy/elm metaphor describing his brother's treachery to Titania's use of that metaphor to describe her embrace of Bottom, then moved from Bottom's recollection of that embrace as a dream back to *The Tempest* and Caliban's experience of dreamlike riches. But whereas the two moments from *A Midsummer Night's Dream* provide two vantage points on the same blissful encounter, the two instances from *The Tempest* are quite remote from one another: Prospero tensely reconstructing the past treachery of his brother; Caliban, his slave, poignantly describing the near escape into dreamlike bliss the island can provide for him with its music. Can the connections to and within *A Midsummer Night's Dream* I have been trying to make illuminate the relationship between these two moments in *The Tempest*?

The psychological connection that has presented itself so far sees Bottom's account of his dream and Caliban's of his dreamlike relation to the island's musical abundance as fantasies deriving from early infantile relations to a nurturing Other, relations that provide the field upon which later fantasies are articulated. The early nurturing environment, if it is sufficient to ensure the infant's survival, will countenance the emergence of polarized fantasies of omnipotence and of total helplessness; of fusion with a benign, nurturant world and of annihilation by a hostile, rejecting world; of good objects and of bad objects located indeterminately inside and outside of a subjectivity still establishing its boundaries; of being loved unconditionally, and returning it in bliss, and of being hated without limit, and of returning that in rage. Introjection and projection – taking bits of the world in and making them parts of one's experience of one's person and taking parts of one's person and casting them into a world of not-self – are dominant psychic mechanisms, shaping a sense of one's person along the coordinates of need, satisfaction/frustration, pleasure/unpleasure, security/distress, bliss/rage.

Bottom's and Caliban's lyrical dreamlike riches share a base in the sensual and nurturant qualities of this level of psychic experience. Prospero's image of the ivy that hid his princely trunk and sucked out his vital spirit suggests a base in the negative register of early infantile experience. If we look just at the action components of the metaphor – the ivy embraces the elm, hiding it, and sucks the verdure from it – the connections come into focus. Holding and sucking, the principal actions conveyed in Prospero's metaphor, are basic to the formative beginnings of an individual. D.W. Winnicott gives the name 'holding phase' to the very earliest stage of infantile existence: the physical experience of being held is central to and prototypical for the infant's relations to an environment that attends to all its needs (Winnicott 1965, 44–50). Freud calls 'sucking at his mother's breast, or at substitutes for it', the 'child's first and most vital activity' (Freud 1953–74, VII: 181). In the action of sucking, sexual pleasure originates and is split off from need satisfaction: when the sucking that seeks to satisfy the infant's hunger produces pleasurable sensations desirable in their own right, 'the need for repeating the sexual satisfaction now becomes detached from the need for taking nourishment' (Freud 1953–74, VII: 182). With the activity of sucking, the infant is initiated into human sexuality. As it negotiates experience within what Winnicott calls the 'holding environment', the infant 'comes to have an inside and an outside, and a body-scheme' (Winnicott 1965, 45).[2]

Psychic manoeuvres that characterize fantasies and dreams account for the transformations necessary to get from the infantile situation to Prospero's metaphor. Whereas the holding environment locates the infant in a world in which the subject can begin to know itself through the attention the world returns, Prospero speaks of the ivy that 'hid' him (or at least hid that part of him designated by 'princely trunk') from the world. The holding is malevolent rather than facilitating – a withholding. Its action is generated by projection and reversal: the sucking fundamental to the infant's hold on life becomes the action of the ivy that 'sucked my verdure out'. Angry, destructive feelings, associated with frustrations of sucking and feeding, are projected into a fantasied attack by the other.

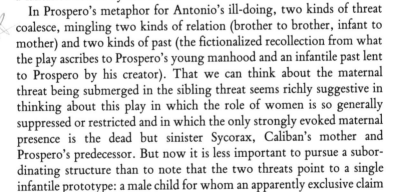

In Prospero's metaphor for Antonio's ill-doing, two kinds of threat coalesce, mingling two kinds of relation (brother to brother, infant to mother) and two kinds of past (the fictionalized recollection from what the play ascribes to Prospero's young manhood and an infantile past lent to Prospero by his creator). That we can think about the maternal threat being submerged in the sibling threat seems richly suggestive in thinking about this play in which the role of women is so generally suppressed or restricted and in which the only strongly evoked maternal presence is the dead but sinister Sycorax, Caliban's mother and Prospero's predecessor. But now it is less important to pursue a subordinating structure than to note that the two threats point to a single infantile prototype: a male child for whom an apparently exclusive claim on the love of his mother is disrupted, not by a father, but by the arrival of a younger brother and by what appears to be the withdrawal of the mother's attention away from him into her preoccupation with the newborn son. Not surprisingly, Shakespeare's drama never represents this situation directly – that is, in the experience of very young children. But the basic structure – a male's love for a female is disrupted by a second male – is pervasive and powerful.

Oberon is in a situation like this when Titania's devotion to the Indian boy disrupts his sexual bond to her. Oberon disposes of his problem by passing on his situation to the Indian boy, whose claim on Titania's love is displaced by Bottom's, who can then be displaced by Oberon. The task is easy enough for Oberon, supernaturally secure in his own exotic manhood, and with a strong prior sexual bond to Titania to renew. The disruption of Prospero's bond to Miranda by the appearance of a young suitor is of a different sort. *The Tempest* must dramatize, not the comic renewal of a sexual bond that has been inter-rupted, but a father's relinquishing to another, younger man, the daughter upon whom his life has been centred ever since his exile to the island, and whose entry into adult sexuality must be her exit from his world.

As with *King Lear*, the jealous intensity of a father's investment in his daughter shapes the bond the younger man will interrupt. Like Lear, Prospero has gone to elaborate lengths to control the conditions of the marriage. Lear, however, tries to use the ritual division of his kingdom to ensure that Cordelia will go on loving her father all, even after her dynastic marriage to another man about to be ritualistically chosen by him; her refusal to cooperate in his plan sets in motion the play's tragic action. Prospero arranges to bring Ferdinand to his island as his chosen husband for Miranda, and he oversees a courtship between them that follows exactly his plan for it; their complicity and his willingness or capacity to make a gift of his daughter to the younger man make possible the play's comic outcome. But what enables Prospero to do what Lear could not? Or, what enables Shakespeare to move from the destructive exploration of Lear's love for Cordelia to the comic outcome of Prospero's love for Miranda?

There are certainly signs that Prospero is not wholly free of what drives Lear to act so tyrannically at the prospect of giving up Cordelia. Though he assures the play's audience that he could not be more pleased to welcome Ferdinand into the family, Prospero renders the young man powerless, threatens him with violence, mocks him in his apparent loss of a father, enslaves and imprisons him, and finally, when making a gift of his daughter, puts a curse on their relationship should they have sex before he binds them in marriage. And Shakespeare seems to want to make things as easy as possible for Prospero, on this count at least: Ferdinand is clearly a right-thinking young man, susceptible to the pieties Prospero enforces, chaste and worshipful in his love for Miranda, and appropriately awed by her magician father. But if one assumes the action of *The Tempest* opens on to the destructive potentiality realized in *King Lear*, it is not yet clear how these measures can protect the movement towards marriage from comparable violence.

Caliban's function as a nasty double to Ferdinand provides one way of defusing the anxieties in the marital situation: it lets Prospero disown and repudiate his own incestuous longing for Miranda and lets him expend his rage against a potential usurper on a vilified embodiment of brute sexuality. I think even more important, however, are the ways in which the play provides multiple situations shaped by the structure that organizes the comic movement toward marriage. Usurpation, of course, is everywhere in *The Tempest*: Antonio's past treachery when he stole Milan from Prospero; Caliban's conviction that Prospero has robbed him of an island properly his by inheritance from his mother; Prospero's charge that Ferdinand usurps his father's place as king of Naples; the plot to kill Alonso and make Sebastian king of Naples; the plot to murder Prospero, which would give Stephano both the island and Miranda. The two I want to focus on, and which I think are most crucial to the action, concern Prospero's charges against his brother and Caliban's experience of losing the island's bounty – Prospero's ivy/elm metaphor and Caliban's 'cried to dream again' situation.

Although Prospero condenses fantasies of maternal threat and sibling threat into a single metaphor, the action of the play for the most part separates them out again – into Antonio's treachery, which points back especially to the extensive sibling violence of the very early histories, and into the evil legacy of Sycorax, the mother as powerful witch and Satan's partner in sex, heir to Joan de Pucelle, Queen Margaret, and Lady Macbeth. Here separation serves a double function of isolation: by keeping the threat posed by Antonio's betrayal separate from that posed by Sycorax's legacy of malevolent female power and debased sexuality, and by keeping both separate from the romance of Ferdinand and Miranda, it protects the marriage plot from the explosive violence engendered by the actions of *Othello* or *Antony and Cleopatra* or *The Winter's Tale*, where brothers or friends come to be seen as usurping enemies and beloved women are repudiated as whores.

I think, however, that the play's most complex, cruel and tender development of a pervasive Shakespearian structure of usurpation and betrayal is in the presentation of Caliban. Caliban's experience of betrayal closely parallels Prospero's story of an inherited claim usurped by someone he trusted and treated generously: 'This island's mine by Sycorax my mother,/Which thou tak'st from me' (I.ii.331–2). Caliban's relation to the island's bounty has been interrupted by the usurper Prospero. But Caliban's story of his past introduces a period between Prospero's arrival and Caliban's effort to rape Miranda in which the intruder Prospero has been the object of his love. In this interim period, the fantasy of maternal bounty is located in the relationship to the intruder, who stroked Caliban, made much of him, taught him how to read and how to name his world. Indeed, Caliban's story of trust and reciprocity recalls the infantile roots common to his situation and Prospero's more directly than anything Prospero says.

The generosity of Caliban's initial response to Prospero dramatizes a procedure, which Anna Freud called altruistic surrender, that compensates with exaggerated tenderness for resentment toward a rival for parental love; the subject seeks his own fulfilment in his service to another; the usurper is embraced and adored (Freud 1966: 123–34). Altruistic surrender is built deeply into the extravagant generosity and adoration that Shakespeare the poet lavishes on the fair friend of the Sonnets, and into the poet's inclination towards extreme and sometimes almost savage self-effacement when that seems the only way to sustain his love. Caliban keeps the impulse towards adoration and generosity alive in *The Tempest*, not only through his recollection of his once worshipful regard for Prospero, but in his readiness to bring adoration and allegiance to Stephano: 'Hast thou not dropped from heaven?' 'I do adore thee.' 'I'll kiss thy foot. I'll swear myself thy subject' (II.ii.131, 134, 146). But where the Sonnets poet debases himself to celebrate the glory of the friend, 'Myself corrupting, salving thy amiss' (Sonnet 35, l. 7), the play debases Caliban, makes a monster of him.

On this island where Prospero subordinates everything to his power, and trusts no one, attitudes of trust and worshipful regard are given extensive thematic development. Gonzalo's fantasy of a sovereignless utopia on the island assumes that trust can replace power as society's basic mode of relating. Ferdinand believes Miranda must be the goddess the island's spirits attend, and he quickly devotes himself to a worshipful love for the sake of which he is happy enough to endure enslavement and imprisonment by Prospero. Miranda thinks Ferdinand must be 'A thing divine' (I.ii.419); at the end, she sees her famous 'brave new world' in the tarnished old order Prospero has reconstituted on the island. In these instances, Prospero's hard-nosed distrust is played against forms of sentimentality or *naïveté* that manage to ennoble, even while identifying the limits of, the characters who express them. Prospero's relationship to the debased Caliban is more complex. Caliban's pathetic tendency to enslave himself in the service of self-liberation is played against Prospero's wise but tough mastery. But Caliban's openness to, and need for, trust, joy and self-surrender can be set against Prospero's willed estrangement from that part of a human life brought into existence through the nurture of a trusted Other. Slave Caliban dreams about riches ready to drop upon him; master Prospero dreams about an 'insubstantial pageant faded' (IV.i.155), a world that recedes into dreamlike emptiness, and about death. Caliban embodies not only the lust and crude violence, but also the access to trust and spontaneity Prospero has repudiated in himself.

Having waded far enough into the troubled waters of authorial allegory to identify Caliban partially with the impulse toward adoration and subjection in the *Sonnets*, I find it tempting to situate Caliban's powerful lyricism against the aggressive theatricality by which Prospero manipulates the action of the play as if it were his play to write. I believe it makes sense to think of the astonishing, distancing control Shakespeare achieves through the drama as crucial to protecting his temperament from the potentiality for adoring self-surrender that many of the sonnets embody. Prospero uses his magic art to manifest that kind of dramatic control from within his position as character/on-stage director; he controls Caliban, and distances himself from him, with particular brutality.

I think, however, the play makes this distinction only to collapse it in the end. If Prospero in some fashion represents Shakespeare's power as dramatist, Caliban represents an impulse as basic to his theatrical art as Prospero's executive power. Where Prospero accomplishes sharply defined social and political purposes in the drama he stages through his magic, Caliban seeks his fulfilment in showing his world to others and sharing it with them. 'I loved thee,/And showed thee all the qualities o'th' isle' (I.ii.336–7), he reminds Prospero. 'I'll show thee every fertile inch o'th' island', he assures Stephano: 'I'll show thee the best springs'; 'Show thee a jay's nest'; 'Wilt thou go with me?' (II.ii.142, 154, 163, 166). Caliban, in short, seeks himself in the pleasure he gives others; gives fundamentally by showing and surrendering to others the world he has a special claim to; and takes pleasure for himself in a kind of worshipful abjection that accompanies the giving: 'I'll kiss thy foot' (II.ii.146). It is an impulse built into Shakespeare's relation to the theatre. As the character Prospero dissolves into the actor who speaks the Epilogue, begging forgiveness and indulgence, it is the impulse that needs to find its recognition and reward in the audience's applause, 'or else my project fails,/Which was to please' (Epilogue, V.i.330–1).

W.B. Yeats once described his 'fancy that there is some one myth for every man, which, if we but knew it, would make us understand all he did and thought' ('At Stratford-on-Avon', in Yeats 1961: 107). Yeats's notion is an extreme version of the sameness and difference issues raised in the first section of this essay: it makes everything each of us does into a variant or elaboration of a core theme. Indeed, Norman Holland has put Yeats's formulation to very interesting psychoanalytic use in developing his own claim that a core identity or identity theme, developed in an infant's early relations to a maternal provider, acts as a kind of master key to any individual's thought and behaviour.[3] I do not wish to make a claim for the comprehensive interpretative power of a single myth or theme in the manner of either Yeats or Holland. But I think that Yeats's formulation of a unifying myth that controls variation in Shakespeare points to a pattern that links up suggestively with patterns I have been discussing in moving from *A Midsummer Night's Dream* to *The Tempest*.

Yeats (1961: 107) wrote: 'Shakespeare's myth, it may be, describes a wise man who was blind from very wisdom, and an empty man who thrust him from his place, and saw all that could be seen from very emptiness.' Yeats sees this myth being worked out in the succession of Hamlet, 'who saw too great issues everywhere to play the trivial game of life', by the soldier Fortinbras. But his chief instance, in this essay prompted by his having just viewed six of the English history plays acted 'in their right order' (Yeats 1961: 97), is 'in the story of Richard II, that unripened Hamlet, and of Henry V, that ripened Fortinbras'. Yeats's clear sympathies are with the otherworldly Richard II, whom he situates on one side of this opposition, and not with the all-too-worldly figure who occupies the pragmatic side:

> instead of that lyricism which rose out of Richard's mind like the jet of a fountain to fall again where it had risen, instead of that fantasy too enfolded in its own sincerity to make any thought the hour had need of, Shakespeare has given [Henry V] a resounding rhetoric that moves men as a leading article does to-day.
>
> (Yeats 1961: 108)

Yeats's curious celebration of Richard the poet-king as 'lovable and full of capricious fancy' (Yeats 1961: 105) but blinded by an excess of wisdom, along with his strong distaste for Henry V as a heartless and ultimately inconsequential politician, sentimentalizes the English history plays. It also introduces an evaluatory register into the myth Yeats associates with Shakespeare that greatly diminishes its interpretative power. If we pull that evaluative register out, the opposition between Richard and Henry V looks rather like the opposition between Caliban's lyricism and Prospero's aggressive theatricality, mentioned earlier.

I do not wish to claim that Caliban is a 'wise man who was blind from very wisdom' – although a powerful trend within criticism of *The Tempest* has long been occupied with a recognition that there is something in Caliban's way of relating to the world that is both precious and incompatible with the sort of order Prospero brings to the island, variants of the mix of attitudes built into the Renaissance notion of the noble savage.[4] Nor do I wish to argue exactly that Prospero, who 'thrust [Caliban] from his place' on the island, is 'an empty man, and saw all that could be seen from very emptiness'. I do, however, find Yeats's use of the idea of emptiness here quite resonant, especially so since he makes it central to Shakespeare's own vantage point on human life: 'He meditated as Solomon, not as Bentham meditated, upon blind ambitions, untoward accidents, and capricious passions, and the world was almost as empty in his eyes as it must be in the eyes of God' (Yeats 1961: 106–7).

To formulate his Shakespearian myth in terms of an opposition between Richard II and Henry V, Yeats, of course, elides two crucial figures. Richard II is not thrust from his position by Henry V, but by Henry Bullingbrook, who thus becomes Henry IV. In order for his son Hal to become Henry V, the figure who must be thrust aside is Falstaff. If the figures missing from Yeats's account are restored, this opposition is worked out doubly in the movement from *Richard II* to *Henry V*: Richard II/Bullingbrook–Henry IV and Falstaff/Prince Hal–Henry V. In both cases, the dominating figure is the one with the superior power to manipulate history theatrically. Richard II is, of course, theatrical to the point of histrionics, but it is Bullingbrook who has the controlling theatrical imagination, who uses theatricality, not for expressive, but for political purposes. And although nobody loves play-acting more than Falstaff, it is Prince Hal who uses theatre for effective political purposes, who makes Falstaff an actor in the political scenario he orchestrates throughout both parts of *Henry IV* to validate his power when he becomes King Henry V.

Both Richard II and Falstaff, like Caliban, are subdued by superior masters of theatre. Do they have anything else in common? I think what they share is a psychological heritage I tried to associate with Bottom and Caliban, a psychological rootedness in themes characteristic of very early phases of infantile development. These connections can be clarified by returning briefly to Bottom and Caliban.

Bottom, too, wants to be an actor; he, too, is manipulated by a man of superior theatrical power when Oberon casts him in the role of Titania's beloved; he, too, will be thrust from his place in Titania's arms after he has served the theatrical effect Oberon seeks by making the Queen of Fairies fall in love with an ass. Bottom's extraordinary good fortune is to inhabit an unusually benign version of this situation. It is as if Bottom recovers in Titania's doting, nurturant love a symbolic replication of the infantile past that would account for the buoyant narcissism of his grown-up character, whereas Caliban can know those nurturant riches only in the longing created by their failure to survive the realm of dream. Bottom's ready self-love is complemented and completed in Titania's adoration of him; Caliban's need to know himself through his surrender of self to a worshipped other who will accept his service reflects his situation in a world where he can only know his place through the hatred and contempt of others. Only in Bottom's hunger for play-acting do we get any hint of the neediness that will drive Caliban to seek recognition through a new and adored master in Stephano. But if bully Bottom is ultimately empowered by his experience, others who share his slot in the opposition I am tracing are not.

Bottom's robust egotism is completed through his inadvertent stumbling into the magical world of Titania; Richard's grandiose but brittle egotism is grounded on a magical identification of his person with a mystical conception of kingly omnipotence. It is an identification in which even Richard can never quite believe, except in so far as he can play the role of omnipotent king before an audience eager to validate his illusion. Because he has no identity apart from this identification, he seeks out those who will sustain his illusion with flattery. When the inevitable crisis approaches, he swings wildly back and forth between assertions of himself as the invulnerable because 'anointed king' (*Richard II*, III.ii.55) and approaches to what finally is completed in his knowledge of himself as 'nothing' (V.v.38) when the grandiose illusion has been shattered by Bullingbrook. What reaches from one extreme to the other is Richard's language, which he uses for purposes quite different from those of any other character in *Richard II*. The 'lyricism' that Yeats associates with Richard springs from his use of language, not to negotiate a world, but to constitute a self, alternatively through illusions of omnipotence and through a kind of masochistic cherishing of every nuance of his psychic distress.

Richard's necessary failure to merge with an ideal of kingly omnipotence engages the same level of psychic development as is invoked by the happy fantasy Bottom enacts in *A Midsummer Night's Dream*. Bottom's rough and ready narcissism rests on a deep trust of self and world that enables him both to inhabit the seeming omnipotence of his position within Titania's dream-world and to sustain himself when the dream is over. Richard's inability to know himself apart from his identification with his dream of kingly omnipotence represents a failure to carry a securely internalized sense of trust into and through the individuation process.

'I have long dreamt of such a kind of man', says the newly crowned Henry V to Falstaff, 'So surfeit-swelled, so old and so profane,/But being awaked, I do despise my dream' (*2 Henry IV*, V.v.45–7). But the prince has been dreaming with his eyes open, always shaping the dream to his own shrewdly conceived and theatrically executed political purpose. That is what he does best. It is Falstaff who has been blinded to reality by his own dream of the prince as king and himself as the king's beloved favourite. Like Caliban, who welcomed the exiled Prospero to his world and 'showed [him] all the qualities o'th' isle' (*Tempest* I.ii.337), Falstaff has welcomed the self-exiled prince to his tavern world and shared it with him. 'When thou cam'st first,/ Thou strok'st me and made much of me', Caliban reminds Prospero, 'and then I loved thee' (I.ii.332–3, 336). The wonderfully childlike situation evoked here by Caliban's recollection of Prospero's arrival on the island could hardly be more different from the sophisticated and sometimes rather savage give and take that has long marked the curious bond of Falstaff and Hal. But different as their relationship has been, Hal has, in his own way, made much of Falstaff as well, and Falstaff has, in his own way, responded with love: 'My king, my Jove, I speak to thee, my heart' (*2 Henry IV*, V.v.42).

Like Richard and Falstaff, Caliban plays a part in a script controlled by another, but he brings to that part a spontaneous expressiveness he shares with no one else in *The Tempest*. Characters who open themselves most fully to those inner dimensions of psychic experience often speak the most widely and vividly expressive poetry in the plays, the poetry that conveys the texture of joy or agony, of rage or bliss, of a self fulfilled or left desolate. They also make themselves vulnerable to those who distance themselves from, or carefully mediate their relationship to, the force of such inner impulses.

Such a distancing process is exactly what Prospero narrates to Miranda as his past history at the opening of *The Tempest*. For him it is a movement from trust through betrayed trust to the assertion of power and control. Prospero, overthrown by his brother when he was himself lost in his imaginative engagement with magic, 'transported/And rapt in secret studies' (I.ii.76–7), his library a 'dukedom large enough' (I.ii.110), has made himself over as a figure of power. His power is that of a dramatist who has waited for years for those characters to arrive whom he needs to act his script.

One Shakespearian genealogy for Prospero would emerge from the theatrical manipulators of those figures I have tried to link to the lyrical impulse manifest in Caliban: Oberon in *A Midsummer Night's Dream*, Bullingbrook and Henry V in the history plays. It would be a group that emphasizes, whether for good or for ill, the effective integration of psychic components in selves geared towards accommodation of, and action taken to, shape social reality. Instead I would like to look briefly at a group of speeches, spread out over a wide range of Shakespeare's work, including a speech by Prospero, in which the immediacy of social accommodation and mastery recede behind the trope of life as a dream, or as theatre, or as both. In these speeches, theatricality does not represent manipulative mastery and dream does not represent longing or desire.

'All the world's a stage', says Jaques in *As You Like It*, 'And all the men and women merely players' (II.vii.139–40). 'Thou hast nor youth, nor age', Duke Vincentio counsels Claudio in *Measure for Measure*, 'But as it were an after-dinner's sleep/Dreaming on both' (III.i.32–4). 'Life's but a walking shadow', Macbeth says to no one in particular, 'a poor player/That struts and frets his hour upon the stage,/And then is heard no more' (V.v.24–6). Prospero explains to Ferdinand, after the wedding masque is interrupted by his recollection of Caliban's conspiracy:

Our revels now are ended.
                    These our actors,
As I foretold you, were all spirits, and
Are melted into air, into thin air,
And, like the baseless fabric of this vision,
The cloud-capped towers, the gorgeous palaces,
The solemn temples, the great globe itself,

Yea, all which it inherit, shall dissolve,
And, like this insubstantial pageant faded,
Leave not a rack behind. We are such stuff
As dreams are made on, and our little life
Is rounded with a sleep.

(IV.i.148–58)

These speeches do not demonstrate theatrical control over an action, but something of how the world looks from the vantage point of Shakespearian drama when it is fully theatricalized. Each is spoken by a character who has rigorously distanced himself in one way or another from direct engagement in human intimacy and from direct responsiveness to powerful inner feelings. Of course, each of these speeches plays a complex dramatic function in the action to which it belongs. What is important to note here, however, is that all these very different characters, in their very different dramatic situations – in a comedy, a problem comedy, a tragedy and a romance – are making the same kind of point: they see life as merely theatre, as no more substantial than a dream.

Jaques, the melancholy satirist who covets the fool's role; Duke Vincentio, the disguised ruler who has stepped out of his political role and is playing at being priest; the murderous tyrant Macbeth, who has cut all close ties to the living and has 'almost forgot the taste of fears' (V.v.9); and Prospero, who has just married off his daughter – all become, in these speeches, poets of desolation. These are not versions of the 'empty man' Yeats believed Fortinbras and Henry V to be, but their haunting expressions of a fundamental emptiness in human life recalls Yeats's claim that 'the world was almost as empty in [Shakespeare's] eyes as it must be in the eyes of God' ('At Stratford-on-Avon', in Yeats 1961: 107).

The emptiness evoked in Jaques's summary of the seven ages of man lies at the centre of his melancholy; it reflects the distance imposed between himself and the world by his satiric spirit. Duke Vincentio's 'absolute for death' speech expresses the emptiness of a character whose most compelling motive for action is to distance himself from what makes the other characters of *Measure for Measure* human, vulnerable, and flawed. Macbeth's 'walking shadow' is split off from the futile hysterics of his engagement with the enemy; the remote and hollow theatricality of his meditative voice and the desperate violence of his actions present themselves as the double legacy of the disintegration of his merger with Lady Macbeth.

What about Prospero? What can account for the sudden retreat from the immediacy of action in this character who has controlled, with astonishing precision, the minute-by-minute activities of every other notable character in the play?

Prospero's great speech emerges from the only moment in the play when he is not actively controlling the lives of all the other characters in it. He speaks it when he has been startled to realize that, having allowed himself to become absorbed in the wedding masque, he has forgotten to attend to 'that foul conspiracy/Of the beast Caliban and his confederates/Against his life' (IV.i.139–41). He offers the speech to Ferdinand, who with Miranda has been startled by his agitation, as reassurance:

FERDINAND This is strange. Your father's in some passion
    That works him strongly.
MIRANDA   Never till this day
    Saw I him touched with anger, so distempered.
PROSPERO You do look, my son, in a moved sort,
    As if you were dismayed. Be cheerful, sir;
    Our revels now are ended. . . .

(IV.i.143–8)

After he has brought his vision of life as the stuff dreams are made on to completion, Prospero himself comments on his 'distempered' state:

                    Sir, I am vexed.
    Bear with my weakness, my old brain is troubled.
    Be not disturbed with my infirmity.

Gently and humbly, he offers Miranda and Ferdinand the use of his cell for rest:

    If you be pleased, retire into my cell,
    And there repose.

But he still feels the aftermath of his strange agitation:

                    A turn or two I'll walk
    To still my beating mind.

(IV.i.158–63)

This lingering distractedness that completes Prospero's speech presents yet a new voice. He has himself demanded rapt attentiveness of Miranda and Ferdinand at the beginning of the masque: 'No tongue! All eyes! Be silent!' (IV.i.59). The only other interruption of the masque comes when Ferdinand questions him about the nature of the actors: 'May I be bold/To think these spirits?' (IV.i.119–20). Prospero explains: 'Spirits, which by mine art/I have from their confines called to enact/My present fancies' (IV.i.120–2). After Ferdinand rejoices at the paradisal prospect of spending his life where 'So rare a wondered father' (IV.i.123) resides, Prospero again calls for silent attentiveness, this time with just a touch of anxiety that something could go wrong:

> Sweet, now, silence!
> Juno and Ceres whisper seriously.
> There's something else to do. Hush, and be mute,
> Or else our spell is marred.
>
> (IV.i.124–27)

Then, within the masque, Iris summons 'temperate nymphs . . . to celebrate/A contract of true love' and 'sunburned sickle-men' to join them 'in a graceful dance' (IV.i.132–3; 134; 138 s.d.). A particularly elaborate stage direction describes what happens then:

> *Enter certain Reapers, properly habited. They join with the nymphs in a graceful dance, towards the end whereof Prospero starts suddenly and speaks, after which, to a strange hollow and confused noise, they heavily vanish*

What precipitates the rapid decay of the dance is Prospero's sudden recollection: 'I had forgot that foul conspiracy/Of the beast Caliban . . .' (IV.i.139–40). When Miranda and Ferdinand are alarmed by Prospero's agitation, he tries to calm them with the eloquent nihilism of 'Our revels now are ended'. Then immediately we hear this master of energy and execution sounding old, out of control, weak and infirm – 'vexed' and 'troubled'.

Critics have understandably found it difficult to understand either why Prospero should be so agitated by the thought of Caliban and company,[5] since Ariel clearly has those pathetic conspirators under firm control, or exactly why the serene nihilism of this speech should be designed to bring cheer to the newly-wed couple. But perhaps the nature of the recollection that has broken Prospero's absorption in the masque is less significant than the uniqueness of Prospero's discovery that he has indeed been so absorbed, that for the first time in the play he has forgotten to attend to his plans. Or perhaps Caliban springs to mind here for some other reason than the danger he and his fellows pose to Prospero's life. And perhaps the purposes the speech accomplishes for its speaker are more prominent than its intended effect on Prospero's immediate audience.

The interrupted masque culminates the marriage plot, which drives the overall action of the play. Miranda has arrived at sexual maturity on an island in which the only two-legged males are her father and Caliban. Neither is an appropriate mate. Caliban has earlier posed a sexual threat to Miranda. As Prospero puts it: 'thou didst seek to violate/The honour of my child' (I.ii.347–8). Caliban is hardly repentant about this thwarted transgression:

> O ho, O ho! Would't had been done!
> Thou didst prevent me – I had peopled else
> This isle with Calibans.

(I.ii.349–51)

In his hopeful new servitude, Caliban concedes Miranda to Stephano: 'she will become thy bed, I warrant,/And bring thee forth brave brood' (III.ii.102–3). But Caliban remains powerfully associated in Prospero's mind with the sexual threat to Miranda. This threat has defined the social structure of the island ever since it was made. Expelled from Prospero's cell and 'confined into this rock' (I.ii.360), Caliban's enslavement dates from and perpetually punishes his aborted rape of Miranda.

Prospero replaces Caliban, a 'thing most brutish' who tried to rape Miranda, with Ferdinand, a 'thing divine' (I.ii.356, 419) who sees Miranda as the goddess of the island. Caliban's degraded sexuality gives way to the idealized and idealizing Ferdinand, all by Prospero's careful design. The psychoanalytic allegory that is being worked out here looks something like this: Prospero's repressed sexual desire for his daughter is purged by his projection of it on to the loathsome Caliban; Ferdinand, ritualistically identified with Caliban by being temporarily imprisoned and enslaved as Prospero's log-carrier, is both punished in advance for the sexuality he brings to Miranda and ritualistically purged of the identification with Caliban's degraded sexuality when he has, with appropriate humility, 'strangely stood the test' (IV.i.7); Prospero maintains his control over Miranda's sexuality with his management of the steps leading to a marriage in which he gives her to the young suitor.[6]

The processes of control by splitting off and projection at work here are characteristic of Prospero, and they are turned towards what is, for him, the central issue in the play and in his life – the sexual maturation of Miranda and the impossible situation this creates for the two of them on the island. But these defensive processes cannot simply erase the deep connections that underlie them, nor can they undo what the passage of time has done to bring Miranda into young womanhood. Prospero sees the circumstances that allow him to bring the Italian ship to the island as depending on an 'accident most strange', 'bountiful Fortune' and a

'most auspicious star' (I.ii.178, 182). But the deeper necessity for the
events of the play is Miranda's maturation. Prospero dramatizes the
urgencies of this most time-conscious play in terms of his astrological
art, but the clock that ultimately drives the play is a natural one, the
biological clock in Miranda's body. And if Ferdinand is going to be the
solution to the problem, he must, for all the idealizing that is going on,
be a sexual solution; he must enact a desire that corresponds to the
repressed desire in Prospero, earlier played out in degraded form in
Caliban's attempt to rape Miranda.

Prior to the masque, Prospero is still struggling to control the conflicts deriving from his recognition of the need to marry Miranda to an
appropriate mate and his repressed desire to keep his daughter for
himself. He controls entirely the circumstances of the marriage,
offering Miranda as 'a third of mine own life', 'my rich gift', 'my gift',
'my daughter', possessing her in his language even while making her
Ferdinand's 'own acquisition/Worthily purchased' (IV.i.3, 8, 13–14).
Should Ferdinand 'break her virgin-knot' (IV.i.15) prior to the ceremony Prospero has arranged, however, the marriage will be destroyed
by the father's curse:

> barren hate,
> Sour-eyed disdain, and discord shall bestrew
> The union of your bed with weeds so loathly
> That you shall hate it both.
>
> (IV.i.19–22)

Ferdinand provides the appropriate reassurance that nothing can convert
'Mine honour into lust' (IV.i.28), and, when warned again a few
moments later about 'th' fire i' th' blood', insists that 'The white cold
virgin snow upon my heart/Abates the ardour of my liver' (IV.i.53,
55–6).

The marriage masque is itself constructed to dramatize an idealized
image of marriage as a perfect harmony that somehow elides the sexual
dimension.[7] The famous exclusion of Venus and Cupid from the
ceremony explicitly averts 'Some wanton charm' (IV.i.95), but the
effect is to exclude sexuality altogether, which can only, in Prospero's
controlling imagination, be imaged as degraded.

What is presented, in Ferdinand's language, as 'a most majestic
vision, and/Harmonious charmingly', does, as Prospero says, 'enact/
My present fancies' (IV.i.118–19, 121–2). This majestic vision, however, expresses only part of Prospero's present fancies, the idealized part,
whereby he can keep at a distance the repressed desires for Miranda that
form the unconscious dimension of his fancies. When the 'graceful

dance' of the reapers and nymphs is violently interrupted, when Prospero 'starts suddenly and speaks' about 'that foul conspiracy/Of the beast Caliban and his confederates/Against my life' (IV.i.139–41), and the dancers, 'to a strange hollow and confused noise, . . . heavily vanish' (IV.i.138 s.d.), what is dramatized is the disruptive convergence of what Prospero has worked so hard to keep separate. Prospero's sudden memory of Caliban's plot against his life represents the intrusion of Prospero's own repressed desires into the idealizing process of the marriage masque.

The masque itself provides the verbal cue for Prospero's response. After 'certain nymphs' have entered, Iris calls forth their dancing partners, rustic field-workers:

You sunburned sickle-men, of August weary,
Come hither from the furrow and be merry;
Make holiday; your rye-straw hats put on,
And these fresh nymphs encounter every one
In country footing.

(IV.i.134–8)

Iris calls for a rustic dance, described as 'graceful' in the subsequent stage direction. But the language calling for that action provides the link to the underside of Prospero's imagination: 'encounter . . ./In country footing' gives us a remarkably dense, redundant, sexual pun, recalling some of the most famous punning moments in Shakespeare.

One is Hamlet's bawdy exchange with Ophelia prior to the play within the play about 'country matters' (III.ii.108). In Partridge's (1968: 87) reckoning, 'country matters' here means 'matters concerned with *cu*t*; the first pronouncing-element of *country* is **coun**'. 'Coun', or 'count', of course, is given its most notorious independent exercise in *Henry V*, with the English lesson Princess Katherine gets from Alice her gentlewoman:

KATHERINE Comment appelez-vous les pieds et la robe?
ALICE *De foot*, madame, et *de cown*.
KATHERINE *De foot* et *de cown*? O Seigneur Dieu! Ils sont les mots de son mauvais, corruptible, gros, et impudique, et non pour les dames d'honneur d'user. . . . Foh! *De foot* et *de cown*!
(*Henry V*, III.iv.44–51)

Here 'foot' for French 'foutre' – 'to copulate with' (Partridge 1968: 108) – is added to the pun on 'count'.

As it is, indeed, in *The Tempest*. For all the effort to dissociate sexuality from the marriage masque, Iris's instructions to the reapers – 'these fresh nymphs en*count*er every one/In *country foot*ing' – release into the masque the debased sexuality associated with Prospero's repressed desire, and with Caliban. Caliban here represents the return of the repressed for Prospero, and the intractable permanence of the repressed as well, its resistance to the demands of civilized morality:

> A devil, a born devil, on whose nature
> Nurture can never stick; on whom my pains,
> Humanely taken, all, all lost, quite lost.
>
> (IV.i.188–90)

'The minute of their plot/Is almost come' (IV.i.141–2), Prospero says in his distraction. What I am trying to argue is that the intrusion of the Caliban plot to murder Prospero into the dance that culminates the marriage masque of Ferdinand and Miranda makes a kind of deep psychological sense. It is not, I believe, the threat to Prospero's life that is at issue here, but the threat to his psychic equilibrium posed by his repressed incestuous desires. In surrendering himself to the progress of the masque, in letting himself become absorbed into a process that does 'enact/My present fancies', Prospero loses conscious control over the direction in which his 'fancies' lead him. The '*country foot*ing' of the reapers and the nymphs comes to represent for him the repressed sexual dimension of his longing for his daughter, and the violent dissolution of the dance breaks the hold of the masque turned to nightmare. Prospero's understanding of the interruption as his sudden memory of Caliban's plot both disguises the threat and identifies it, since it is Caliban as a representation of his own repressed sexuality that figures unconsciously into the memory.

The exquisite poetry of 'Our revels now are ended' expresses Prospero's full recoil from his dangerous absorption in his 'present fancies'. The masque has drawn him into a process that, for the first time in the play, eludes his control, draws him into a closeness with deeply repressed dimensions of himself – not only his desire for Miranda but his very capacity to give himself over to an experience that follows a logic deeper than his conscious manipulations. The psychological result, as he recovers himself, and before he turns to the business of resuming control over the action, is a movement in the opposite direction from control. After the marriage masque has drawn him too deeply into its symbolic action, Prospero retreats to a vantage point where nobody is in control and where it does not much matter.

Prospero's lyrical vision of the world as 'insubstantial pageant' in some respects recalls Caliban's account of his dream of imminent riches that are all but his, but that waking deprives him of. 'I am full of pleasure' (III.ii.114), Caliban says, when he thinks all will work out with Stephano. It is a momentary perception, ill grounded, but its expression catches the whole orientation of Caliban's character. This orientation is most fully expressed in his account of the 'Sounds, and sweet airs, that give delight and hurt not' (III.ii.135), of the clouds he thinks will 'open and show riches/Ready to drop upon me' (III.ii.139–40) – the experience to which he gives himself in his dreams, and for which, upon awakening, he cries to dream again.

My notion here is that Prospero's marriage masque captures him in something of the same way that Caliban is captured by his dream of imminent but elusive riches. It is the closest this power-dominated man comes to a point where it would make sense for him to say, with Caliban, 'I am full of pleasure'. In his absorption in the masque, which represents his 'present fancies', that pleasure proves to be disruptive. Suddenly vulnerable to a threat from within himself, Prospero for the first time finds himself in a situation where he cannot address his crisis by magically manipulating the external world. He cannot act on, cannot even acknowledge directly, the sexual component of his need for Miranda – though he will, later, in a famous and problematic statement, say of Caliban: 'this thing of darkness I/Acknowledge mine' (IV.i.275–6). And he cannot stop the socially inflected but ultimately natural clock that has brought Miranda to sexual maturation and that demands that he surrender her to another. In short, Prospero, the master manipulator, the nearly omnipotent controller of the action of this play, finds himself in a position beyond the limits of his control, a position of helplessness before his own need and before developments in his world that will not yield to his magic.

Prospero's immediate response is not to cry to dream again. Nor is it to reassert the sort of control that has been crucial to his life on the island. Instead, Prospero retreats to a vantage point from which neither the nature of his feelings nor the control he exercises over his world matters. Where Caliban, in his dream, envisions a world heavy with riches ready to drop upon him, Prospero envisions a receding world, of no more substance or consequence than 'this insubstantial pageant faded', dissolving, without a trace, into nothingness. His life, those of his daughter, her suitor, the usurping visitors to the island on whom he still seems to plan vengeance – a little world of people about whom Prospero has made the finest distinctions, ranging from his precious daughter to his pernicious brother, from the venerable Gonzalo to the despised Caliban – all are simply 'such stuff/As dreams are made on'. Their lives, all lives, add up to a 'little life/. . . rounded with a sleep' (IV.i.155–8).

When Prospero the master of magical power confronts his own helplessness in the face of a situation beyond the limits of his control, he retreats to a vantage point in which action no longer matters, where the precise distinctions and discriminations and the minute-by-minute timing that have characterized his relation to the world are dissolved in the blank emptiness of eternity. On the one hand, this vision of all of life as an insubstantial pageant faded is the extreme form of theatricality as a defence, Prospero's version of Macbeth's poor player who struts and frets his hour upon the stage, and then is heard no more. But the tone or feeling of the speech could hardly be more different from that of Macbeth's. Prospero describes an emptiness as radical as Macbeth's, an emptiness that suggests Yeats's notion of Shakespeare meditating on a world 'almost as empty in his eyes as it must be in the eyes of God'. But Prospero's speech conveys something very different from the embittered desolation of Macbeth. It is offered to comfort Miranda and Ferdinand; and it seems to bring comfort to Prospero, to break the agitation of his thought of Caliban.

Part of Prospero's comfort, of course, derives simply from the distancing this vantage point provides, the relief of watching his inner conflict and the vexations of managing his world recede into oblivion. But the comfort provided seems to be more richly textured than the comfort of the world's absence. And Prospero's speech, unlike Macbeth's, seems shielded from the perception of life's emptiness as a source of despair, or of terror.

It is harder to point to what there is in the language of this speech that accounts for this more positive sense of comfort and reassurance. But I think important keys are in the lines that bring Prospero's vision of the world's emptiness to a culmination:

> We are such stuff
> As dreams are made on, and our little life
> Is rounded with a sleep.

It seems to me that there may be some sense in which 'stuff' brings as much substantiality to 'dreams' as 'dreams' brings ephemerality to 'stuff'. There is, moreover, a kind of gentleness about this utterance, a tenderness even, quite uncharacteristic of Prospero elsewhere in the play. But I think more important is what happens in the last clause. The plain sense of the passage is that human lives emerge out of a dark, sleeplike void and pass back into it at death and that these brief lives are of small matter in this everlasting movement from nothing to nothing. But 'our' in 'our little life' seems to play against the sense of dispossession that the speech has turned on. The word 'little' does not suggest paltriness or insignificance here so much as the vulnerability of tininess. I associate 'little life' here with infancy, a little living person. The phrase 'little life . . ./. . . rounded with a sleep' seems to present a kind of holding, almost a caressing image, the little life held by the sleep, or held in ways that facilitate sleep, protecting it from the hurly-burly of the larger world. And 'rounded' here seems to me to convey something of the same tenderness that we can find in this account from *A Midsummer Night's Dream*: 'For she his hairy temples then had rounded/With coronet of fresh and fragrant flowers' (IV.i.48–9), describing Titania's tender and protective dotage over Bottom.

In short, the speech has submerged within it the tender infant–mother paradigm I earlier associated with Bottom's fulfilment through Titania. In this phase of Shakespeare's development, I think it suggests a point of connection to the two romances from which it most differs: to the promise for renewed life associated with Marina's infancy in *Pericles* and Perdita's in *The Winter's Tale*. Within *The Tempest*, it points back to the nostalgic evocations of Miranda's infancy, both to her distant memory, 'rather like a dream than an assurance/That my remembrance warrants' (I.ii.45–6), of being attended by feminine presences in Milan, and to Prospero's memory of the courage he gathered from Miranda's infantile presence on the 'rotten carcase of a butt' (I.ii.146) that brought them to the island in their exile: 'O, a cherubin/Thou wast that did preserve me' (I.ii.152–3).

Within the play, it also reaches out to Caliban's dream of maternal riches about to drop upon him. If Caliban's sexuality unconsciously represents to Prospero his repressed incestuous longing for Miranda, Caliban's psychological orientation toward a nurturant, giving world represents for Prospero a comparably repressed wish to turn oneself over in trust to a world understood as the heritage of the infantile world of oneness with maternal bounty. Forgoing this wish has defined Prospero's post-Milan world of magic, power, mastery. Obliquely, but poignantly, following his recognition of his helplessness before his own desires and developments in his world, and in the course of an imaginative vision of universal emptiness, Prospero touches base with that wish. It is, I think, an important moment for him, one that contributes crucially to the gestures that culminate his role in the play: his surrender of his magical power, his foregoing of his plan for vengeance, his final, formal release of Miranda to Ferdinand, his acknowledgement of Caliban, and his readiness to prepare himself for death in Milan, 'where/Every third thought should be my grave' (V.i.310–11) and where his own little life will be rounded with a sleep.

III

There is something perhaps disingenuous, even perverse, about including 'history' in the title of this essay, since I have almost completely ignored those historical and political lines of enquiry that have dominated critical discussions of The Tempest in recent years. My purpose has been to emphasize a different sort of history, what Loewald calls the historicity of the individual. A fuller reading of the play would be responsive both to how the play is situated within its historical moment and to how it is situated in what is distinctive to Shakespeare's psychological development.

Many recent readings have rigorously emphasized the importance of the play's relation to the colonialist enterprise. In response to such readings, Meredith Skura has pointed to ways of integrating psychological and historical concerns in discussions of The Tempest. Skura (1989: 69) writes:

> Shakespeare's assimilation of elements from historical colonialist discourse was neither entirely isolated from other uses or innocent of their effects.

But she goes on to say:

> Nonetheless, the colonialism in his play is linked not only to Shakespeare's indirect participation in an ideology of political exploitation and erasure but also to his direct participation in the psychological after-effects of having experienced the exploitation and erasure inevitable in being a child in an adult's world.

Skura's essay is an impressive effort, not just to resituate psychological considerations in a critical discourse that has come to be dominated by political considerations, but also to show how psychological and political considerations can complement each other.

Clearly the dominant political and ideological currents of a historical moment do not make everyone just like everyone else who inhabits that moment. They do not even make all members of one class or another just like everyone else who belongs to that class. They do not make all institutional shift from a particular, historically situated theatre to texts that can be 'endlessly reproduced, circulated, exchanged, exported to other times and places' (Greenblatt 1988: 160).

I turned to Hans Loewald at the beginning of this essay because his little book provides a compelling statement of the historicity that is built into individual development. We are separated from Shakespeare by massive historical differences. Historically based criticism can show us what Shakespeare has in common with his own age and how that historical commonality is alien to ours. Loewald and psychoanalysis can provide some ways to approach both what, on the one hand, is distinctive to Shakespeare within his own age and what, on the other hand, can bridge the gap between his historical moment and ours.

Psychoanalysis does this because it focuses on what the individual brings to the encounter with history, out of which the subject is constituted. We do not share with Shakespeare the historical moment that produced the Globe Theatre and the beginnings of a British colonialist venture that would affect the entire world. The particularities of that moment belong to history – they are not reproducible, and we cannot fully inhabit them, however powerful our historical imaginations. But like Shakespeare, we do lead lives that began in a situation of total infantile helplessness and dependence, lives that were given distinctive form as our unfolding capacities for human development encountered first the familial world and then the broader social world we were born into. And like Shakespeare, we go on re-encountering, renegotiating, and re-forming that formative past for as long as we live. Our history may separate us from Shakespeare, but what Loewald calls our individual historicity is crucial to what makes his work matter to us as something more than the representation of a lost historical moment. As we refine the historicist project of placing Shakespeare in his historical moment as distinct from our own, it seems to me important as well to develop a critical vantage point that does not sever all connections between the life Shakespeare led, the lives his works dramatize, and the lives we continue to lead in the historical moment and the particularized familial circumstances that have shaped us.

SUPPLEMENT

NIGEL WOOD: Would it be wide of the mark to suggest that this study provides a form of Shakespearian psychobiography, that is, that *The Tempest* is a symptom of its author's growth to 'historicity'? If so, what form of authorial intention are you laying claim to here?

residents of the same region just like everyone else in that re
they do not make all members of the same family just like
else in that family. Of course, all these considerations are
historically shaped ideologies, class structure, regional d
familial characteristics, all, obviously, shape people in both ena
limiting ways. But if such considerations do not make virtually
all members of the category they comprise, then something else
in the discussion as well.

The Elizabethan/Jacobean stage belongs to history. All wh
cipated in the shaping of what was distinctive to it were shaped
historical moment. But what the dramatists shared because of bel
to the same age cannot account for what differentiates one dra
from another, cannot account for what is distinctive to the we
Shakespeare, or Marlowe, or Jonson, or Marston, or any of the
individualized styles that came into focus through the theatres com
to them.

Nor does the enormous historical divide that separates us f
Shakespeare put his works out of our reach, make their concerns s
alien to us. Accounting for this is a serious critical problem, of cou
The ahistorical explanation for this phenomenon is that Shakespea
work provides us with a supreme representation of universal hum
nature, transcending history. Older historical accounts saw our affini
to Shakespeare as largely illusory, based on an illegitimate appropriatio
that so blurred difference into identity that the Shakespeare we read o
view and think we understand has little to do with what Shakespear
wrote, what he meant to his age.

Raymond Williams efficiently sketches the development and the
effective critical bankruptcy of both of these kinds of explanations in the
Afterword to *Political Shakespeare*. Williams sees the 'most practical and
effective new direction . . . in analysis of the historically based conventions of language and representation: the plays themselves as socially and
materially produced, within discoverable conditions; indeed the texts
themselves as history' (Dollimore and Sinfield 1985: 239). Other critics
have turned to analysis of how history itself has mediated the relationship of succeeding generations of readers to Shakespeare's work, as in
Greenblatt's (1988: 160) understanding of how 'collective enterprises,
including the educational system in which this study is implicated, have
focused more on the text than the playhouse'. Both critics are concerned
to place Shakespeare's work historically, Williams in the 'multivocal'
and 'inherently interactive' development of dramatic form in Renaissance England (Dollimore and Sinfield 1985: 238), Greenblatt in the

RICHARD P. WHEELER: I have not tried to bring what are usually regarded as biographical considerations into the picture at all – except in so far as attributing the plays (in the main) to a single author and accepting certain claims about chronology amount to biographical considerations. But, of course, these are biographical considerations. Would it affect my argument (and more generally, my whole sense of these plays) significantly if someone proved conclusively that, say, *A Midsummer Night's Dream* and *The Tempest* were written (in the main) by different authors? Or if someone proved conclusively that they were written by the same author, but that *The Tempest* was written in the mid-1590s and *Dream* was written in about 1611? The answer to both questions is, of course, *yes*. In the first instance, the answer is *yes* because I find in the two plays shared patterns that as shared patterns seem to me to belong compellingly to the relative unity I associate with an individual human subject. They belong, that is, to a patterned construction of a psychological human subject that I put together in reading these and other Shakespearian plays. They also present patterns I associate more generally with the drama of early modern England, as do plays by Marlowe, Jonson, Marston, and so on, but it is the more particularized, Shakespearian patterns that are pertinent here. In the second instance, the answer is *yes* because it seems to me that *The Tempest* belongs to a later phase of Shakespeare's development than *Dream*. In *Shakespeare's Development and the Problem Comedies* (Wheeler 1981), I tried to put together some main outlines of that developmental picture.

So, yes, what I present here could be called a form of Shakespearian psychobiography. The claims I am making about *The Tempest* and about Shakespeare presume that the plays were produced by a person who once was a child, and that he, like other persons, was shaped by his childhood past. I assume that Shakespeare re-encountered the shaping power of his childhood past in his ongoing life, and that these imaginative encounters shape the psychological patterns that I find being reworked in the drama.

NW: In many of those readings of the play that stress its contemporary debate with colonialist literature, Caliban is sometimes a figuring of an English/Irish phenomenon, the 'masterless man', who, according to Paul Brown (among others) in his contribution to *Political Shakespeare*, is the 'ungoverned and unsupervised man without the restraining resources of social organisation, an embodiment of directionless and indiscriminate desire' (Dollimore and Sinfield 1985: 52). It seems here that your focus on the repetitions of the *Tempest* narrative can provide a view of a whole community's collective psyche. Is that stretching an analogy too far? If not, what might the relationship between Prospero and Caliban tell us about the early Jacobean period?

RPW: Paul Brown's article in *Political Shakespeare* emphasizes those elements of early modern English society in *The Tempest* that point to 'the play's involvement in the colonialist project' (Dollimore and Sinfield

1985: 48). He wants to localize the concerns of the play within 'a moment of *historical* crisis' and to read the play as 'not simply a reflection of colonialist practices but an intervention in an ambivalent and even contradictory discourse'. Included in that discourse were the social phenomena of 'masterless men' and the 'wild men' or 'savage men' of medieval legend. Brown finds that 'a sexual division of the other into rapist and virgin is common in colonial discourse' (Dollimore and Sinfield 1985: 62), and one way *The Tempest* reveals its participation in that discourse is the construction of Caliban as the savage man whose sexuality must be subdued lest he again try to rape the virginal wonder Miranda. The vilified, degraded qualities in Caliban that must be punished and controlled, with the idealized qualities of Miranda that must be protected, function to justify a political programme that includes the enslavement of Caliban and the patriarchal regulation of sexuality in the play; in the English colonialist enterprise, such considerations justify the subjugation of whole groups of people identified as alien or other. All these observations seem to me quite telling interpretations of where the psychological themes of the play intersect with key political themes of its historical moment – of what Brown calls 'the ideological contradictions of its *political* unconscious' (Dollimore and Sinfield 1985: 69).

My problem with this and kindred readings of the play is their tendency to fold the unconscious totally into the political and historical. Let me put this another way. I believe *The Tempest* was written by an individual human subject who lived at a particular historical moment and did his work in the service of institutions that were saturated with the political ideology of the time. What a reading like Brown's does is submerge, at one extreme, the individual, and, at the other extreme, the human, in the historical and the ideological. Like Skura (1989), whom I also cited in my essay (p. 158), I am more concerned with how, on the one hand, *The Tempest* dramatizes more individualized patterns of development (including a history of non-colonialist precedents for dimensions of the Prospero–Caliban–Miranda relationship) that suggest what is distinctive to Shakespeare as opposed to patterns that generalize colonialist ideology, and how, on the other hand, *The Tempest* fits into patterns of human development (including degradation and idealization) that are larger or more general than what can be confined to the play's particular historical moment. I believe that coherently lining up the individual, the historical, the ideological, and the human is an enormously difficult project. Brown has more faith than I do in what is accomplished along these lines by Fredric Jameson's notion of the political unconscious.

NW: Your depiction of Prospero as striving to attain a vantage point from which 'neither the nature of his feelings nor the control he exercises over his world matters' (p. 155) might be taken to be the *return* to the bad ruler who, 'neglecting worldly ends' (I.ii.89), had invited usurpation. This could still be maintained, in my view, even when Prospero's Epilogue is considered. Is there some didactic lesson here for guardians of the law (as some claim Vincentio provides in *Measure for Measure*) or, alternatively, in a way that renders clear statements beside the point, a more open exploration of the contradictions felt to be endemic in power?

RPW: I am not sure I am talking about the return of the bad ruler, but I think I am talking about the return of a long repudiated impulse that played a deeper role in Prospero's life when he neglected worldly ends and before his betrayal by his brother. But it returns with a difference. The Prospero who trusted too easily and too much gave himself over to the positive pleasure of 'being transported/And rapt in secret studies' (I.ii.76–7); the Prospero who can no longer trust any power beyond his own can only surrender himself to an evocation of universal emptiness, the satisfactions of that surrender sliding back in, as it were, against the grain of the nihilistic vision, and without fully breaking his vigilance. If there is a clear didactic lesson here, I don't see it. But there may be something here about 'the contradictions felt to be endemic in power'. Paul Brown thinks that 'Caliban's dream' ultimately represents the '*apotheosis* of colonialist discourse', a 'utopian moment where powerlessness represents a *desire for powerlessness*', revealing 'a radical ambivalence at the heart of colonialist discourse' (Dollimore and Sinfield 1985: 66). What I have described about Prospero's 'revels now are ended' speech, which I have tried to link to Caliban's dream, could perhaps be called a 'desire for powerlessness', a desire to be lost in a great expanse of nothingness in which there is nothing to exert power over. For Prospero, this situation represents a withdrawal from impulses within himself that he has earlier repudiated through repression and projection. To the extent that power is always exercised over projected dimensions of the self, and the desire for powerlessness represents flight when the control power manifests over those dimensions has broken down, then something like 'contradictions felt to be endemic in power' are at issue.

NW: I'm interested in your distinction between 'theatricality' and what an audience might perceive as 'dramatic'. Would you maintain this perception as valuable outside the Shakespearian canon? Or is it especially true in this period and this author?

RPW: As I am using the terms, Caliban is dramatic, Prospero is theatrical. Othello is dramatic, Iago is theatrical – Othello comes to enact his drama in a perceived reality that has been drastically reshaped and controlled by Iago, and that control and reshaping belong to what I am referring to as theatrical. Mark Antony is dramatic and both Cleopatra and Octavius Caesar are theatrical, each trying to the end to produce the script in which Antony's meaning will be fixed. My usage strains ordinary usage somewhat: for example, histrionic Richard II and the inveterate actor Falstaff – both abundantly theatrical in obvious ways – are dramatic; Bullingbrook and

Prince Hal are theatrical, masters of a political theatre that uses for political ends the roles Richard and Falstaff play. The theatrical characters aggressively stage-manage their respective dramatic realities; they use theatrical means to control the actions, the significance, and often the perceptions of other characters in ways that further their own designs. These theatrical characters are not always particularly candid about their powers and inclinations. 'I love the people/But do not like to stage me to their eyes' (I.i.67–8), says the Duke in *Measure for Measure*, who will culminate his (often shaky) theatrical control over the play by staging himself as the returning hero. The character who stage-manages the play from within the play has a distinctive history within the Shakespearian canon, but the theatrical/dramatic distinction as I am using it is by no means restricted to Shakespeare, or to Renaissance drama, or, for that matter, to the theatre.

Endpiece

NIGEL WOOD

ALONSO   *I long*
  To hear the story of your life, which must
  Take the ear strangely.

PROSPERO   *I'll deliver all,*
  And promise you calm seas, auspicious gales,
  And sail so expeditious that shall catch
  Your royal fleet far off. My Ariel, chick,
  That is thy charge. Then to the elements
  Be free, and fare thou well.

(V.i. 311–18)

Does Ariel fly off, happily enfranchised – that is, after one last chore?
Unlike Puck, in *A Midsummer Night's Dream*, Ariel is not allowed a last
statement to the audience. But then, Ariel has been about to be freed
from his bonds for almost the whole play, and on at least two occasions
could be understood to correct Prospero's prejudices: at I.ii. 282–5,
where it is feasible to find Ariel correcting Prospero's assumption that
Caliban is sub-human; and the more familiar reminder of common
humanity at V.i. 20. If Caliban were not so obviously a candidate for
the mutinous rebel, we might regularly look at Ariel's plight a little
more closely. As early as Act I, scene ii Prospero finds or dubs him
'Moody', when he reminds his master of the promise to 'bate' him a

year's service and grant him his liberty earlier than originally promised. Ariel brings up the matter of his 'worthy service' wherein he has told 'no lies, made no mistakings, served/Without or grudge or grumblings' (I.ii. 244; 247–50), an objection to which Prospero makes no direct answer: 'Dost thou forget/From what a torment I did free thee?' (I.ii. 250–1). Power, which has the capacity to remake history, can also, it would seem, have obligation depend on convenience. Prospero again promises freedom at I.ii. 499–500 and then at IV.i. 265–7, V.i. 87 and V.i. 95–6. Ariel reminds him that the time of release is due at V.i. 4–5. There is a growing insistence on Ariel's desire for such liberty at the same time as Prospero's reluctance to grant it as his project cannot otherwise prosper.

At the moment of final (although still promised) release Sam Mendes (Royal Shakespeare Company, Stratford-upon-Avon, 1993) had Ariel spit – obviously and accurately – in his master's face, a significant prelude to Prospero's Epilogue ('*Now* my charms are all o'erthrown, . . .' (V.i. 319)?). This one theatrical gesture had the effect of releasing the audience's grasp on the earlier events of the play – to take altered account of the blank, neutral acquiescence on Ariel's part and the growing pleasure on Prospero's that his art had provided him a kind of managerial fulfilment. Let success be Prospero's dower – and little else. In the *Sunday Times* (London, 15 August 1993), John Peter, while on the whole engaged with and appreciative of the play's political potential, found this *geste* unacceptable:

> I prefer to think of this as a temporary aberration of taste, and hope that it will be cut at once [it was not]. I mention it because it touches on one of the crucial themes of the play. For if Prospero is not a sad senior citizen, he is not a moral circus master either, and his relationships with his servants are laden with moral and political meaning. The spitting episode is catastrophic, not only because it is vulgar but also because it goes right against everything both in Shakespeare's text and in Mendes's own production.

Irving Wardle (*The Independent on Sunday*, London, 15 August 1993) recognized that the spit was an 'effective shock', yet a gratuitous one: 'shocks come cheap when they have no preparation and no consequences'. This was not a universal view – see Paul Taylor, *The Independent* (London, 13 August 1993) who found it hinted at earlier – but Malcolm Rutherford (*Financial Times*, London, 13 August 1993) reacted against it as a production that 'smack[ed] excessively of English literary criticism', an 'entirely cerebral' activity in itself and out of place when it invades the world of the theatre.

The point to my detailing this particular production and the reaction to it is to provide neither an alternative review nor personal reminiscence (although I found the production entirely enjoyable and the spit permissible), but rather to illustrate certain assumptions about just what *The Tempest* might be. Individual productions are in their nature evanescent and cannot furnish a reliable yardstick, so it would be fruitless to commend or fault anyone's recall. These verdicts do, however, draw some authority from a point of textual stability about what are permissible theatrical liberties and what may not be. Unprepared shocks can be perfectly legitimate (un-Aristotelian) theatre, and they can unbalance a play that we thought we knew. One of the immediate effects of replacing as the climactic moment of Act V either Prospero's farewell to his art, or his attempt to conjure up one last spirit of reconciliation, by the novel expedient of directing our attention on to Ariel's reaction to (colonial?) mastery is that it is more a political than a humanist or theological focus. Shakespeare may be for all time because his texts are eminently susceptible to (doubtless anachronistic) revaluation, and for each culture the point to all revision is to enable the hitherto 'invisible' text to become prominent, this none more so than when *The Tempest* is staged outside the boundaries of WASP culture – see Thomas Cartelli's 'Prospero in Africa: *The Tempest* as colonial text and pretext', in Howard and O'Connor (1987: 99–115); Nixon (1987); Loomba (1989, 142–58).

Peter goes on to claim that Prospero is a 'magician', a 'playwright' and the island's ruler, 'in loving command of a creative spirit'. We have already seen how tendentious the image of the benevolent Shakespeare/Prospero might be, and, given this assumption, how this particular release of Ariel might strike us as forced and against the grain (Peter's 'vulgar'). Rutherford's regret at the production's lack of 'mysteries' which should not be easily explicable may be itself a reaction against 'master-explanations', yet colonialism is now very much on the agenda of much *Tempest* criticism. This could be an obvious conclusion, if you were simply to describe the contours of the plot: Prospero is a colonizer of 'his' island, and he subjects the original inhabitants in the same measure as he frees them from a former bondage. At the same time, it certainly is no truism to find colonial assumptions in the very linguistic and dramatic weave of the text, and then relate them to wider cultural ideals.

Post-colonial readings I here take to involve a concentration on the relations of civility and savagery, of authority and subjection, on an international or inter-cultural scale. This surely not directly addressed to strictly Renaissance preoccupations with the Good Ruler, but to latter-day democratic instincts, the way that sympathies for Shylock's strategies or Hamlet's delay as well as Caliban's savagery have nowadays had a more serious hearing. How savage is Caliban, and how dutiful is Ariel? The corollary to this is, how *gratuitously* despotic is Prospero? In performance, one could extend this serious questioning to the role of Miranda, too – how persuaded can we be that she is, indeed, about to inherit a brave new world away from her father's dominance, or is her innocence too vulnerable to survive the 'real' world that Prospero is weary to reinherit? As, for example, Skura (1989), Howard Felperin and Richard Wheeler (in this volume, pp. 47–56; 158–60) have made clear, the 'new point is that *The Tempest* is a political act' (Skura 1989: 45). For Skura, this is a perspective that takes a lot on trust: 'In 1611 there were in England no literary portrayals of New World inhabitants and certainly no fictional examples of colonialist discourse' (Skura 1989: 57). We therefore are forced to regard this trace of colonialist discourse as 'prophetic' rather than descriptive, as Charles Frey (1979: 31) notes, and as motivated by psychic fears as political propositions. Deborah Willis strives to draw a distinction between texts where there is a more or less overt anatomy of such power relations and those where the symbolic includes such an analysis as well as much else as well, for example, the idea that the 'true threatening "other" is not Caliban, but Antonio' (Willis 1989: 280).

For a text to display a political core of interest is not at the same time to declare that it is tied to a specific historical moment to which it ultimately refers. Thus, while there is some mileage for the view that *The Tempest* incorporates, even alludes to, say, the manuscript letter by the Virginia Company's William Strachey on the hurricane off the Virginia coast and landfall in Bermuda in 1609, or Shakespeare's friendship with Company members, it is not often the case that New Historicists or cultural historians actually make the exclusive point that what has survived is in fact a play *à clef*, offering an easily decodable 'intervention'. Returning the play 'to history' can be regarded as a more vulnerable move if this is how its motivation is represented, and so it should come as no surprise if those antagonistic to such a move prefer its being viewed so reductively. Paul Brown's goal in his essay, '"This thing of darkness I acknowledge mine": *The Tempest* and the discourse of colonialism' (in Dollimore and Sinfield 1985: 48–71), is to represent the text as 'radically ambivalent', exemplifying 'not some *timeless*

contradiction internal to the discourse by which it inexorably under-
mines or deconstructs its "official" pronouncements, but [rather] a
moment of *historical* crisis' (Dollimore and Sinfield 1985: 48). The struggle for 'powerful' meaning, that is, the structuring of significance
assigned to language and myth to promote some specific set of interests,
is, however, not played out allegorically, but in the implicit effects of
drama as well as 'text', where a particular discourse is a struggle for
meaning not its prepackaged site (see Dollimore and Sinfield 1985:
66–7). A similar concept is advanced by Francis Barker and Peter
Hulme, when they make the point that 'instead of *having* meaning,
statements should be seen as *performative of* meaning; not as possessing
some portable and "universal" content but, rather, as instrumental in
the organization and legitimation of power-relations' ('Nymphs and
reapers heavily vanish', in Drakakis 1985: 197).

In practice, Brown is careful to regard Prospero's dominance as not
just down to magic but also the 'strong' narrative he has to tell about
the past, the way it can operate as 'a reality principle' through which
he can correct and subordinate island society (Dollimore and Sinfield
1985: 66). This discloses anxiety as well as dominion, for the audience
witnesses the effort and art needed on Prospero's part to keep this image
uncontaminated. He must keep the sub-plot in its place, as Barker and
Hulme point out, lest it expose the manufactured quality of the division
itself (Drakakis 1985: 202–3; Hulme 1986:120–8). In this, it is as much
about a pressing Jacobean Irish question as the New World.

What has been altered in this 'colonial' *Tempest*? Howard Felperin,
in this volume and in his examination of '*The Tempest* in our time'
(Felperin 1990), is wary of the claims often advanced on its behalf.
Instead of humanist ideologies (Prospero as Shakespeare or as a recur-
rently troubled Authority), we still have an 'allegorical romance' which
may be (note the qualification) just as narrow in its interests as earlier
formalist approaches (Felperin 1990: 170–6). What Brown, Barker and
Hulme all accomplish, however, is a questioning of the orthodox
methods by which effects or conclusions may be drawn from available
empirical 'causes'. The search for these reasons need not just lead us to
an author's conscious intention, but also to the primary sources that
constitute the picture we now form of past cultures. At the same time,
however, as we conclude that such evidence is 'primary', we might conclude that it is also 'preliminary' and need not function as an absolute
limit or foundation for all ensuing readings. Cultures as well as
individuals have 'official' versions of their identity, which they often
hope will be taken on trust by either their contemporaries or future

generations. It would be surprising if play texts were exempt from this – and if they did not provide some indications, too, of an 'unofficial' supplement which is decipherable only by our now hoping to reregister far less regulated and verifiable aesthetic effects and their motivation. This latter task could be taken to be a distinctive critical activity.

The Tempest confronts us also with the critical proposition that artistic modes or genres are almost always calculated to have a contemporary impact, even when they appeal to posterity and even when they provide the most indirect forms of mimesis, such as in romances or myths. Philip Brockbank, in his seminal essay on '"The Tempest": Conventions of Art and Empire', reminds us that

> Long before we pursue 'meanings' (after the play, brooding upon it) we recognize that the allegory is anchored in the instant realities of human experience. Its aetherial affirmations are hard-won, spun out of substantial material. The truths which offer themselves as perennial are made very specifically out of and for the England and the theatre of Shakespeare's own time.
>
> (Brown and Harris 1966: 184)

In his rigorous account of otherwise hidden *formal* similarities between the colonial tracts and *The Tempest*, Stephen Greenblatt has identified specific social anxieties that the play both stages and 'manages', and reminds us that the route there has not taken us past 'the reflections of isolated individuals musing on current events but with expressions whose context is corporate and institutional' (Greenblatt 1988: 148). This collection of essays shows the influence of this critical emphasis of the 1980s while at the same time providing significant modification and, in Charles Frey's case, trenchant refutation: the discovery of 'significant aesthetic reality' a challenge to the 'generalizing drives of theory' (this volume, p. 72). I have already referred to Howard Felperin's distrust of those global explanations which may end up being more hopeful than grounded in the experience of the whole play. For John Turner, a clear and detailed look at this romance material enhances our view of just what Jacobean society felt it lacked: a semblance of agreed order which could, ultimately, banish anarchy. For Richard Wheeler, Hans Loewald's value lies in his ability to refocus critical attention on to the individual and how he/she has been shaped by history, and thus how we may attend to the distinctive shapes that Shakespeare created for his own sense of personal history. My introduction reaches out to what I take to be specifically Jacobean theatrical experiences and how we may regard such information in our own judgements as to what is now a relevant or comprehensible *Tempest*. The Boatswain in I.i. 21–6 may have a point: 'these elements' may perhaps only be commanded 'to silence' and 'the peace of the present' preserved by 'authority' – but ultimately even Prospero craves indulgence.

Notes

Introduction

1 In a play that does not seem to be adapted from one basic text, any episode that can be identified as an allusion takes on a special importance. Gonzalo's speech uses phrases from John Florio's translation (1603) of Michel de Montaigne's essay 'Of the Cannibals' (c.1588, pub. 1592). Montaigne's primitivistic 'savages' are simply other than our civilized selves – cruel yet uncorrupted by luxuries:

> They are even savage as we call those fruits wild which nature of herself and of her ordinary progress hath produced, whereas indeed they are those which ourselves have altered by our artificial devices and diverted from their common order we should rather term savage.
> (as reprinted in Orgel 1987: 230)

Europe's cruelty is amply shown in the schemes of Antonio and Sebastian.

2 Especially in Act II, scene iii. The possible staging of the play (and an enthusiastic defence of it) has been outlined by Powell (1984: 62–83). See also Guffrey (1984) for an exploration of the contemporary political climate.

3 There is a clear connection in Warton's mind between Shakespeare's Ariel and Belinda's etherial guardian Sylph in Pope's *The Rape of the Lock* (1712; 1714) (see Vickers 1974– , 4: 62–3). Warton concludes, 'we are transported into fairy land; we are rapt in a delicious dream, from which it is misery to be disturbed; all around is enchantment!' (Vickers 1974– , 4: 64).

4 This is a significant step towards Coleridge's positive definition of 'poetic faith'. Characters such as Ariel vanquish 'our common notions of philosophy' that come to the aid of mere 'historic faith' (Coleridge 1960, 2: 135).

5 Robert Browning's 'Caliban Upon Setebos; or, Natural Theology in the Island' (*Dramatis Personae*, 1864) is an extended excursus on the limits imposed on knowledge by a reasoning based just on natural evidence, that is, unaided by the power of revelation. Caliban expresses his idea of a divinity – Setebos – solely in terms of his own senses, which help depict a world bereft of sweetness and light (ll. 200–69; Browning 1979: 257–9). His knowledge may be partial, yet there is the doubt as to whether the sophisticated mind may fare better.

6 This reading of Prospero's closing attitude is very much part of the radical appraisal of the 'relevant' Shakespeare pursued by Kott (1964). Far from a utopia, Kott (1964: 188) regards the island as an arena where Shakespeare's 'history of the world is played out, in an abbreviated form. It consists of a struggle for power, murder, revolt and violence'. It is therefore superreal rather than fantastic. It also ought to be emphasized that Shakespeare did *not* end his writing here, collaborating with John Fletcher on three plays, *Henry VIII*, *The Two Noble Kinsmen* and (the now lost) *Cardenio*.

7 Orgel (1987: 1–4) summarizes the evidence for and against the play's being designed for Court performance. The direct evidence is sketchy, as Gary Schmidgall recognizes, but does not prevent his drawing broad, suggestive but ultimately strained correspondences between *The Tempest* and better-documented courtly work. The most obvious practical result is the necessary polarization of the ignorant and mendacious Caliban and the mage Prospero (see Schmidgall 1981: 188–214, 217–50; see also Bergeron 1985: 113–17, 178–203).

8 A definitive account of the Blackfriars Theatre's status as a superior 'public' venue is given by Gurr (1987: 164–9). It is to be supplemented by his later, more extensive comments on *The Tempest* in particular (Gurr 1989), and R.A. Foakes's 'Playhouses and Players', in Braunmuller and Hattaway (1990: esp. 24–32).

9 This is the Folio reading. There are two other versions: the 1603 Quarto, which is more specific (where 'the principall publicke audience' are turned to 'private playes/And to the humour of children' [Sig. E3ʳ] and the second Quarto (1604), where there is hardly any mention of it at all. The strongest conjecture is that Q1 might have been a provincial touring version, perhaps F imperfectly remembered. By 1604, such a topical reference may have seemed outdated. See Patterson (1989: 13–31) and Farley-Hills (1990: 7–40).

10 Fitzdotterel is no reliable commentator; indeed, he is dubbed the 'ass' of the title, 'in spite of providence', by Manly at the comic climax (V.viii. 154). The whole passage from Act I, scene vi is too protracted (to my mind) to be explained away by heavy-handed satire at his expense:

Today, I go to the Blackfriars Playhouse,
Sit i' the view, salute all my acquaintance,
Rise up between the acts, let fall my cloak,
Publish a handsome man, and a rich suit
(As that's a special end, why we go thither,
All that pretend, to stand for't o' the stage)
The ladies ask who's that? (For, they do come
To see us, love, as we do to see them)
                    (I.vi. 31–8; Jonson 1981–2, 4: 142)

11 Players operated without a developed 'guild' system, as 'hired' men.
    When travelling, their undefined status was a hazard, as they could be
    apprehended under the Henrician statutes against 'vagabonds' (1530–1).
    'Masterless men' were vulnerable. The Elizabethan reaffirmation of these
    measures (in the Act of 29 June 1572) can be read as a more directed attack
    on itinerant players: those proscribed included anyone 'having not land or
    master . . . [and those who] can give no reckoning how he or she doth
    lawfully got his or her living'. Examples included 'fencers, bear-wards,
    common players in interludes, and minstrels' (Chambers 1923, 4: 269–70).
    For an extensive and accessible account of how the profession of player
    improved in the late Elizabethan and Jacobean periods, see Bentley
    (1984: 3–24).
12 Hence it is that commentators on *The Tempest* have so often stressed its
    musical qualities (see Lindley 1984: 47–59). This masque trope is also a
    specific comment on the very situation it helps produce, as Marcus (1981: 7)
    succinctly puts it: 'the form taken by the masque becomes an original and
    often sturdily independent statement about the situation it commemorates.
    The masque's occasion is the key to its unity and to its autonomy as art'.
    A useful conspectus of primary material and its recent interpretations can
    be found in Graham Parry's 'The politics of the Jacobean masque', in
    Mulryne and Shewring (1993: 87–117).
13 The descent of Jupiter and the apparitions that encircle Posthumus in
    Cymbeline (Act V, scene iv) not only usher in his freedom, but also signal,
    according to the Soothsayer, 'the fingers of the powers above' that
    'tune/The harmony of this peace' (V.iv. 467–8). The reunions at the close
    of *The Winter's Tale* succeed the music and rapt attention that attends the
    'resurrection' of Hermione. As Paulina notes (with only a little special
    pleading), there are 'precious winners all' (V.iii. 131).
14 There is frequently, however, a realization that a public role has here
    thwarted a private vocation. See Corfield 1985, 43: 'Prospero himself has
    failed his test. Instead of pursuing appropriate theurgic ends, he has chosen
    to "court" the "auspicious star" so as to pursue a revenge plot'; Black 1991,
    29–41; Rosador 1991, 1–13.
15 I here take it as unproven whether V.N. Voloshinov's *Marxism and the
    Philosophy of Language* (1973) was actually written by Bakhtin. See Laing

(1978: 38–9); Eagleton (1991: 194–6); and Young (1985–6). That they shared the same concerns about language in society is incontestable.

16 A helpful review of the arguments in favour of and against Divine Right can be found in Sommerville (1986: 9–85). For a fuller picture of the unpolitical classes, see Underdown (1985: 9–72); Patterson (1989: 32–51); Weimann (1978: 15–30). On Shakespeare's probable support for (and recognition of the limitations of) 'a petitioning society', see Patterson (1992: 57–79).

17 Selden actually changed his mind in the second edition (Selden 1631: 4–5, 11).

18 Although published posthumously in 1640, it is prefaced by Jonson's 'To the Reader', which explains the 'analogy' he intends between this collection ('lesser poems, of later growth') and his earlier collection, The Forest in the Works (1616) (Jonson 1975: 122).

19 Parfitt (Jonson 1975: 508) makes the point that 'To Penshurst' could possibly have served a political aim of James's: to portray provincial life as integral to the state, so that more of the aristocracy might remain where they could take a full part in the necessary regional administration. On the other hand, one can hardly ignore the poem's comment on courtly excess, which has to be taken along with any possible service of subtextual 'courtly' aims.

20 It should be remembered that Cerimon resurrects Thaisa in Pericles – not by magic, but by the learned use of nature: while it is a 'secret art', it involves a study of 'the blest infusions/That dwells in vegetives, in metals, stones;/And [so he] can speak of the disturbances that/Nature works . . .' (III.ii. 32, 35–8). Medea's renovation of Aeson is one of the less than reassuring instances of devotion in love cited by Jessica with Lorenzo in The Merchant of Venice (V.i. 12–14). The argument that Shakespeare may have been imitating Ovid here, rather than alluding to the passage, has been refuted by Bate (1993: 8–11, 254–63).

21 This is more fully explored in Orgel (1984), Kahn (1981: 193–225) and in David Sundelson's 'So rare a wonder'd father: Prospero's Tempest', in Schwartz and Kahn (1980: 33–53).

1 Political Criticism at the Crossroads

1 Marx wrote:

> The difficulty we are confronted with is not . . . that of understand-ing how Greek art and epic poetry are associated with certain forms of social development. The difficulty is that they still give us aesthetic pleasure and are in certain respects regarded as a standard and unattainable ideal.
>
> A Contribution to the Critique of Political Economy (Marx 1970, 217).

The passage is usefully, if defensively, discussed by Eagleton (1976b: 11–13).

2 Althusser (1971: 222–5) writes:

> Art (I mean authentic art, not works of an average or mediocre level) does not give us a knowledge in the strict sense; it therefore does not replace knowledge (in the modern sense: scientific knowledge), but what it gives us does nevertheless maintain a certain specific relationship with knowledge. This relationship is not one of identity, but one of difference.

He goes on to describe the difference as an 'internal distancing' from the ideology the text 'seemingly bathes in'.

3 See, for example, Coleridge's ninth lecture from his *Lectures on Shakespeare and Milton* (1811):

> In this play Shakespeare has especially appealed to the imagination, and he has constructed a plot well adapted to the purpose. According to his scheme, he did not appeal to any sensuous impression . . . of time and place, but to the imagination, and it is to be borne in mind, that of old, and as regards scenery, his works may be said to have been recited rather than acted – that is to say, description and narration supplied the place of visual exhibition: the audience were told to fancy what they only heard described: the painting was not in colours but in words . . .
>
> (Coleridge 1960, 2: 130)

4 The critical literature performing this work is already substantial and still growing. I concentrate, in the following pages, on the influential essays by Greenblatt, 'Learning to Curse: Aspects of Linguistic Colonialism in the Sixteenth Century', in Chiappelli (1976, 2:561–80), and Barker and Hulme, in Drakakis (1985), but a more extensive bibliography can be found in Felperin (1990) and Vaughn and Vaughn (1991).

5 Ariel's midnight trip to the 'still-vexed Bermudas' (I.ii. 229); Gonzalo's use of the word 'plantation' (II.i. 141) which occurs nowhere else in Shakespeare; according to Caliban, the local god is Setebos (I.ii. 372; V.i. 261), a Patagonian deity; the possible metathesis of the generic name for indigenous Caribbean inhabitants, 'canibal', in Caliban. Despite E.E Stoll's (1927: 485) influential scepticism – 'There is not a word in *The Tempest* about America' – only passing acquaintance is needed with contemporary Bermudan pamphlets to establish strong stylistic links with New World colonial literature even if there is (a) also mention of the Mediterranean (Naples, Tunis and Algiers) and (b) little geographic focus in the references – see Kermode (1957: xxvi–xxx); Frey (1979) and Hulme (1986: 91–4).

6 First cited in this connection, to the best of my knowledge by Greenblatt,

in Chiappelli (1976, 562), subsequently by Barker and Hulme, in Drakakis (1985, 197) and Hulme (1986, 1).

7 It is perhaps significant that it is Miranda who first regards the 'slave' Caliban as a 'villain' (I.ii. 309), and supplies the strongest denunciation (350–52). Prospero then outdoes her: 'poisonous slave' (319), 'most lying slave' (344) and 'Hag-seed' (364). Trinculo immediately regards the gaberdine/Caliban as a commercial opening as potentially lucrative as the display of 'a dead Indian' (II.ii. 32), while Stephano likens him to the tribe of 'savages and men of Ind' (57).

8 Note that I have quietly emended the Folio's 'I *thank* thee, Ariel' to 'I *think* thee, Ariel'. In order to retain the Folio's reading, editors (including Kermode) are forced to redirect this part of Prospero's line to Ferdinand and Miranda, towards whom his courtesy would seem less out of character than it does towards the spirit he treats so masterfully. It makes more sense to me to assume a simple misprint ('thank' for 'think'), since the emended half-line perfectly expresses Prospero's relation to Ariel – as Ariel himself confirms in the subsequent line by his reply: 'Thy thoughts I cleave to. What's thy pleasure?'

9 Such idolatry derived as much from the terms provided by Servius's commentary and *Life* plus that of Aelius Donatus as close textual reading. Dryden's testament to Virgil's greatness in his *Dedication* to his translation of the *Aeneid* (1697) is hardly hyperbolic, where he concludes that the 'heroick Poem, truly such, is undoubtedly the greatest Work which the Soul of Man is capable to perform' (Dryden 1955– , 5: 267). Shakespeare's debt to Virgil is most exhaustively studied in Nosworthy (1948), Pitcher (1984) and, with a *caveat* about resemblance as opposed to downright influence, A.D. Nuttall's 'Virgil and Shakespeare' in Martindale (1984: 71–93).

10 As noted by, among others, Segal (1989: 168), Orpheus was rediscovered by Renaissance humanists as an individual intellect:

> The Renaissance recovery of the distinction between mythical and historical time again places Orpheus in a remote, idealized setting. Orpheus the magician or the rescuer of souls once more becomes Orpheus the artist and the civilizer ... He embodies [the] cultural ideal of a human figure who combines the discovery of natural and divine mysteries with emotional depth and intensity, intellect, the arts, and love for his fellow men.

See also Giuseppe Scavizzi, 'The myth of Orpheus in Italian Renaissance art, 1400–1600' and Patricia Vicari, 'The triumph of art, the triumph of death: Orpheus in Spenser and Milton', both in Warden (1982:111–62, 207–30).

11 Though frequently alluded to by Shakespeare's contemporaries, this telling

fact is strangely ignored by modern critics. I am indebted to Jeffrey Knapp for bringing it to my attention, while drawing out of it quite different historical implications. See Knapp (1992).

12 The clearest expressions of this core Marxist idea can be found in *Toward the Critique of Hegel's Philosophy of Right* (1844): 'The only *practically* possible liberation of Germany is liberation from the standpoint of *the* theory which proclaims man to be the highest essence of man'. (Marx and Engels 1959: 306); the *Theses on Feuerbach* (1845) *passim* (Marx and Engels 1959: 283–6); and *The German Ideology* (1846): 'Where speculation ends – in real life – there real, positive science begins: the representation of the practical activity, of the practical process of development of men. Empty talk about consciousness ceases, and real knowledge has to take its place' (Marx and Engels 1959: 289). For a thorough examination of how this might affect cultural critique, see Althusser (1969: 164–93).

3 Reading by Contraries

1 See, in particular, Bettelheim (1978: 6–11) for the meaning given to this phrase.

2 See Bettelheim (1978: 313–14, nn. 11–12) for some of the classic psychoanalytic literature on the fairy tale.

3 Perhaps the best discussion of this idea, central to Winnicott's work, is to be found in his 1960 paper, 'The theory of the parent–infant relationship', in Winnicott (1979: 37–55). It is an idea with much potential for literary studies.

4 In similar vein, Frye (1957: 193) describes the quest-romance as 'the search of the libido or desiring self for a fulfilment that will deliver it from the anxieties of reality but will still contain that reality'.

5 Orgel (1987: 30–1) summarizes the importance of the 'political marriage' to the play.

6 Orgel (1987: 49) has good words on the play's ambiguous presentation of virginity, as either 'a royal bargaining chip' or a power holding 'the promise of civilization and fecundity'.

7 See my essay 'Purity and Danger in D.H. Lawrence's "The Virgin and the Gipsy"', in Kalnins (1986) for a parallel argument with supporting references.

8 Phillip Brockbank, '"The Tempest": Conventions of art and empire', in Brown and Harris (1966: 195).

9 Interesting discussions of Shakespeare's dramatization of his colonial sources are to be found in Brockbank's essay in Brown and Harris (1966) and in Greenblatt (1988, 129–63, esp. 147–58).

10 Starkey (1987: 9). See also Neil Cuddy, 'The revival of the entourage: the Bedchamber of James I, 1603–1625', in Starkey (1987: 173–225).

11 For another version of this argument, see Graham Holderness's chapter on *The Tempest* in Holderness *et al.* (1990: 136–94).

12 As with bawds and justices of the peace, Wycherley (1968: 6) writes of himself and his fellow dramatists, 'the vices of the age are our best business'.

13 Wells, quoting these lines from the last book of *Aethiopica*, suggests that they might 'almost serve as an epigraph to the last plays' (Brown and Harris 1966: 51–2).

4 Fantasy and History

1 For an account of the uses to which Freud put the term 'repression' see Laplanche and Pontalis (1973: 390–4). Freud uses the term to designate both a specific, albeit prototypical, defensive manoeuvre and the larger domain of the defences generally. I am using the term here in its narrower range, which Laplanche and Pontalis (1973: 390) specify as follows:

> Strictly speaking, an operation whereby the subject attempts to repel, or to confine to the unconscious, representations (thoughts, images, memories) which are bound to an instinct. Repression occurs when to satisfy an instinct – though likely to be pleasurable in itself – would incur the risk of provoking unpleasure because of other requirements . . . It may be looked upon as a universal mental process in so far as it lies at the root of the constitution of the unconscious as a domain separate from the rest of the psyche.

2 Drive-centred theories and object–relations theories of psychoanalysis have their respective points of departure in this situation – the emergence of infantile sexuality within the nurturant environment that provides both the first objects of desire and the object relation in which the infant's primary sense of being in the world is anchored.

3 See Holland's chapter on the poet H.D., called 'A Maker's Mind', in Holland (1973: 5–59).

4 Recent readings of the play as either a complicit celebration of or a subversive indictment of the colonialist enterprise complicate and extend that trend. When Caliban complains to Prospero that his 'profit' from learning the Europeans' language is 'I know how to curse' (I.ii. 362–63), Greenblatt (1990: 25) writes: 'Ugly, rude, savage, Caliban nevertheless achieves for an instant an absolute if intolerably bitter moral victory.' For Paul Brown, even the dream that seems to give Caliban something he 'may use to resist, if only in dream, the repressive reality which hails him as villain', is ultimately the expression of desire generated by and within colonialism: 'the colonialist project's investment in the processes of euphemisation of what are really powerful relations here has produced a utopian moment where powerlessness

represents *a desire for powerlessness*' ('"This thing of darkness I acknowledge mine": *The Tempest* and the discourse of colonialism', in Dollimore and Sinfield (1985: 65, 66).

5 Skura (1989: 60–5), however, points tellingly to several situations in Shakespeare's earlier drama that provide parallels to this moment when the exiled, manipulative, paternalistic duke erupts in anger in response to a figure who embodies qualities he has repudiated in himself: Antonio to Shylock in *The Merchant of Venice*; Duke Senior to Jaques in his satiric mood ('thou thyself hast been a libertine') in *As You Like It*; Duke Vincentio to Lucio in *Measure for Measure*; the newly crowned Henry V to Falstaff in *2 Henry IV*.

6 The psychoanalytic components of this narrative have been distributed variously in different psychoanalytic accounts, but they have been in place since 'Otto Rank [in *Das Inzest-Motiv in Dichtung und Sage* (1912)] set out the basic insight' (Holland, 1966: 269).

7 Prospero's pageant presents a mythic utopian vision which Skura (1989: 68) compares to Gonzalo's 'more socialized' utopia and to Caliban's dream: all three 'recreate a union with a bounteous Mother Nature. And like every child's utopia, each is a fragile creation, easily destroyed by the rage and violence that constitute its defining alternative – a dystopia of murderous vengeance; the interruption of Prospero's pageant is only the last in a series of such interruptions.'

References

Unless otherwise indicated, place of publication is London.

Adelman, Janet (1992) *Suffocating Mothers: Fantasies of Maternal Origin in Shakespeare's Plays, 'Hamlet' to 'The Tempest'*. New York.

Althusser, Louis (1969) *For Marx*, trans. Ben Brewster.

Althusser, Louis (1971) *Lenin and Philosophy and Other Essays*, trans. Ben Brewster. New York.

Auden, W.H. (1968) *Collected Longer Poems*.

Auerbach, Erich (1953) *Mimesis: the Representation of Reality in Western Literature*, trans. Wiilard Trask. Princeton, NJ.

Bate, Jonathan (1986) *Shakespeare and the English Romantic Imagination*. Oxford.

Bate, Jonathan (1989) *Shakespearean Constitutions: Politics, Theatre, Criticism, 1730–1830*. Oxford.

Bate, Jonathan (ed.) (1992) *The Romantics on Shakespeare*. Harmondsworth.

Bate, Jonathan (1993) *Shakespeare and Ovid*. Oxford.

Benjamin, Walter (1968) *Illuminations*, trans. Harry Zohn, ed. Hannah Arendt.

Bentley, G.E. (1948) 'Shakespeare and the Blackfriars Theatre', *Shakespeare Survey*, 1: 38–50.

Bentley, G.E. (1984) *The Profession of Player in Shakespeare's Time, 1590–1640*. Princeton, NJ.

Berger, Harry Jr (1969) 'Miraculous harp: a reading of Shakespeare's *Tempest*', *Shakespeare Studies*, 5: 253–83.

Bergeron, David (1985) *Shakespeare's Romances and the Royal Family*. Lawrence, KS.

Bettelheim, Bruno (1950) *Love is Not Enough: The Treatment of Emotionally Disturbed Children*. New York.

Bettelheim, Bruno (1978) *The Uses of Enchantment: The Meaning and Importance of Fairy Tales*. Harmondsworth.

Bettelheim, Bruno (1982) *Freud and Man's Soul*.

Bevington, David (ed.) (1980) *The Works of William Shakespeare*. Glenview, IL.

Black, James (1991) 'The latter end of Prospero's commonwealth', *Shakespeare Survey*, 43: 29–41.

Blake, William (1988) *The Complete Poetry and Prose of William Blake*, rev. edn, ed. David V. Erdman. New York.

Bleich, David (1978) *Subjective Criticism*. Baltimore, MD.

Bowie, Malcolm (1993) *Psychology and the Future of Theory*. Oxford.

Braunmuller, A.R. and Hattaway, Michael (eds) (1990) *The Cambridge Companion to Renaissance Drama*. Cambridge.

Bristol, Michael (1985) *Carnival and Theater: Plebeian Culture and the Structure of Authority in Renaissance England*. New York.

Bronson, Bertrand H. and O'Meara, Jean M. (eds) (1986) *Selections from Johnson on Shakespeare*. New Haven, CT.

Brook, Peter (1968) *The Empty Space*. Harmondsworth.

Brower, Reuben (1951) *The Fields of Light: An Experiment in Critical Reading*. New York.

Brown, John Russell and Harris, Bernard (eds) (1966) *Later Shakespeare*.

Browning, Robert (1979) *Robert Browning's Poetry*, ed. James F. Loucks. New York.

Caudwell, Christopher (1946) *Illusion and Reality: A Study of the Sources of Poetry*. New York.

Chambers, E.K. (1923) *The Elizabethan Stage*, 4 vols. Oxford.

Chiappelli, Fredi (ed.) (1976) *First Images of America: the Impact of the New World on the Old*. 2 vols, Berkeley, CA.

Cohen, Ralph (ed.) (1989) *The Future of Literary Theory*. New York.

Coleridge, Samuel Taylor (1960) *Coleridge: Shakespearean Criticism*, 2 vols., 2nd edn, ed. Thomas Middleton Raysor.

Coleridge, Samuel Taylor (1987) *Lectures 1808–1819: On Literature* ed. R.A. Foakes (in *The Collected Works*, Vols 5: I and 5: II). Princeton, NJ.

Corfield, Cosmo (1985), 'Why does Prospero abjure his "rough magic"?', *Shakespeare Quarterly*, 36: 31–48.

de Grazia, Margreta (1981) '*The Tempest*: Gratuitous movement or action without kibes and pinches', *Shakespeare Studies*, 14: 249–65.

Dobson, Michael (1991), '"Remember/First to possess his books": The appropriation of *The Tempest*, 1700–1800', *Shakespeare Survey*, 43: 99–107.

Dobson, Michael (1992) *The Making of the National Poet: Shakespeare, Adaptation and Authorship, 1660–1769*. Oxford.

Dollimore, Jonathan and Sinfield, Alan (eds) (1985) *Political Shakespeare: New Essays in Cultural Materialism*. Manchester.

Dowden, Edward (1875) *Shakspere – His Mind and Art.*

Drakakis, John (ed.) (1985) *Alternative Shakespeares.*

Dryden, John (1955–) *The Works of John Dryden*, ed. Edward Niles Hooker and H.T. Swedenberg Jr, Berkeley, CA.

Eagleton, Terry (1976a) *Criticism and Ideology: A Study in Marxist Literary Theory.*

Eagleton, Terry (1976b) *Marxism and Literary Criticism.*

Eagleton, Terry (1991) *Ideology: An Introduction.*

Eccleshall, Robert (1978) *Order and Reason in Politics: Theories of Absolute and Limited Monarchy in Early Modern England.* Hull and Oxford.

Edwards, Paul (ed.) (1967) *The Encyclopedia of Philosophy.* New York.

Farley-Hills, David (1990) *Shakespeare and the Rival Playwrights, 1600–1606.*

Felperin, Howard (1990) *The Uses of the Canon: Elizabethan Literature and Contemporary Theory.* Oxford.

Freud, Anna (1966) *The Ego and the Mechanisms of Defence.* (rev. edn). New York.

Freud, Sigmund (1953–74) *The Standard Edition of the Complete Psychological Works*, ed. J. Strachey, 24 vols.

Freud, Sigmund (1954) *The Origins of Psychoanalysis: Letters to Wilhelm Fliess, Drafts and Notes, 1887–1902*, eds Marie Bonaparte, Anna Freud and Ernst Kris, trans. E. Mosbacher and J. Strachey.

Frey, Charles H. (1979) '*The Tempest* and the New World', *Shakespeare Quarterly*, 30: 29–41.

Frey, Charles H. (1988) *Experiencing Shakespeare: Essays on Text, Classroom and Performance.* Columbia, MO.

Frye, Northrop (1957) *The Anatomy of Criticism.* Princeton, NJ.

Frye, Northrop (ed.) (1959) *The Tempest* Baltimore, MD.

Frye, Northrop (1965) *A Natural Perspective: The Development of Shakespearean Comedy and Romance.* New York.

Goldman, Lucien (1964) *The Hidden God: A Study of Tragic Vision in the Pensées of Pascal and Racine.* London.

Greenblatt, Stephen (1988) *Shakespearean Negotiations: The Circulation of Social Energy in Renaissance England.* Oxford.

Greenblatt, Stephen (1990) *Learning to Curse: Essays in Early Modern Culture.* New York.

Greene, Thomas M. (1982) *The Light in Troy. Imitation and Discovery in Renaissance Poetry.* New Haven, CT.

Griffiths, Trevor (1983) '"This island's mine": Caliban and colonialism', *Yearbook of English Studies* 13; 159–80.

Guffrey, George (1984) 'Politics, weather, and the contemporary reception of the Dryden–Davenant Tempest', *Restoration*, 8: 1–9.

Gurr, Andrew (1987) *Playgoing in Shakespeare's London.* Cambridge.

Gurr, Andrew (1989) '*The Tempest*'s tempest at the Blackfriars', *Shakespeare Survey*, 41: 91–102.

Hamilton, Donna B. (1990) *Virgil and* The Tempest: *The Politics of Imitation.* Columbus, OH.

Hartman, Geoffrey H. (1991) *Minor Prophecies: The Literary Essay in the Culture Wars*. Cambridge, MA.

Hawkes, Terence (1986) *That Shakespeherian Rag: Essays on a Critical Process*.

Hazlitt, William (1930–4) *Complete Works*, ed. P.P. Howe, 21 vols.

Heliodorus (1895) *An Aethiopican History, written in Greek ...*, *By Thomas Underdowne, anno 1587*, intro. Charles Whibley (Vol. 5 of *The Tudor Translations*, ed. W.E. Henley).

Holderness, Graham, Potter, Nick and Turner, John (1990) *Shakespeare: Out of Court*.

Holland, Norman (1966) *Psychoanalysis and Shakespeare*. New York.

Holland, Norman (1973) *Poems in Persons: An Introduction to the Psychoanalysis of Literature*. New York.

Hooker, Richard (1989) *Of the Laws of Ecclesiastical Polity*, ed. Arthur Stephen McGrade. Cambridge.

Howard, Jean and O'Connor, Marion (eds) (1987) *Shakespeare Reproduced: The Text in History and Ideology*. New York.

Hulme, Peter (1986) *Colonial Encounters: Europe and the Native Caribbean, 1492–1797*.

Jameson, Fredric (1972) *The Prison-House of Language: A Critical Account of Structuralism and Russian Formalism*. Princeton, NJ.

Jameson, Fredric (1979) 'Reification and utopia in mass culture', *Social Text*, 1: 130–48.

Jameson, Fredric (1981) *The Political Unconscious: Narrative as a Socially Symbolic Act*. Ithaca, NY.

Jameson, Fredric (1988) *The Ideologies of Theory: Essays 1971–1986*. 2 vols. London.

Jonson, Ben (1975) *The Complete Poems*, ed. George Parfitt. Harmondsworth.

Jonson, Ben (1981–2) *The Complete Plays of Ben Jonson*, ed. G.A. Wilkes, 4 vols. Oxford.

Kahn, Coppélia (1981) *Man's Estate: Masculine Identity in Shakespeare*. Berkeley, CA.

Kalnins, Mara (ed.) (1986) *D.H. Lawrence: Centenary Essays*. Bristol.

Kavanagh, Thomas (ed.) (1989) *The Limits of Theory*. Stanford, CA.

Kay, Carol M. and Jacobs, Henry E. (eds) (1978) *Shakespeare's Romances Reconsidered*. Lincoln, NB.

Kermode, Frank (ed.) (1957) *The Tempest*.

Knapp, Jeffrey (1992) *An Empire Nowhere: England, America, and Literature from Utopia to The Tempest*. Berkeley, CA.

Knight, G. Wilson (1932) *The Shakespearean Tempest*.

Knight, G. Wilson (1947) *The Crown of Life*.

Kott, Jan (1964) *Shakespeare Our Contemporary*. trans. B. Taborski.

Laing, Dave (1978) *The Marxist Theory of Art: An Introductory Survey*. Brighton.

Laplanche, J. and Pontalis, J.B. (1973) *The Language of Psychoanalysis*, trans. Donald Nicholson-Smith. New York.

Layton, Lynne and Schapiro, Barbara Ann (eds) (1986) *Narcissism and the Text: Studies in Literature and the Psychology of the Self*. New York.

Lawrence, D.H. (1971) *Fantasia of the Unconscious*. Harmondsworth.

Limon, Jerzy (1990) *The Masque of Stuart Culture*. Newark, DE.

Lindley, David (ed.) (1984) *The Court Masque*. Manchester.

Linklater, Kristin (1992) *Free Shakespeare's Voice*. New York.

Loewald, Hans (1978) *Psychoanalysis and the History of the Individual*. New Haven, CT.

Loomba, Ania (1989) *Gender, Race, Renaissance Drama*. Manchester.

Lyly, John (1902) *The Complete Works of John Lyly*, ed. R. Warwick Bond, 3 vols. Oxford.

Macherey, Pierre (1966) *A Theory of Literature Production*, trans. Geoffrey Wall.

McDonald, Russ (1991) 'Reading *The Tempest*', *Shakespeare Survey*, 43: 15–28.

McIlwain, C.H. (ed.) (1918) *The Political Works of James I*. Cambridge, MA.

Malinowski, Bronislaw (1954) *Magic, Science and Religion, and Other Essays*. New York.

Malone, Edmond (1808) *Account of The Incidents from which The Title and Part of the Story of Shakespeare's Tempest were derived*.

Mannoni, O. (1964) *Prospero and Caliban: The Psychology of Colonization*, trans. Pamela Powesland. New York.

Marcus, Leah (1981) 'Masquing occasions and masque structure', *Research Opportunities in Renaissance Drama*, 24: 7–16.

Martindale, Charles (ed.) (1984) *Virgil and His Influence: Bimillenial Essays*. Bristol.

Marx, Karl and Engels, Friedrich (1959) *Marx and Engels: Basic Writings on Politics and Philosophy*, ed. Lewis Feuer. New York.

Marx, Karl (1970) *A Contribution to the Critique of Political Economy*. Moscow.

Masaki, Tsuneo (1991) 'Shakespeare's use of the New World in *The Tempest*'. Unpublished paper delivered at the meeting of the International Shakespeare Association, Tokyo.

Maus, Katherine Eisaman (1982) 'Arcadia lost: politics and revision in *The Tempest*', *Renaissance Drama*, 13: 189–209.

Miller, Gregory A., Levin, Daniel N., Kozak, Michael J. and Cook, Edwin W. (1987) 'Individual differences in imagery and the psychophysiology of emotion', *Cognition and Emotion*, 1(4): 367–90.

Milton, John (1971) *Paradise Lost*, ed. Alastair Fowler.

Montaigne, Michel de (1991) *Montaigne: The Complete Essays*, ed. M.A. Screech. Harmondsworth.

Mullaney, Stephen (1988) *The Place of the Stage: License, Play, and Power in Renaissance England*. Chicago.

Mulryne, J.R. and Shewring, Margaret (eds) (1993) *Theatre and Government under the Early Stuarts*. Cambridge.

Murry, J. Middleton (1936) *Shakespeare*.

Nicoll, Allardyce (1952–9) *A History of English Drama*, 6 vols. Cambridge.

Nilan, Mary M. (1972) 'The Tempest at the turn of the century', Shakespeare Survey, 25: 113–23.

Nixon, Rob (1987) 'Caribbean and African appropriations of The Tempest', Critical Enquiry, 13: 557–78.

Nosworthy, J.M. (1948) 'The narrative sources of The Tempest', Review of English Studies, 24: 281–94.

Orgel, Stephen (1965) The Jonsonian Masque. Cambridge, MA.

Orgel, Stephen (1975) The Illusion of Power: Political Theater in the English Renaissance. Berkeley, CA.

Orgel, Stephen (1984) 'Prospero's wife', Representations, 8: 1–13.

Orgel, Stephen (1987) 'Introduction' in The Tempest, ed. Stephen Orgel. Oxford, pp. 1–87.

O'Toole, John (1992) The Process of Drama: Negotiating Art and Meaning.

Ovid (1961) Shakespeare's Ovid, Being Arthur Golding's Translation of the Metamorphoses, ed. W.H.D. Rouse.

Papanicolaou, A.C. (1989) Emotion: A Reconsideration of the Somatic Theory. New York.

Parker, G.F. (1989) Johnson's Shakespeare. Oxford.

Partridge, Eric (1968) Shakespeare's Bawdy, 2nd edn.

Patterson, Annabel (1989) Shakespeare and the Popular Voice. Oxford.

Patterson, Annabel (1992) Reading between the Lines. Madison, WI.

Pitcher, John (1984) 'A theatre of the future: The Aeneid and The Tempest', Essays in Criticism, 34: 193–215.

Pliner, Patricia (ed.) (1979) Perception of Emotion in Self and Others. New York.

Powell, Jocelyn (1984) Restoration Theatre Production.

Rabkin, Norman (1981) Shakespeare and the Problem of Meaning. Chicago.

Rader, Melvin M. (ed.) (1979) A Modern Book of Esthetics: An Anthology, 5th edn. New York.

Rosador, Kurt Tetzeli von (1991) 'The Power of Magic: From Endimion to The Tempest', Shakespeare Survey, 43: 1–13.

Salingar, Leo (1974) Shakespeare and the Traditions of Comedy. Cambridge.

Schmidgall, Gary (1981) Shakespeare and the Courtly Aesthetic, Berkeley, CA.

Schwartz, Murray M. and Kahn, Coppélia (eds) (1980) Representing Shakespeare: New Psychoanalytic Essays. Baltimore, MD.

Scot, Reginald (1964) The Discoverie of Witchcraft.

Segal, Charles (1989) Orpheus: The Myth of the Poet. Baltimore, MD.

Selden, John (1614) Titles of Honor.

Selden, John (1631) Titles of Honor (2nd edn).

Sidney, Sir Philip (1973) A Defence of Poetry, ed. J.A. Van Dorsten. Oxford.

Skura, Meredith Anne (1989) 'Discourse and the individual: the case of colonialism in The Tempest', Shakespeare Quarterly, 40: 42–69.

Smith, Irwin (1966) Shakespeare's Blackfriars Playhouse. New York.

Sommerville, J.P. (1986) Politics and Ideology in England, 1603–1640.

Sprague, Arthur Colby (1944) Shakespeare and the Actors. Cambridge, MA.

Starkey, David (ed.) (1987) The English Court: from the Wars of the Roses to the Civil War.

Stoll, E.E. (1927) 'Certain fallacies and irrelevancies in the literary scholarship of the day', *Studies in Philology*, 24: 483–508.

Styan, J.L. (1975) *Drama, Stage and Audience*. Cambridge.

Teague, Francis (1985) *The Curious History of Bartholomew Fair*.

Tennenhouse, Leonard (1986) *Power on Display: The Politics of Shakespeare's Genres*. New York.

Thomson, Peter (1983) *Shakespeare's Theatre*.

Tilley, M.P. (1950) *A Dictionary of Proverbs in England in the Sixteenth and Seventeenth Centuries*. Ann Arbor, MI.

Tillyard, E.M.W. (1938) *Shakespeare's Last Plays*.

Todorov, Tzvetan (1973) *The Fantastic: A Structural Approach to a Literary Genre*, trans. Richard Howard. Cleveland, OH.

Trilling, Lionel (1972) *Sincerity and Authenticity*. Cambridge, MA.

Underdown, David (1985) *Revel, Riot and Rebellion: Popular Politics and Culture in England, 1603–1660*. Oxford.

Vaughan, Alden T. and Vaughan, Virginia Mason (1991) *Shakespeare's Caliban: A Cultural History*. Cambridge.

Vickers, Brian (ed.) (1974–   ) *Shakespeare: The Critical Heritage*.

Voloshinov, V.N. (1973) *Marxism and the Philosophy of Language*, trans. L. Matejka and I.R. Titunik. New York.

Warden, John (ed.) (1982) *Orpheus: the Metamorphosis of a Myth*. Toronto.

Watt, John (1989) *Individualism and Educational Theory*. Dordrecht.

Weimann, Robert (1978) *Shakespeare and the Popular Tradition in the Theater*, ed. Robert Schwartz. Baltimore, MD.

Wheeler, Richard (1981) *Shakespeare's Development and the Problem Comedies*. Berkeley, CA.

Wikander, Matthew H. (1991) '"The Duke my father's wrack": The innocence of the Restoration Tempest', *Shakespeare Survey*, 43: 91–8.

Williams, Raymond (1977) *Marxism and Literature*. Oxford.

Willis, Deborah (1989) 'Shakespeare's Tempest and the discourse of colonialism', *Studies in English Literature, 1500–1900*, 29: 277–89.

Winnicott, D.W. (1965) *The Maturational Processes and the Facilitating Environment*.

Winnicott, D.W. (1974) *Playing and Reality*. Harmondsworth.

Wordsworth, William (1979) *The Prelude 1799, 1805, 1850: Authoritative Texts, Context and Reception, Recent Critical Essays*, ed. Jonathan Wordsworth, M.H. Abrams and Stephen Gill. New York.

Wordsworth, William (1988) *Selected Prose*, ed. John O. Hayden. Harmondsworth.

Wycherley, William (1968) *The Plain Dealer*, ed. Leo Hughes.

Yeats, W.B. (1955) *Autobiographies*.

Yeats, W.B. (1950) *The Collected Poems of W.B. Yeats*.

Yeats, W.B. (1961) *Essays and Introductions*.

Young, Robert (1985–6) 'Back to Bakhtin', *Cultural Critique*, 2: 71–92.

Further Reading

1 Political Criticism at the Crossroads

Comprehensive bibliographies of Marxist literary criticism can be found in Lee Baxandall, *Marxism and Aesthetics* (New York, 1968) and Chris Bullock and David Peck, *Guide to Marxist Literary Criticism* (Bloomington, IN, 1980). The following short list is intended merely as a set of useful points of departure for the student curious to explore further the topics at issue here:

Diacritics, 12 (Fall, 1982).
A special issue devoted to Jameson and his then recent *The Political Unconscious*. It contains a fascinating interview with Jameson and a range of responses to his work.

William C. Dowling, *Jameson, Althusser, Marx: An Introduction to* The Political Unconscious (Ithaca, NY, 1984).
A lucid, yet detailed, exposition of the complexities of Jameson's and Althusser's thought and the relations between the two. It is at the same time an eminently undogmatic and accessible introduction to Marxism for the open-minded student.

Terry Eagleton, *Marxism and Literary Criticism* (Berkeley and Los Angeles, 1976).
The most pedagogical and least polemical of his many expositions of contem-
·ary Marxist criticism in the wake of Althusser.

Fredric Jameson, *Marxism and Form* (Princeton, NJ, 1971).
An early, but still seminal, work of Jameson's on the dialectical tradition of modern Marxist criticism, and a preliminary staging of his own development of it.

Raymond Williams, *Marxism and Literature* (Oxford, 1971).
A succinct and thoughtful introduction to the defining concepts of Marxism and Marxist criticism by one of its foremost British exponents in this century.

2 Embodying the Play

Morris Berman, *Coming to Our Senses: Body and Spirit in the Hidden History of the West* (New York and London, 1989).
A history of 'ascent psychology' and the loss of somatic awareness in 'our' culture. Background and sourcebook for theories of kinaesthetic education and experiential reading.

Charles H. Frey, *Experiencing Shakespeare: Essays on Text, Classroom, and Performance* (Columbia, MO, 1988).
Advocates and exemplifies experiential or process-oriented reading and teaching of Shakespeare.

Terence Hawkes, *The Shakespeherian Rag: Essays on a Critical Process* (London, 1986).
Argues, especially in the chapter 'That Shakespeherian Rag', for dialogical, improvisatory responses both to linguistic and paralinguistic (tonal, non-discursive) dimensions of Shakespeare.

Kristin Linklater, *Freeing Shakespeare's Voice* (New York, 1992).
Encourages a freer, more richly embodied, more energetic and, arguably, more authentic (Elizabethan, stage-worthy, true) perception and performance of Shakespeare's language.

3 Reading by Contraries

Philip Brockbank, '"The Tempest": conventions of art and empire', in *Later Shakespeare*, Stratford-upon-Avon Studies 8 (London, 1966) pp. 183–201.
An excellent introduction to the play as an exploration of contemporary colonial practice; the essay is particularly good in its analysis of Shakespeare's uses of his sources.

Stephen Greenblatt, *Shakespearean Negotiations: The Circulation of Energy in Renaissance England* (Oxford, 1988), pp. 129–63.
An interesting study of Prospero's use of 'salutary anxiety' in *The Tempest*,

showing how the play both enacts and unsettles patriarchal dreams of absolute power.

Stephen Greenblatt, 'Learning to curse: aspects of linguistic colonialism in the sixteenth century', in Fredi Chiappelli (ed.), *First Images of America: The Impact of the New World on the Old* (Berkeley, 1976) vol. II, pp. 561–80.
   A fascinating discussion of the contrast between lettered and unlettered culture both in *The Tempest* and in early modern imperial practice.

Trevor R. Griffiths, '"This island's mine": Caliban and colonialism', *The Yearbook of English Studies*, 13: 159–80 (1983).
   A thorough history both of colonial readings and colonial productions of *The Tempest*.

Stephen Orgel, *The Illusion of Power: Political Theater in the English Renaissance* (Berkeley, CA, 1975).
   A good modern text on the history and development of the masque, with useful pages on *The Tempest*.

Annabel Patterson, *Shakespeare and the Popular Voice* (Oxford, 1989), pp. 154–62.
   A recent short history of the ironic readings of *The Tempest*.

David Starkey (ed.), *The English Court from the Wars of the Roses to the Civil War* (London, 1987).
   A fascinating history of structural developments within the English Court, full of useful hints for approaching Tudor and Jacobean representations of the court in literature.

4 Fantasy and History

Sigmund Freud, *A Case of Hysteria: Three Essays on the Theory of Sexuality, and Other Works.* Volume 7 of *The Standard Edition of the Complete Psychological Works*, ed. J. Strachey (London, rev. ed., 1962).
   Although I have not focused directly on Freud's writings on the libido, this standard account of how our sexuality is achieved, not innate, is still central to the debate on society's role in the definition of acceptable desires, and so the prohibition of those that are anti-social. See especially, 'Fragment of an analysis of a case of hysteria'.

Norman N. Holland, 'Caliban's Dream', *Psychoanalytic Quarterly*, 37: 114–25 (1968). Reprinted in M.D. Faber, ed. *The Design Within* (New York, 1970), pp. 522–33.
   Holland uses Caliban's dream of riches dropping from clouds to illuminate play's preoccupation with conflicts between freedom and authority. These al concerns of the Freudian anal development stage colour Caliban's nce to Prospero and his acceptance of Stephano as a new master whom

he encourages to commit the archetypal Oedipal crime by killing Prospero and taking Miranda. For Holland, the play confirms Freud's premise that a dream appearing in a literary work will reflect and enrich the unity of that work as a whole.

Peter Homans, 'Epilogue: When the Mourning is Over: Prospero's Speech at the End of *The Tempest* as a Model of Individuation', in *The Ability to Mourn: Disillusionment and the Social Origins of Psychoanalysis* (Chicago, 1989), pp. 344–48.

Homans concludes his exploration of the cultural origins of psychoanalysis with the assertion that analysts see their work and themselves more clearly in art than in theory. *The Tempest* explicitly depicts the individuation process and the transitional space between the inner psychological and outer cultural realities. The structure of Prospero's epilogue indicates the start of individuation as he concedes his power to the audience, deconstructing the boundary between audience and play.

William Kerrigan, 'Life's Iamb: The Scansion of Late Creativity in the Culture of the Renaissance', in *Memory and Desire: Aging-Literature-Psychoanalysis*, ed. Kathleen Woodward and Murray M. Schwartz (Bloomington, IND., 1986), pp. 168–91.

Countering Keats's passive concept of youth, Kerrigan defines a 'positive capability' or *furor poeticus* characteristic of late-in-life creativity displayed by Shakespeare, Milton, and other Renaissance figures. Prospero's fury exemplifies the third Oedipal conflict of man's life in which relinquishing his daughter to her mate confronts him with death. Prospero himself evokes the superego, and much of the play's magic substitutes for the guilt that would prevent crime.

Hans Loewald, *Psychoanalysis and the History of the Individual* (New Haven, CT., 1978).

Already described in my essay. Its value lies in its reference to an individual's lived existence and personal history and significance of psychoanalysis in ordering it.

Stephen Orgel, 'Prospero's Wife', *Representations*, 8: 14–29, (1984).

Following a critique of the reading of the play as case history, Orgel presents psychoanalytic literacy criticism as a form of reader response. The subject of Prospero's magic as an antithesis to the absent and unspoken in the text is explored in five instances deleting the feminine: Prospero plays the role of father/mother; Prospero magically dominates the family lacking mate relations; Prospero's self-created power parallels the historical power of Elizabeth I and James I, both of whom used questionable claims to the throne; Prospero's magic cancels the power of Sycorax and appropriate that of Medea, whose words he appropriates via allusion.

Meredith Skura, 'Discourse and the individual: the case of colonialism in *The Tempest*', *Shakespeare Quarterly*, 46: 42–69 (1989).

Not just a critical treatment of recent exclusively sociological readings, but a carefully considered account of how references to colonialism are part of a larger set of problems worked out in the play about more personal areas of psychological development, such as infantile utopian fantasies.

David Sundelson, '"So Rare a Wonder'd Father": Prospero's *Tempest*', in *Representing Shakespeare: New Psychoanalytic Essays*, ed. Murray M. Schwartz and Coppélia Kahn (Baltimore, MD., 1982, 33–53).

In a play about the anxieties and conflicts over paternal authority, paternal narcissism usurps the maternal role. Prospero plays midwife to Ariel and denies Caliban's matrilineal claim to the island. Prospero's parodic rival, Stephano, mimics the breast with his bottle, and the gaberdine episode parodies childbirth. Ferdinand, the only threat to paternal rule, surrenders to Prospero's demands for ritualistic servitude, providing the father a symbolic victory that allows him to surrender the pleasure of his daughter.

Index

ENGLISH PEOPLE
THE EXPERIENCE OF TEACHING AND LEARNING ENGLISH IN
BRITISH UNIVERSITIES

Colin Evans

English People is a portrait of the subject 'English' as it is experienced by teachers
and students in British Higher Education. The author has interviewed staff and
students in the Universities of Cardiff, Newcastle, Oxford and Stirling and
in the former Polytechnic of North London (now the University of North
London). These 'English People' speak of the impact of Theory, of Feminism,
of the experience of reading and writing, of the problems of teaching literature,
of the peculiarities of Oxford and of compulsory Anglo-Saxon, of post-colonial
literature and of academic leadership in a time of financial pressure.

English People is also an example of the way in which nations attempt to
produce unity out of ethnic diversity by using the national education system
and especially the subject which has the name of the national language. It
questions whether 'English' can still produce unity and whether it has unity
itself. Is 'English', like the British Isles, a varied archipelago and not a land
mass? Has it deconstructed itself out of existence?

The book is about students and teachers who have made this choice of subject
and career, and is fascinating reading for past, present and aspiring students
and teachers of English, in universities, colleges and schools. It is also relevant
to anyone interested in Higher Education and its organization.

Contents
*Part 1: Joining – Origins – Choice – Reading and writing – Teaching and learning –
Life in an institution – Part 2: Dividing – Male/female – Theory – Discipline –
English, Englishes and the English – Postface – Appendix – Notes – Bibliography –
Index.*

256pp   0 335 09359 0 (Paperback)   0 335 09361 2 (Hardback)

WHICH SHAKESPEARE?
A USER'S GUIDE TO EDITIONS

Anne Thompson, with Thomas L. Berger, A.R. Braunmuller, Philip Edwards and Lois Potter

Which Shakespeare? offers a concise and authoritative survey of the competing editions, providing readers and potential buyers with the basic information they need to choose the edition most appropriate to their requirements. It covers both editions of the complete works and editions of the individual plays, and will become a standard reference work for students, academics, those working in the theatre and the general Shakespeare reader. All of the co-authors are respected editors and critics of Shakespeare.

Contents
Introduction – The complete works – Individual works

208pp   0 335 09035 4 (Hardback)

MACBETH

John Turner

Macbeth is called by actors 'the Scottish play'; but how far is it about mediaeval Scotland, and how far about aspects of the human condition that still concern us today?

John Turner offers a close reading of the play which discusses these questions in the light of two contrasting productions, each available on video. Polanski's film is set in mediaeval Scotland, a study of aristocratic competition in feudal times; but Trevor Nunn's TV film of his RSC production aspires to be timeless, a study of human society throughout the ages, caught in its recurrent crisis of violence and sacrifice.

This guide shows how the different meanings found 'in' *Macbeth* depend upon the different choices made in production and the different languages used in criticism. John Turner explores the play's depiction of mediaeval history; discusses the relationship between its imagined feudal past and its contemporary Jacobean present; and explores how, in its openness and playfulness, it may be seen to image a universal human condition that brings history itself into play. The book provides a stimulating introductory guide for students of *Macbeth*.

Contents
Introduction – Part one: Duncan's Scotland: The violent hierarchy – The weird sisters – Duncan – Part Two: Duncan's Scotland denatured – Macbeth and Lady Macbeth (I): The murder and the motive – Macbeth and Lady Macbeth (II): Tyranny and revolt – Malcolm – Conclusion – References – Suggestions for further reading – Index.

144pp   0 335 09448 1 (Hardback)   0 335 09447 3 (Paperback)